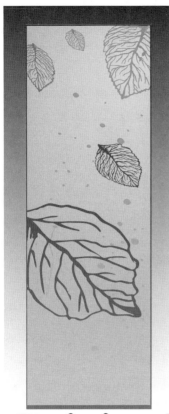

Critical Incidents
in Integrating
Spirituality
into Counseling

edited by Tracey E. Robert and Virginia A. Kelly

AMERICAN COUNSELING
ASSOCIATION

5999 Stevenson Avenue • Alexandria, VA 22304 • www.counseling.org

Critical Incidents in Integrating Spirituality into Counseling

Copyright © 2015 by the American Counseling Association. All rights reserved. Printed in the United States of America. Except as permitted under the United States Copyright Act of 1976, no part of this publication may be reproduced or distributed in any form or by any means, or stored in a database or retrieval system, without the written permission of the publisher.

10   9   8   7   6   5   4   3   2   1

American Counseling Association
5999 Stevenson Avenue • Alexandria, VA 22304

Associate Publisher • Carolyn C. Baker

Digital and Print Development Editor • Nancy Driver

Production Manager • Bonny E. Gaston

Copy Editor • Kimberly W. Kinne

Cover design by Bonny E. Gaston

Library of Congress Cataloging-in-Publication Data
Critical incidents in integrating spirituality into counseling/Tracey E. Robert and Virginia A. Kelly, editors.
    pages cm
    Includes bibliographical references and index.
    ISBN 978-1-55620-336-7 (pbk. : alk. paper)
1. Counseling—Religious aspects.   2. Spirituality—Psychological aspects. 3. Psychology and religion.   I. Robert, Tracey.   II. Kelly, Virginia A.
    BF636.68.C75 2015
    158.3—dc23   2014016244

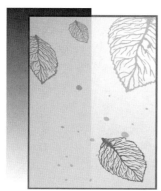

Table of Contents

Section II Spirituality and Wellness

Section III Spirituality and Specific Disorders

Section IV Substance Abuse

Section V Career

Section VI Diverse Populations

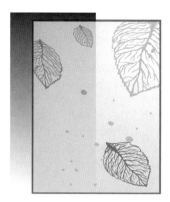

Foreword

Working from the premise that spirituality is at everyone's core, that we all are, in the words of French philosopher and Jesuit priest Pierre Teilhard de Chardin, "spiritual beings having a human experience," editors Tracey E. Robert and Virginia A. Kelly proffer a cutting-edge, practical must-read that effectively integrates critical incidents, spirituality, and counseling in a variety of settings with diverse populations across the entire developmental spectrum. Moreover, *Critical Incidents in Integrating Spirituality Into Counseling* not only readily falls under the umbrella of professional counseling, but it also adds to the clinical and conceptual knowledge base of an important specialty area.

Drs. Robert and Kelly have long been well-respected proponents of the interface of the sacred with the secular in mental health, and they acknowledge the guidance of pioneers in the field, many of whom are contributors to this book. Furthermore, the editors' leadership, research, and service in such organizations as the Association for Spiritual, Ethical, and Religious Values in Counseling (ASERVIC) and the International Association of Addictions and Offender Counselors establish their "walking the talk."

The editors place the book in a historical context, noting the relevant debates over religion, spirituality, and psychotherapy of such luminaries as Freud, Jung, and James. In addition, Drs. Robert and Kelly acknowledge the profound and courageous leadership of pioneering ASERVIC board members during times in which many in the mental health field looked askance at those who dared to posit that a person's spiritual and religious beliefs potentially affected his or her psychological and physical well-being. One might ask how it is even possible to divorce a client from his or her belief system.

Described by the editors as a casebook, this helpful manual's intended audience would easily include counselors in training, counselors in the field, counselor educators, psychologists, social workers, psychiatrists, psychiatric nurses, and other mental health professionals, as well as pastoral counselors and those with pastoral counseling training in a variety of religious settings. Not only can this easy-read be used as a text or companion to a text, it can also be recommended as a handy professional reference to be kept permanently in one's library.

The book is organized into seven theme-based sections, each with a specific clinical focus. These sections include a look at incidents or cases from a developmental perspective ranging from childhood, including school counseling issues, to adolescence; to young, middle, and mature adulthood; to the end of life. This latter stage is often viewed as an uncomfortable topic, yet it is vital to address it. A second section presents such issues as trauma, abuse, and disaster from a wellness model. Another denotes the relationship between spirituality and specific disorders, including sexual addiction and eating disorders. Because the topics of substance abuse and dependence are so important, they are in a separate section. Alcoholics Anonymous, which is arguably the most powerful spiritually based psychotherapeutic movement, provides the background for a cogent case, followed by the presentation of another scenario in the context of families and addiction. Another section focuses on job loss and on career issues over the life span—including career choice, career planning, and career search—all of which are especially relevant given the current macroeconomic situation. A separate section on dilemmas in the context of diversity factors deals with such wide-ranging topics as religious identity; individuals who are lesbian, gay, bisexual, transgender, or questioning (LGBTQ); military families; offenders; and the integration of religion into counseling. Finally, spiritual interventions, such as meditation, prayer, and group work and trauma, end the book.

As previously noted, the book is written in casebook style and is viewed by the editors as a potential companion to texts for courses on spirituality and counseling. This useful, applied format does indeed "bridge the gap between theory and practice." First, a contributor presents a situation, a crisis, a critical incident, or a dilemma with a spiritual or religious dimension. Next, this same expert practitioner describes spiritually based interventions he or she used. Questions for possible alternative strategies or treatment are then posed. Finally, another expert practitioner responds with additional input and critique, and the editors themselves then reflect on the case with the goal of conceptual integration and subsequent therapeutic benefit.

With regard to author instructions, Drs. Robert and Kelly requested that contributors adhere to the spiritual competencies of ASERVIC. According to ASERVIC, these competencies, revised in 2009 and endorsed by the American Counseling Association (ACA), "are intended to be used in conjunction with counseling approaches that are evidence based and that align with best practices in counseling" (ASERVIC, 2009, preamble). As with the format of this casebook, the ASERVIC competencies follow a developmental design; address and respect diversity; incorporate assessment, diagnosis, and treatment; allow for counselor introspection and reflection; and respect and honor client values, beliefs, background, personhood, and humanity. Furthermore, authors were advised to take into careful consideration the revised *ACA Code of Ethics* (ACA, 2014) and the ACA-endorsed *AMCD Multicultural Counseling Competencies* (Association for Multicultural Counseling and Development [AMCD], 2004).

This useful book also addresses several of the Council for Accreditation of Counseling and Related Educational Programs (CACREP) core content areas, including those of assessment, helping relationships, and social and cultural diversity. Thus, for those counselor educators concerned with its fit into the CACREP curriculum, *Critical Incidents in Integrating Spirituality Into Counseling* could easily be incorporated into such courses as Advanced Techniques and Practice, Interventions and Ethics, and Diversity Issues, among others.

Over 50 in number, the contributors include a virtual who's who of counselors with expertise in the integration of counseling and spirituality. Many are seasoned authors, renowned practitioners, esteemed counselor educators, and professional association leaders. It is apparent from reading the book that all contributors must view professional counseling as a true vocation, a calling. The cases and critical incidents contained in the book are objectively, yet humanely, presented. These cases describe suffering beings in various and sundry dilemmas who are guided to wholeness through a variety of spiritually based techniques and resources in a therapeutic relationship that values, affirms, and normalizes without moralizing, judging, or criticizing.

The editors' stated goal for *Critical Incidents in Integrating Spirituality Into Counseling* is to "offer counselor educators, students, and clinicians a highly useful educational tool that helps them incorporate the entirety of human experience into the counseling process for more effective teaching and practice" (p. xii). This they do with aplomb! In essence, this casebook ably assists professional counselors as they respond to their clients' initial push of despair and pull of hope.

—*Christopher M. Faiver*
Professor Emeritus
John Carroll University

References

American Counseling Association. (2014). *ACA code of ethics.* Alexandria, VA: Author.

Association for Multicultural Counseling and Development. (2004). *AMCD multicultural counseling competencies.* Retrieved from http://www.counseling.org/docs/competencies/multcultural_competencies.pdf?sfvrsn=5

Association of Spiritual, Ethical, and Religious Values in Counseling. (2009). *Competencies for addressing spiritual and religious issues in counseling.* Retrieved from http://www.aservic.org/resources/spiritual-competencies/

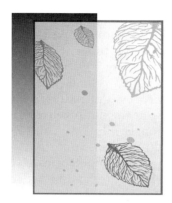

Preface

"We are not human beings having a spiritual experience; we are spiritual beings having a human experience," wrote French philosopher Pierre Teilhard de Chardin in his 1959 book *The Phenomenon of Man*. Spirituality has been defined in various ways over the years—the search for the sacred, a process of human re-formation, the internal experience of individual persons. Spiritual or religious beliefs often express a key human need: the search for meaning and purpose in life. In describing this search, Burke and Miranti (1992) stated, "The very core of our existence depends on one's ability to remain centered and focused while struggling to exercise the freedom to grow and transcend life's difficult choices" (p. ix).

Increasingly, recognition of the spiritual domain as central to human experience has become integral to counseling practice (Council for Accreditation of Counseling and Related Educational Programs [CACREP], 2001, 2009). Integration of religion and spirituality into counseling and therapy has been debated for more than 100 years by the likes of James, Freud, and Jung (Hage, Hopson, Siegel, Payton, & DeFanti, 2006). The Association of Spiritual, Ethical, and Religious Values in Counseling (ASERVIC), committed to integrating these values into the counseling process, grew from humble beginnings in the 1950s and 1960s. During the late 1970s and 1980s, attention was focused on exploration of religion and spirituality in counseling and recognition of the importance of cultural sensitivity to the client's worldview.

Before 1990, the spiritual domain and religious views of clients were not addressed in most training programs. Then a Summit on Spirituality (1995) that included ASERVIC leaders identified competencies for counselors interested in integrating spirituality and religion into counseling. They developed a description of spirituality as "an animating force in life . . . the capacity and tendency that is innate and unique to all persons . . . and includes one's capacity for creativity, growth, and the development of a values system (p. 30)." The ASERVIC board took leadership of the process and endorsed the competencies and conducted a town meeting at the national conference for discussion with counseling professionals. The result of this meeting was a formal description of spirituality and identification of nine competencies. The development of counselor competencies gave structure to the discussions that had been taking place and provided data to be included in curricula and accreditation standards.

Growing recognition of the importance of the spiritual domain increased the need for training materials and strategies for integrating the new ASERVIC competencies into counseling. Several useful references were published. In 2003, Marsha Wiggins Frame's comprehensive textbook *Integrating Religion and Spirituality Into Counseling* provided a framework for counselor educators that supported counselors-in-training and increased their confidence in addressing a major domain in their clients' lives. In 2005, Craig Cashwell and J. Scott Young described and developed the competencies in their book titled *Integrating Spirituality and Religion Into Counseling: A Guide to Competent Practice,* which serves as a resource for counselor educators, students, and practitioners. This book became required reading in many counselor education spirituality courses and made a significant contribution to the counseling literature. In 2011, Cashwell and Young published a revised edition in response to new research and updated competencies and requests from practitioners and counselors-in-training for clarification and direction on how to integrate spirituality into practice.

We see this casebook, *Critical Incidents in Integrating Spirituality Into Counseling,* as a companion book to these texts and the next step in the evolution of integrating spirituality into the counseling process. Our goal is to offer counselor educators, students, and clinicians a highly useful educational tool that helps them incorporate the entirety of human experience into the counseling process for more effective teaching and practice.

Critical Incidents in Integrating Spirituality Into Counseling uses an applied format that presents a variety of critical incidents/cases. The book is organized in seven theme-based sections: life span issues, spirituality and wellness, specific disorders, substance abuse, career, diverse populations, and frequently used spiritual interventions. Each critical incident/case examines a specific topic related to integrating spirituality into counseling (e.g., emerging adulthood, disaster mental health, sexual addiction, job loss, and Islam identity conflict). Reporting counselors describe the presenting situation and the treatment and interventions they provided. They pose three or four key questions that ask for possible alternative strategies, interventions, or approaches that might include or further integrate spirituality into the process. Practicing counselors and counselor educators with expertise in integrating spirituality into counseling then provide responses to the questions and insights and recommendations related to the presented case. For each case, we then offer our reflections on its significance in the context of the integration of spirituality into counseling, providing a concise summary of beneficial counseling outcomes.

As a classroom tool, *Critical Incidents in Integrating Spirituality Into Counseling* can help counselors-in-training by fostering discussion and case conceptualization and intervention skills. Case studies have been shown to be an effective teaching tool in a variety of disciplines, especially applied fields of study like education and mental health, where processes, problems, and programs can be examined to increase understanding and improve practice. Case studies can serve a number of purposes, including applying tools and facilitating decision making, to bridge the gap between theory and practice. The book also may serve as an easy reference for practitioners in the field.

We selected authors known for their expertise and research in various specialties within the counseling field. Many have advanced the integration of spirituality into counseling through their work in ASERVIC, a division of the American Counseling Association (ACA). In their responses, the authors were asked to address the *ACA Code of Ethics* (2014) and the ACA-endorsed Multicultural Counseling Competencies (Arredondo & Toporek, 2004).

Of note, a review of the literature reveals a struggle to define spirituality in research-based studies—studies that are intended to provide strategies for competent practice. Many studies have indicated that definitions vary because the nature of spirituality is personal and assessing and measuring the construct can be difficult. However, with the ASERVIC competencies as a guide, counselors must know the difference between spirituality and religion for effective practice.

For the purposes of this book, we define *spirituality* as the pursuit of meaning and purpose in life, often individual to clients, including the influence of their belief system and worldview and their values as they face the challenges of life events. We define *religion* as a belief that is associated with a world religion or specific philosophy, such as Buddhism, and is outwardly manifested by organized practices and sacred texts. Applying our definition of spirituality to include meaning and purpose in life and values allows counselors to address the belief systems of nonaffiliated and nonreligious clients, which is an important part of adhering to the ACA ethical and multicultural competencies. We hope this book helps counselors recognize the differences between spirituality and religion and how to use the two constructs to enhance the counseling process.

Also, wellness, a foundational construct of the counseling profession, places spirituality at the person's core. Ignoring this domain can result in a lack of understanding of the client's worldview and an insensitivity to multicultural issues. Both can be detrimental to the counseling effort.

In counseling, as in many disciplines, the only constant is change. The counseling field has evolved in recent years to accommodate clients' changing needs and increasingly has recognized the important role the spiritual domain can play in meeting them. Since the 1990s, when ASERVIC developed competencies to help professionals address spiritual and religious issues in counseling, the field also has recognized the need for more and better training and strategies for integrating the competencies into counseling. We hope this book will make a positive contribution to the literature by helping counseling professionals keep up with the always changing challenges and rewards of bringing spirituality into counseling.

Critical Incidents in Integrating Spirituality Into Counseling takes a practical, hands-on approach to exploring spirituality in counselor education and practice. Overall, we see the use of this tool as a potentially rewarding next step in the movement toward the integration of human and spiritual experience.

—*Tracey E. Robert and Virginia A. Kelly*

References

American Counseling Association. (2014). *ACA code of ethics.* Alexandria, VA: Author.

Arredondo, P., & Toporek, R. (2004). Multicultural counseling competencies = ethical practice. *Journal of Mental Health Counseling, 26*, 44–55.

Burke, M. T., & Miranti, J. G. (Eds.). (1992). *Ethical and spiritual values in counseling.* Alexandria, VA: Association for Religious and Values Issues in Counseling.

Cashwell, C. S., & Young, J. S. (Eds.). (2005). *Integrating spirituality and religion into counseling: A guide to competent practice.* Alexandria, VA: American Counseling Association.

Cashwell, C. S., & Young, J. S. (Eds.). (2011). *Integrating spirituality and religion into counseling: A guide to competent practice* (2nd ed.). Alexandria, VA: American Counseling Association.

Council for Accreditation of Counseling and Related Educational Programs. (2001). *2001 standards.* Retrieved from http://www.cacrep.org/2001standards.html

Council for Accreditation of Counseling and Related Educational Programs. (2009). *2009 standards.* Retrieved from http://www.cacrep.org/doc/2009 standards with cover.pdf

Hage, S. M., Hopson, A., Siegel, M., Payton, G., & DeFanti, E. (2006). Multicultural training in spirituality: An interdisciplinary review. *Counseling and Values, 50,* 217–234.

Summit on Spirituality. (1995, December). *Counseling Today,* p. 30.

Teilhard de Chardin, P. (1959). *The phenomenon of man.* New York, NY: Harper & Row.

Wiggins Frame, M. (2003). *Integrating religion and spirituality into counseling: A comprehensive approach.* Pacific Grove, CA: Brooks/ Cole.

About the Editors

Tracey E. Robert, PhD, LPC, NCCC, is an associate professor and director of clinical training in the Counselor Education Department at Fairfield University, Fairfield, CT. She is a past president of the Association of Spiritual, Ethical, and Religious Values in Counseling (ASERVIC) and currently serves as president of the North Atlantic Regional Association for Counselor Education and Supervision. Tracey received ASERVIC's Graduate Student National Research Award in 2003 for her dissertation work on the relationship between spiritual well-being and job satisfaction among working adults. She designed and implemented an 18-credit certificate program for Integrating Spirituality and Religion into Counseling.

• • •

Virginia A. Kelly, PhD, LPC, is an associate professor in the Counselor Education Department at Fairfield University, Fairfield, CT. Ginny is a past president of the International Association of Addictions and Offender Counseling and of the North Atlantic Regional Association for Counselor Education and Supervision. She received Chi Sigma Iota's Outstanding Researcher award and has published a monograph on integrating spirituality into counseling.

About the Contributors

Anjabeen Ashraf, PhD, North Carolina State University, Raleigh, NC
Bobbie A. Birdsall, PhD, Boise State University, Boise, ID
Cecile Brennan, PhD, John Carroll University, University Heights, OH
Ford Brooks, EdD, Shippensburg University, Shippensburg, PA
Mary Alice Bruce, PhD, University of Wyoming, Laramie, WY
Larry D. Burlew, EdD, Montclair State University, Upper Montclair, NJ
Matthew Carlson, MEd, professional school counselor, Orting High School, Orting, WA
Craig S. Cashwell, PhD, LPC, NCC, ACS, the University of North Carolina at Greensboro, Greensboro, NC
Jane C. Chauvin, PhD, University of New Orleans, New Orleans, LA
Sharon E. Cheston, EdD, LCPC, Loyola University Maryland, Columbia, MD
Abigail H. Conley, PhD, Virginia Commonwealth University, Richmond, VA
Jennifer M. Cook, PhD, M.Div, LPC, NCC, Marquette University, Milwaukee, WI
Stephanie Dailey, EdD, LPC, NCC, ACS, Argosy University, Arlington, VA
Richard G. Deaner, PhD, LPC, NCC, Georgia Regents University, Augusta, GA
Robert A. Dobmeier, PhD, LMHC, CRC, the College at Brockport, State University of New York, Brockport, NY
Taysier El-Gaili, MSc, candidate, CAS, Loyola University Maryland, Baltimore, MD

Donna Fletcher, MA, LPC, LADC, Child and Family Guidance Center of Greater Bridgeport, Bridgeport, CT

Ryan D. Foster, PhD, LPC, NCC, Marymount University, Arlington, VA

Misty M. Ginicola, PhD, Southern Connecticut State University, New Haven, CT

Jane Goodman, PhD, Oakland University, Rochester, MI

Paige Greason, PhD, LPCS, NCC, Wake Forest University School of Medicine, Winston-Salem, NC

Bryce Hagedorn, PhD, LMHC, NCC, MAC, QCS, University of Central Florida, Orlando, FL

Stephanie F. Hall, PhD, LPC, Monmouth University, West Long Branch, NJ

Janice Miner Holden, EdD, LPC-S, LMFT, NCC, ACMHP, University of North Texas, Denton, TX

Victoria Holroyd, PhD, private practice, Virginia Beach, VA

Diana Hulse, EdD, LPC, NCC, Fairfield University, Fairfield, CT

A. Michael Hutchins, PhD, LPC, private practice, Tucson, AZ

Lisa R. Jackson-Cherry, PhD, LCPC, NCC, ACS, Marymount University, Arlington, VA

Gerald A. Juhnke, EdD, LPC, NCC, MAC, ACS, the University of Texas at San Antonio, San Antonio, TX

Virginia A. Kelly, PhD, LPC, Fairfield University, Fairfield, CT

Michele L. Kielty, PhD, LPC, James Madison University, Harrisonburg, VA

Melissa Luke, PhD, Syracuse University, Syracuse, NY

Joel Clark Mason, DMin, Drew University, Madison, NJ

Mary Jo Mason, PhD, LPC, Sacred Heart University, Fairfield, CT

Holly Mensching, MA, NCC, private practice, New Canaan, CT

Dana Michie, MA, LMFT, private practice, Wilton, CT

Geri Miller, PhD, LPC, LCAS, ABPP, Appalachian State University, Boone, NC

Judith G. Miranti, EdD, LPC, LMFT, NCC, Xavier University, New Orleans, LA

E. Christine Moll, PhD, LMHC, Canisius College, Buffalo, NY

Oliver J. Morgan, PhD, NCC, LMFT, University of Scranton, Scranton, PA

Keith Morgen, PhD, LPC, NCC, ACS, Centenary College, Hackettstown, NJ

Sylvia C. Nassar-McMillan, PhD, LPC, NCC, ACS, North Carolina State University, Raleigh, NC

Jocelyn Novella, MA, LPC, Sacred Heart University, Fairfield, CT

Nicole B. O'Brien, PhD, LMFT, Fairfield University, Fairfield, CT

Eileen R. O'Shea, DNP, RN, CHPPN, Fairfield University, Fairfield, CT

Summer M. Reiner, PhD, LMHC, NCC, ACS, the College at Brockport, State University of New York, Brockport, NY

Edina L. Renfro-Michel, PhD, LPC, ACS, Montclair State University, Upper Montclair, NJ

Leila F. Roach, PhD, LMFT, LMHC, NCC, Stetson University, DeLand, FL

Tracey E. Robert, PhD, LPC, NCCC, Fairfield University, Fairfield, CT

Catherine B. Roland, EdD, Georgia Regents University, Augusta, GA

Joyce Shea, DNSc, APRN, Fairfield University, Fairfield, CT

W. Matthew Shurts, PhD, Montclair State University, Upper Montclair, NJ

Anneliese A. Singh, PhD, LPC, University of Georgia, Athens, GA

Christopher A. Sink, PhD, LMHC, NCC, Seattle Pacific University, Seattle, WA

Cheri Smith, PhD, LPC, Southern Connecticut State University, New Haven, CT

Hallie Sylvestro, MA, NCC, the University of North Carolina at Greensboro, Greensboro, NC

Kim M. Tassinari, MA, LPC, NCC, doctoral candidate, Montclair State University, Upper Montclair, NJ

J. Scott Young, PhD, LPC, NCC, the University of North Carolina at Greensboro, Greensboro, NC

Mark E. Young, PhD, University of Central Florida, Orlando, FL

Acknowledgments

We thank the more than 50 contributors who shared their experiences, their expertise, and their passion for integrating spirituality into the counseling process. The recommendations and insights they offer provide counselors with a wealth of understanding and tools for working more effectively with a diversity of client groups.

Thanks to Carolyn Baker, associate publisher for the American Counseling Association, for her interest in this project and her invaluable guidance and support. We also thank all of those who work in the counseling field for providing their clients with the strategies and support to meet life's challenges.

We would like to acknowledge those who have shared their vision and guided and supported us on our journey, including Ann Marie Wallace, Mary Thomas Burke, Jane Chauvin, Judy Miranti, Sharon Cheston, Craig Cashwell, Ellen Cook, Marsha Wiggins, and J. Scott Young.

A special thanks to our families—Leo, Eric, and Leah Robert; Drew, Kathy, and Charlie Kelly; and Mike Wallace—for their love and support.

Section I

Life Span Issues

Chapter 1 # Children

Case
Donna Fletcher

Will, a 12-year-old White boy, came to see me with his family. He had been exhibiting oppositional defiant behavior at both home and school and had been suspended from school several times for being disruptive. Will was quick to anger and had a negative attitude toward all. He often tried to dominate his siblings.

Background

Will lived in a northeastern state with his mother, age 35, and three brothers, ages 14, 10, and 8. He attended a local Catholic school and was raised with Catholic traditions.

Will and his brothers had grown up with an alcoholic father. The family had gone through a major trauma when Will's youngest brother died at the age of 2. Eight at the time, Will never fully processed his feelings about the loss of his brother. This tragedy also brought his father further into the throes of addiction, and his parents eventually separated.

Incident

Will's father took his sons to visit his parents in a southern state for Thanksgiving. Before leaving to return home, he drank excessively. While on the highway, he had a horrific car accident that left Will with an injured arm and his brothers with severe wounds that required surgeries. Will was the only one in the car who was conscious after the accident, and he was able to get out of the demolished vehicle to seek help. The boys were sent home, and their father was sent to jail and later to a drug treatment program in the South.

Discussion

When my client first came to see me, he exhibited posttraumatic stress disorder symptoms, including night terrors and flashbacks as well as avoidant behaviors. Much of the initial work involved helping him process the traumas of the accident and the loss of his brother years prior.

Using a trauma-focused cognitive–behavioral model, I provided psychoeducation around "What is trauma?" as well as the possible emotional and behavioral effects. Will learned that his negative reactivity was connected to his past traumas and that his anger was rooted in sadness about the death of his brother as well as his father's abandonment of him and his family. To cope, he learned relaxation techniques and ways to identify, talk about, and regulate his feelings.

Will had taken on the role of father for the family and was hyper-focused on earning money at odd jobs, such as mowing lawns and delivering papers, to help the family with finances. As a result, he felt empowered and domineering, yet he became very resentful.

I used structured family therapy to help put Will's mother back in control at the head of the family, which allowed Will to be a child again. At the same time, he struggled with his feelings about his father, who had moved back to an apartment nearby. His father had supervised visits on a limited basis, and his mother was preparing to divorce him. Although Will was angry with his father, he had mixed feelings toward him, including both love and hate.

In addition to all of the above-mentioned losses, the family had to leave their home and move into a small apartment because of financial problems. Will's mother was away from the home often because she worked and was going to school. She received a great deal of support and assistance from people at her church.

Will's mother told me that her greatest coping mechanism was prayer and that she did this at times with the four boys. The value of prayer to the family and especially to Will became apparent to me one day while I was in a family session with all of the boys.

We had been trying to play games to build family connection, but Will, in his usual way, dominated his brothers and his behavior led to several arguments. The boys started disagreeing on their beliefs about their father and became tearful.

When Will was asked what could help him feel calmer, he began to pray the "Our Father" out loud, and the other boys joined him. I knew the prayer and also joined them. It was one of the most poignant moments in my career as a counselor, and I too was brought to tears. At the end of the prayer, the boys all appeared calmer and began chattering and playing together.

I learned from this experience the importance of helping clients feel safe in therapy and free to express their spirituality. It is also important for the counselor to feel comfortable allowing clients to take the lead. In addition, the therapist must have a clear understanding of his or her own spirituality.

My therapeutic connection with this family was strengthened because we were able to relate on a spiritual level. Although counselors are taught to disclose on a limited basis, I found that opening up and sharing some of my own spiritual beliefs, having been raised Catholic, actually helped us connect. Together, we understood prayer as a pathway to healing.

Questions

1. Will experienced many losses in his short lifetime. How should a counselor work with grief using a family's spiritual beliefs?
2. How could the counselor help the mother be reinstated as head of this family?
3. What specific spiritual interventions could be used to deal with the trauma in this story?

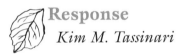 Response
Kim M. Tassinari

The counselor in this case was able to connect with Will on a spiritual level through prayer, and that became a pivotal moment in the therapeutic process. Approaching counseling by incorporating spirituality, therefore, would be therapeutic and healing for Will and his family, especially in working with issues related to grief and loss. I would first approach this case by qualitatively assessing Will's developmental and spiritual levels, gauging the family's spiritual and cultural beliefs, and learning more about Will's interests in order to find meaningful ways to connect with him.

Setting the Stage

Before working with Will and his family, I would reflect on and stay aware of my own spiritual and religious beliefs, especially when integrating spirituality into the therapeutic process (Cashwell & Young, 2011). In addition to these initial steps, I would, as always, provide a warm and safe environment in which Will and his family and I could develop a bond of trust and support. In this case, one with many issues to work through and resolve, the counselor should be commended for making great strides through successfully implementing effective strategies and interventions. I would continue to build levels of trust and further develop specific strategies that are effective for Will and his family.

Proceeding with this case, I would gather more information from Will's mother and Will to explore the family's Catholic cultural background, because Catholic traditions may vary among different ethnicities (McGoldrick, Giordano, & Pearce, 1996; O'Brien, 2010). I would further examine the family's cultural rituals, become familiar with their religious beliefs and practices, and learn how their faith has sustained them through times of difficulty (Cashwell & Young, 2011), always approaching counseling from a cultural context and with cultural humility.

Working With Grief Using Spiritual Beliefs

After working with the family as a unit, I would work with Will individually to learn more about his own spirituality and how his faith and religion speak to him, especially during the most difficult times of his short life. Psychoeducation would be helpful because it would provide him with a level of understanding of his own grief, how the many losses have affected his life, and how grief affects persons differently. This knowledge may help normalize some of his grief and loss reactions and help him see how some of his anger and sadness have manifested in his externalizing behaviors.

From a developmental perspective, Will is crossing into early adolescence, a time of difficulty for most young teenagers and a real challenge for someone like Will, who may be seeking stability in his life (Worden, 2009). In addition, not only is Will struggling with his identity, he might also be experiencing academic issues, peer pressure, and relational issues in school. Therefore, it would be important to consult with Will's school counselor and work collaboratively to ensure that his needs are being met in school (Sink & Devlin, 2011).

Several authors have suggested meaning-making activities that may be helpful for Will as he navigates through his adolescence and makes sense of his losses (Muselman & Wiggins, 2012; Sink & Devlin, 2011). I would try specific meaning-making exercises within the counseling session and work on different themes during each session.

For example, I might have Will write a letter to his father during a session to help Will process and express some of the anger, sadness, and resentment he feels toward him. In addressing the loss of Will's youngest brother, I would explore with Will some of his unresolved grief over this tremendous loss and have him recall positive memories of his brother as well as what others have said about him. For an activity, I might have Will write a short epitaph honoring his deceased brother. Activities such as this are effective in helping persons make sense of and clarify the meaning of grief and loss (Edgar-Bailey & Kress, 2010).

From a faith development perspective, Will also might be experiencing a spiritual transition co-occurring with a life crisis in which his sense of a just world may be shaken because of many losses (Parker, 2011). Therefore, I would explore with Will some of the religious and spiritual texts that have nurtured and comforted him, especially during the most difficult times in his life. The use of specific prayers, particularly those that can help clients find meaning and purpose in loss, can prove to be a valuable model of strength, compassion, and hope and can provide great resources for clients like Will (Pargament, 2007).

My counseling approach has always been strength-based, and one of the things that struck me as I read this case was Will's heroic action after the tragic car accident and how he escaped the demolished vehicle and called for help. Together, we would explore more of Will's strengths, especially how he stepped up to help his family, and look at his potentials and discuss how, in time, he might apply these strengths to a positive pursuit in his future.

Reinstating the Mother as Head of the Family

Many Catholic families have strong religious beliefs (Duba & Ponton, 2012) and a sense of loyalty to family, and they tend to keep family issues private. In this case, Will's mother found it necessary to seek counseling to help strengthen and support her family.

In review, this family endured a tremendous amount of loss and grief because of the tragic loss of Will's youngest brother; the father's addiction, which resulted in his eventual imprisonment and the horrific accident; the loss of their home; and the impending divorce of Will's parents. Throughout these events, parental and child roles became blurred, with Will feeling a need to take on parental responsibilities. I would provide psychoeducation for Will's mother to help her understand the developmental process of adolescents and the possible implications of parentification of a child. This psychoeducation may provide an explanation for her in terms of how her children have been operating differently because of the changes within the family context that required role adjustments (Minuchin & Fishman, 1981).

Using a structural family approach, as the counselor did, I would observe the family dynamics in a session in which all family members are present to get a better understanding of the transactional patterns within the family holon. I also would focus on the parental subsystem to learn the transactions, because I suspect that Will may be drawn repeatedly into the problems of the subsystem. One boundary that might be drawn would allow Will to access both parents yet exclude him from parental functions, such as family decision making

(Minuchin & Fishman, 1981). In addition, I would focus on the sibling subsystem to learn the transactions that take place and to provide support for the subsystem to negotiate clear but crossable boundaries between the brothers.

Overall, power differentials clearly exist, evidenced in Will's mother's lack of control over her family. Will may have sensed this imbalance and felt empowered to take over and step into the role of father—Will's attempt to create and restore equilibrium for himself and his family. I would aim to restructure the entire family system by eventually joining subsystems and provide psychoeducation to help the family understand how they arrived at this imbalance and dysfunction. For example, I might assign tasks within a session, such as having family members communicate and discuss specific issues while I make suggestions. I also might teach Will's mom how to respond differently to her children and have each family member practice alternative behaviors in session and at home.

Spiritual Interventions to Deal With Trauma

Prayer seems to be a source of inspiration for Will and his family. I would try to learn the personal meaning and benefits of praying for this family, how often members pray, and the feelings that emerge after the act of praying. After praying with the counselor in this case, Will and his brothers became more relaxed and at ease. Therefore, I would explore with Will other prayers that bring meaning, comfort, and peace.

Although prayer became a pivotal moment for Will and his counselor, praying overtly with a client should be approached cautiously. Counselors must integrate spirituality in an ethical manner when practicing and not be looked upon as their clients' spiritual advisors (Cashwell & Young, 2011).

In addition to using prayer as a spiritual intervention, I would encourage Will to try meaning-making activities to find a sense of meaning and purpose in the face of adversity (Sink & Devlin, 2011). Activities might include reading poetry, taking a stroll in the woods for deep reflection, conversing with a spiritual mentor, creating a beautiful piece of artwork, and engaging in other reflective processes (Sink & Devlin, 2011).

Several authors have suggested the use of various techniques as a powerful means to gain mastery over crisis and trauma (Edgar-Bailey & Kress, 2010; Wehrman & Field, 2013), such as drawing, painting, creating eco-maps and genograms, using sand tray therapy, and participating in family story telling. I find sand tray therapy to be a powerful and therapeutic technique for use with clients of any age. This activity would help Will develop a sense of identity, reduce and make meaning of his grief and loss, find more effective coping skills, and build healthy relationships in his life.

References

Cashwell, C., & Young, J. S. (Eds.) (2011). *Integrating spirituality and religion into counseling. A guide to competent practice* (2nd ed.). Alexandria, VA: American Counseling Association.

Duba, J., & Ponton, R. (2012). Catholic annulment, an opportunity for healing and growing: Providing support in counseling. *Journal of Psychology & Christianity, 31,* 242–252.

Edgar-Bailey, M., & Kress, V. (2010). Resolving child and adolescent traumatic grief: Creative techniques and interventions. *Journal of Creativity in Mental Health, 5,* 158–176. doi:10.1080/1540138 3.2010.485090

McGoldrick, M., Giordano, J., & Pearce, J. (1996). *Ethnicity and family therapy.* New York, NY: Guilford Press.

Minuchin, S., & Fishman, H. (1981). *Family therapy techniques.* Cambridge, MA: Harvard University Press.

Muselman, D. M., & Wiggins, M. I. (2012). Spirituality and loss: Approaches for counseling grieving adolescents. *Counseling and Values, 57,* 229–240. doi:10.1002/j.2161-007X.2012.00019.x 6676.2012.00046.x

O'Brien, H. (2010). The intergenerational transmission of parenting styles of Irish immigrant mothers. *Journal of Family Social Work, 13,* 395–409. doi:10.1080/10522158.2010.514680

Pargament, K. (2007). *Spirituality integrated psychotherapy.* New York, NY: Guilford Press.

Parker, S. (2011). Spirituality in counseling: A faith development perspective. *Journal of Counseling & Development, 89,* 112–119.

Sink, C., & Devlin, J. (2011). Student spirituality and school counseling: Issues, opportunities, and challenges. *Counseling and Values, 55,* 130–148.

Wehrman, J., & Field, J. (2013). Play-based activities in family counseling. *American Journal of Family Therapy, 41,* 341–352. doi:10.1080/01926187.2012.704838

Worden, J. W. (2009). *Grief counseling and grief therapy* (4th ed.). New York, NY: Springer.

 ## Reflections
Tracey E. Robert and Virginia A. Kelly

In the book *Counseling Children: A Core Issues Approach*, Richard Halstead, Dale Pehrsson, and Jodi Mullen wrote, "For all children, life is a challenging endeavor. Many are constantly experiencing who they are; testing alternative ways to live their lives; and exploring opportunities for love, safety, and joy" (Halstead, Pehrsson, & Mullen, 2011, p. vii). He added, "Some children are forced to cope with overwhelming experiences, resulting in the loss of all of the best aspects of childhood," (p. vii) which aptly describes the plight of 12-year-old Will in this case. Halstead concluded, "It is the counselor's role, of course, to assist children who may be experiencing a whole host of difficulties through no fault of their own" (p. vii).

Spirituality can play a key role in counseling children, according to school counselor and counselor educator Mary Alice Bruce, who has stated that counselors can use strategies that address children's spiritual dimension and create opportunities for spiritual development. A point to keep in mind when using spirituality in counseling children is to remain culturally sensitive and avoid making assumptions that because you share a similar religious background your beliefs and practices may be the same as the client's. Also, being self-aware and monitoring your responses in light of the client's worldview, as was done in this case, fosters ethical practice.

An understanding of the faith development process, in addition to other developmental factors, provides the counselor with additional resources and insights for working with children. A spiritual focus for counseling children can be beneficial in the following ways:

- Use of the child's cultural beliefs and practices can enhance coping skills and the process of meaning making in counseling.
- Integrating spiritual interventions, such as prayer, and expressive arts modalities, such as writing, art, and movement, provides an integrated and holistic approach that can engage children who have experienced trauma and loss.
- Acknowledging the spiritual development of children and integrating this domain into counseling can enhance personal growth and support life transitions.

References

Halstead, R. W., Pehrsson, D., & Mullen, J. (2011). *Counseling children: A core issues approach*. Alexandria, VA: American Counseling Association.

• • •

Chapter 2
Adolescents

Case
Victoria Holroyd

Fifteen-year-old Annika stated that she did not want to stop stealing because, for her, "stealing was as essential as breathing." Diagnosed with depression and an impulse control disorder (kleptomania), she was a repeat offender brought to counseling via an Integrated Domestic Violence (IDV) Court referral. She readily described lifelong beatings she suffered because of a strict parenting style at her home that included more than "one thousand rules." The penalty for breaking any of those rules was a beating, and Annika stated, "If it didn't leave a mark, it didn't make an impact." Occurrences that were held up as "rules" ranged from the petty, such as no poor grades, to the ridiculous, such as no vacuum cleaner tracks evident on the carpet.

Background

Annika's father, a Methodist minister and pastoral counselor, met and married Annika's mother during a mission trip to China. After returning to the United States and earning master's degrees, they settled into an upper-middle-class lifestyle. The maternal grandmother moved to the United States to care for Annika shortly after her birth. The family publicly espoused the Methodist religion, but her mom continued her devotion to Taoism. Annika was raised bilingual and excelled in school. She refused to believe in a God who would place her with a mother who hurt her and a father who, as she stated, was "so cowardly" he failed to protect her.

Annika's father attended the first session and explained that he and his wife were embroiled in a bitter divorce, and he shared his inability to protect his daughter as he was also a victim of physical abuse by his wife. Family counseling had been recommended but not mandated. Dad felt his past training as a Christian counselor was adequate support for him and Annika's mother. The mom, who was born and raised in China, did not believe in counseling as a viable family intervention.

Although Annika's poor hygiene and flat affect silently announced it, she described herself as a depressed loner and her life as hopeless with no expectation of relief or healing. She felt deserving of abuse and described herself as a good daughter who patiently endured the beatings her mother dispensed almost daily.

Religion played a prominent role in the family. Annika's father was a Methodist minister with an active congregation, so Annika faithfully attended both Sunday school and church. Her mother, she claimed, played the role of devoted Christian wife but stayed true to her Taoist roots. Angry at her parents' religious hypocrisy and bitter at God, Annika actively sought to avoid the topic of religion. Nevertheless, religion hung heavy and oppressive over every session and seeped into most conversations.

Incident

IDV courts allow a single judge to hear multiple case types—criminal, family, and matrimonial—that relate to one family in which the underlying issue is domestic violence. In spite of numerous family stressors, it was the risk of placement in a juvenile treatment center for shoplifting that brought Annika to counseling. The reasons for IDV involvement were the following:

- Annika had a third shoplifting offense and was at risk of placement in a residential treatment facility.
- Annika's grandmother, injured in a domestic incident, had pressed charges against Annika's father for assault.
- Annika's mother admitted to beating both her husband and daughter.
- Annika's parents were embroiled in high-conflict divorce proceedings.

Annika readily admitted to stealing items from family, neighbors, friends, and stores for as long as she could remember. The items did not hold meaning or value for her, but she felt a sense of fulfillment immediately before and after the experience. She was proud of her shoplifting skills and would strategically preplan "events" at favorite stores, even though she believed stealing is a sin.

Discussion

Annika's case was intensely complex, with ongoing physical and emotional abuse, emotional abandonment by parents, and impulsive control disorder and mood disorder. Dad's occupation, Mom's culture, and the overarching belief in God as a sham pervaded her belief system and contributed to the diagnoses. Several school counselors and social workers had attempted intervention over the years as did the family pediatrician. However, the family refused medication that was recommended as treatment for her depression and impulse control disorder.

Annika reported that her mother and grandmother were verbally and physically abusive to her father and her for years. In a detached manner, with vivid recall detailing past events from as young as age 3, Annika related horrific stories of daily abuse—of being gripped so tightly she endured broken arms, getting stabbed with a fork for not washing dishes properly, and being whipped with plastic tubing. Emotion showed on her face only when she described her father's beatings; for example, when she assisted him in stitching an open gash on his arm with a thread and needle after his wife cut him.

Annika stated that her father failed to protect her and emotionally abandoned her. Although there was no one to protect her from her mother and grandmother, she remained a staunch defender of both women because of the Chinese values of obedience and reverence. Recognizing the need to address the ongoing familial abuse first, I used trauma-focused cognitive–behavior therapy. This model allowed for an integration of interventions tailored to meet Annika's specific emotional and psychological needs related to the difficulties of trauma. I could then combine this strategy with evidence-based humanistic and familial strategies.

After a year of this treatment, Annika's episodes of kleptomania continued to occur about once a week. She previously self-reported stealing several times a week and at least once a week. If it occurred to her that she had not stolen anything within a few days, she would plan "an outing." I decided on a mindfulness-based treatment model that focused on healing the whole person—mind, body, and spirit—to provide Annika with the skills needed to accomplish and sustain long-term recovery.

Poetry and yoga therapy provided Annika with an outlet to actively express her authentic self and become reconnected to her body and mind in new, creative, and healthy ways. The imagery, emotion, and metaphor of poetry provided opportunities for self-discovery and became a catalyst for healing. Through the practice of yoga, Annika came to understand and love her body as well as the modality's philosophical/spiritual concepts, such as using the connectedness of humankind and yoga as a pathway to freedom. Through the mind–body realm of healing, Annika experienced personal growth that allowed her to explore her own spiritual beliefs safely.

Having been raised to believe in a higher power, Annika saw herself as powerless. A cynic at age 15, she viewed the world as hostile and her life as hopeless. God was an empty, shallow figurehead whom she wanted to believe in but who had abandoned her. In developing her spirituality, she saw that, for her as well as her parents, what a person chooses to believe dramatically affects one's ability to endure the pain necessary for growth and healing and achieve a sense of happiness and peace of mind that is vital to a life well lived.

As Annika's feelings of safety increased, a facility to acknowledge, mourn, and grieve her life and its traumas emerged. This ability allowed her to start the process of creating and rooting herself in meaning and purpose. Using her intellect as a tool, bibliotherapy became a powerful intervention. Spiritual books, especially Joseph Campbell's *Hero With a Thousand Faces,* wove the stories of Osiris, Prometheus, the Buddha, Moses, and Christ into an accessible understanding of the strength and courage that lie within each of us despite our demons, dragons, and obstacles. The voyage of spiritual discovery eliminated the negative attitudes and beliefs toward God and religion that contributed to Annika's pain and helplessness. She ultimately began cultivating new and empowering attitudes and beliefs that gave her hope.

Shifting from a religious viewpoint to a spiritual understanding and connection with Spirit was essential to Annika feeling hope, optimism, and the ability to control events in her life. She could articulate that, although the world was full of pain, loneliness, and fear, it also provided hope, love, and renewal that brought blessings, joy, and happiness. For Annika, this shift from empty to full was transcendent and empowered her to control her impulses and forgo the need to steal. By accessing her own personal sense of spirituality, she derived a mature positivity from realizing the blessings evident—even in the midst of sadness, pain, and loss—in a full and vital life.

Questions

1. What needed to be considered for working with an adolescent whose parent was an important community religious leader?
2. Annika initially rejected her Chinese American cultural and religious upbringing. What culturally sensitive interventions could be incorporated into her treatment plan?
3. There are many avenues through which to create meaning and purpose. Why did the therapist think it was essential for Annika to connect with her spiritual core?

 Response
Mary Alice Bruce

The priority issue in this case is Annika's safety. Initially, I ask how her ongoing safety is ensured by the therapist, who must promote her welfare (American Counseling Association [ACA], 2014, Standard A.1.a.).

Compliance with federal and state laws regarding the mandatory reporting of any child abuse is crucial. In addition, a suicide assessment with an action plan to set up a suicide watch is needed.

With Annika feeling abandoned by her father and reportedly beaten and abused almost daily by her mother, and perhaps her grandmother, no wonder she is depressed, feels hopeless, has poor hygiene, is a loner, and has resorted to illegal behaviors that symbolically involve stealing what has been robbed from her. The therapist must act now to protect Annika from further destruction of her self-image and will to live. She desperately needs for someone or something to step in and protect her as well as meet her needs for belonging and physical/emotional security.

Although Annika expressed her desire to stay with her family, she may not believe she can state her real feelings because of possible retribution if her family members found out about her statement. Ensuring that Annika is in a safe environment is the crucial first step toward her well-being. In fact, depending on the state, the therapist may be able to appeal to the IDV court to mandate family counseling or to mandate foster care while family counseling is ongoing.

Conceptualizing this case, I appreciate the therapist's careful analysis of the complexity of the situational factors. Annika seems to be desperately attempting to fill the void in her soul. Her whole self is robbed; kleptomania and depression may be conceptualized as her maladaptive ways of responding to continuous trauma. Alleviating Annika's symptoms may help her gain strength and hope to move forward step by step into healthier coping behaviors.

As stated, family counseling is essential, and I think of strategic therapy (Haley & Richeport-Haley, 2003) whereby the counselor contacts family members and any others who may be helpful, and then says, "I hear about Annika's ideas about what is happening, and I would like to know your thoughts and ideas about what is really going on. Let's meet." Attempts to bring the family or different family members and friends together may spark some support efforts for Annika. Honoring her family connection in such a manner may enhance the working alliance between her and the therapist.

Working With Children of Ministry Families

With a recognized religious leader as part of the family, as referenced in Question 1, the therapist faces a unique situation as Dad's ministry roles and responsibilities affect all family members (Hileman, 2008). In particular, children of ministry families often do not feel included in social activities with their classmates or may be specifically excluded from activities. Meaningful personal connections with those outside the family may be limited by both parties, who fear judgment.

In addition, family members often hold themselves to high standards of internal goodness and expectations that may be unrealistic. In this case, Dad indicated that his training and skills were such that he did not need to participate in family counseling, but it may have been because of his sense of inadequacy and shame resulting from his own victimization. However, Moon and Shim (2010) found that church leaders often avoid working with family violence because of their lack of training. Close (2010) found that church leaders avoid clinical treatment because they perceive the purpose of their pastoral role as offering support, not therapeutic intervention.

Meanwhile, ministry family members themselves, as well as members of the congregation and community, frequently have preconceived judgments regarding the morality and ethics of family behaviors. Community surveillance of family members may occur regarding their level of dedication to church activities, amount of volunteer work for the church, and appropriateness of daily activities. As a result of such demands, family members may feel trapped and experience dissatisfaction, including loneliness, resentment, and dissonance (Hileman, 2008).

Annika's family seemed to demonstrate a sense of entrapment whereby they attended church services regularly and appeared to be the devoted family members. From Annika's point of view, however, they appeared hypocritical in that they were pretending goodness. At the same time, in his role as a clergyman, Annika's dad provided comfort and strength to others (Close, 2010) yet failed to protect her.

Cultural Sensitivity

Contributing another layer of dissonance for Annika are the Taoist values and beliefs brought forward by her mother and, probably, her grandmother. She may feel caught in the middle. Thus, religion as a major factor of family life being "heavy and oppressive" throughout counseling sessions is not surprising. Kudos to the therapist for facilitating Annika along her spiritual journey by means of a mindfulness-based treatment model encompassing poetry, yoga, and bibliotherapy. As noted in Question 2, a culturally sensitive intervention may be a necessary part of treatment. The time may be right to bring the covert spiritual journey into the light.

With the bleak energy in the room weighing down the personal connection, the therapist can step into the right moment with thoughtful transparency. "I believe now is a good time for us to talk about what is going on in here with us. I feel we are pretending a little bit with each other, since we ignore how religion is really a part of what's going on. Let's just get it out in the open, realizing how it is in your life and then our time together. I want to know how you are putting everything together." With a time of listening and validating, the therapist and Annika may enhance their trust and build her power.

With a myriad of attachment issues swirling, the therapist can allow Annika to express and begin processing the pain, grief, and emotional dissonance that led her into depression. Adolescents who experience reactive attachment disorder need a sense of security (Goldwyn & Hugh-Jones, 2011). This security might be best achieved within the therapeutic relationship between Annika and the counselor. Methodically, the therapist must help her transition toward increased control and organization that can facilitate her move to future security in herself and her world.

The therapist can wonder aloud about ideas and practices of the East and West in a manner that demonstrates care and complements the religious and spiritual expressions in Annika's family. Close (2010) purported that therapists have added a new dimension to their role, acknowledged by the public, in supporting persons who have spiritual struggles and their journey in self-transcendence. The *ACA Code of Ethics* (ACA, 2014, Standard D.1.a.) emphasizes respect for the skills and work of professionals in other fields; thus, rather than seeming to judge Annika's parents, particularly her dad, the therapist can seek to understand how all this fits—or does not fit—together for Annika.

Annika has multiple cultural, religious, and racial identities and, as is typical of her stage of adolescent development (Erikson, 1968), is constantly evolving in her conceptualization of her personal identity and psychological well-being. As part of her treatment plan, the therapist may want to coach her to explore the interconnectedness of her world. Joining with Annika to investigate the paradigms of a variety of cultural groups and values can reinforce the relationship the therapist has with her. Identifying spiritual themes across groups may help Annika manage and integrate her surging identities.

Connecting to the Spiritual Core

Question 3 asked about the importance of connecting with Annika's spiritual core. Numerous studies (Yeh, Borrero, & Shea, 2011; Yick, 2008; Yonker, Schnabelrauch, & DeHaan, 2012) have indicated that spirituality can serve as a protective factor to ease depression as well as enhance well-being, a sense of purpose, and strength for diverse survivors of violence and trauma. Intensifying the spiritual core has been shown to be an effective evidence-based practice that gives hope and empowers those who are experiencing abuse and oppression (Walker & Aten, 2012; Yeh et al., 2011).

Realizing that Annika is striving for meaning in this stage of her development (Erikson, 1968), the therapist used a mindfulness-based treatment model to bring spirituality into focus. Although not perpetuating stereotypes, the therapist offers a space for culturally relevant activities that may serve as solid stepping stones for Annika to express her unique strengths and dreams. While she continues on her spiritual path, she needs continuing social support to "transition through the roles of victim, survivor, and thriver" (Jacinto, Turnage, & Cook, 2010, p. 110).

Expanding the Support Network

Reflecting on Annika's dangerous living environment with a pending divorce and violent family conflicts, I reiterate that she must be in a safe environment that meets her basic needs. Creatively moving Annika from isolation into a caring social network can be the next focus of the therapist's work. The therapist can connect with others to discover school or local community organizations that may be available to give caring support and help Annika move on with her life. As she appreciates her adaptive coping skills and grows, Annika may be able to give to others who need support.

In conclusion, too many youth experience heart-breaking situations. As therapists, we must consider our own wellness and continually enhance our spiritual core to have positive energy for others. Acknowledging and then acting regarding our need for ongoing clinical supervision, knowledge of evidence-based practices, and a personal support network can help us sustain our psychological well-being and clinical competence.

References

American Counseling Association. (2014). *ACA code of ethics.* Alexandria, VA: Author.

Close, R. E. (2010). Ethical considerations in counselor–clergy collaboration. *Journal of Spirituality in Mental Health, 12,* 242–254. doi:10.1080/19349637.2010.518826

Erikson, E. (1968). *Identity, youth and crisis.* New York, NY: Norton.

Goldwyn, R., & Hugh-Jones, S. (2011). Using the adult attachment interview to understand reactive attachment disorder: Findings from a 10-case adolescent sample. *Attachment and Human Development, 13,* 169–191.

Haley, J., & Richeport-Haley, M. (2003). *The art of strategic therapy.* New York, NY: Taylor & Francis.

Hileman, L. (2008). The unique needs of Protestant clergy families: Implications for marriage and family counseling. *Journal of Spirituality in Mental Health, 10,* 119–144. doi:10.1080/19349630802081152

Jacinto, G. A., Turnage, B. F., & Cook, I. (2010). Domestic violence survivors: Spirituality and social support. *Journal of Religion & Spirituality in Social Work: Social Thought, 29,* 109–123. doi:10.1080/15426431003708220

Moon, S. S., & Shim, W. S. (2010). Bridging pastoral counseling and social work practice: An exploratory study of pastors' perceptions of and responses to intimate partner violence. *Journal of Religion & Spirituality in Social Work, 29,* 124–142.

Walker, D. F., & Aten, J. D. (2012). Future directions for the study and application of religion, spirituality, and trauma research. *Journal of Psychology & Theology, 40,* 349–353.

Yeh, C. J., Borrero, N. E., & Shea, M. (2011). Spirituality as a cultural asset for culturally diverse youth in urban schools. *Counseling and Values, 55,* 185–198.

Yick, A. G. (2008). A metasynthesis of qualitative findings on the role of spirituality and religiosity among culturally diverse domestic violence survivors. *Qualitative Heath Research, 18,* 1289–1306. doi:10.1177/1049732308321772

Yonker, J. E., Schnabelrauch, C. S., & DeHaan, L. G. (2012). The relationship between spirituality and religiosity on psychological outcomes in adolescents and emerging adults: A meta-analytic review. *Journal of Adolescence, 35,* 299–314. doi:10.1016/jadolescence.2011.08.010

Reflections

Tracey E. Robert and Virginia A. Kelly

Abandonment leading to significant attachment issues permeates this complex case. Emotionally shut down, Annika has used stealing as a way to fill the hole—as a way to "feel." The complexities regarding religion and culture have further alienated her and disrupted her ability to heal. Her cultural background is at odds with the reality of the events taking place in her life, and the disconnect between being a part of this "religious" family and the reality of being a part of this abusive family have left her believing that God (and, thus, spirituality) are a sham. Incorporating a spiritual focus can enhance the counseling process in the following ways:

- A stronger sense of spiritual connection might inspire hope and a sense that things can get better.
- Spirituality may provide Annika with a context for understanding that her parents, religious or not, are human. Perhaps a focus on a "higher power" can help her disentangle her notion of God from the behavior of her parents.
- A focus on something larger than her family might enable Annika to consider alternative models for relationships—models that could result in loving, predicable, nonviolent relationships for her as she continues to develop.

• • •

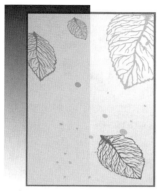

Chapter 3
School Counseling

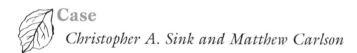

Case

Christopher A. Sink and Matthew Carlson

Sarah, a 16-year-old European American (White) high school student, faced the dilemma of countermanding her parents' religious beliefs and their insistence that she maintain sexual abstinence before marriage. Sarah's high school counselor supported her as she worked through various issues. When she went to see her counselor, she was struggling with the decision she had made to be sexually active with her boyfriend of 9 months.

Background

Sarah was a 10th-grade student when she came to the school counselor for assistance. She lived in a rural community and attended a small public high school. Sarah was raised in a Christian home by two parents who advocated for sexual abstinence before marriage. She had a 14-year-old sister, Suzy, and an older sister, Sadie, 19. Suzy was singing in her parents' church choir and waiting until marriage before engaging in sexual behavior; Sadie was a regular marijuana user and had been sexually active with multiple partners since she was 15.

Sarah's parents had lived in separate bedrooms for 10 years but, for financial and religious reasons, remained married. Later, Sarah's mother filed for divorce, and her father developed a serious medical condition and had two strokes. He had been a long-time marijuana user and tried to hide it from the children. Because his medical and relationship issues had worsened, he sought out his local church for refuge and support. Sarah reported feeling close to her dad and sharing some of his personality traits. Sarah's mother played in a rock band and enjoyed partying almost nightly, particularly when she and the band performed in bars.

Sarah and Suzy had bonded during the time of their parents' impending divorce, and both had chosen to live with their father. Sadie, on the other hand, sided with their mother and informed the other two sisters how wrong they were about her. The counselor was privileged with the knowledge that the father had an undisclosed mental health issue, and both parents reported having depression. The counselor did not know whether their mental health status was formally diagnosed by a professional but surmised that the issues probably were the result of ongoing family turmoil and personal histories.

Incident

Sarah told Sadie, her older sister, of her sexual activity during a moment of vulnerability. One evening, Sadie was supposed to help with the after-dinner cleanup, but she refused and Sarah told her mother. Out of retribution, Sadie blurted to her mother that Sarah was sexually active. Sadie then called their father and informed him of Sarah's sexual behavior. Sarah reported that her father became very angry and delivered a profanity-laced tirade at Sarah, calling her a "whore." Sarah was mortified and extremely upset. The next day, in tears, she went to her school counselor for help.

Discussion

The counselor, who was not aware of Sarah's situation at home, discovered that Sarah was experiencing strong feelings of humiliation and anger. Sarah reported feeling like her close relationship with her father was fractured. She had let him down by engaging in premarital sex.

Sarah expressed serious doubts about her family's faith and religious heritage and the choices she was making in her life. She argued that it was unfair for her father to judge her so harshly when his own "Christian values" were suspect. Sarah said that she was livid with Sadie, indicating that she would not forgive her. She disclosed that her younger sister, Suzy, would now be treated better by her father because she chose abstinence.

The counselor's initial concern was to help Sarah work through her difficulties with her father. They agreed that the counselor would call her father to set up a meeting to discuss the issues with him and try to mediate some resolution between the two of them. Sarah's father did not respond to the counselor's voicemails, and the meeting never took place.

Next, the counselor attempted to help Sarah (a) process how she felt about the inconsistencies between her parents' beliefs and behaviors and (b) explore how her own beliefs and actions aligned with one another. The counselor used cognitive–behavioral techniques (Kendall, 2011) to focus on helping Sarah understand the real nature of the problem. Together, they explored the fact that her parents were not perfect and had let her down on multiple occasions but that this was because of their depression and unhealthy communication style (e.g., loud arguing, disregard for each other's feelings, using the children as pawns in their troubles). It was not a failing of the faith system in which she was raised.

More specifically, the counselor provided Sarah with a safe and facilitative environment in which to clarify what her values were related to Christianity. As a result, Sarah recognized clear differences between her parents' religion and her own beliefs. General sharing in the course of the discussion ensued around various meaningful issues, such as love and sex and gay relationships. During the process, Sarah expressed that she believed two persons who love each other should be able to live however they choose. The counselor used open questioning, a technique from motivational interviewing (Naar-King & Suarez, 2011), to further explore with Sarah what her current involvement was with her parents' faith system.

Sarah attended church periodically with her father in the hope of making him happy. The counselor sensitively pressed her to communicate her feelings of anger and resentment, but she resisted, indicating she was frightened to do so. After further processing, she settled for an awkward relationship with her father rather than confront him about the inconsistencies between his behavior and his beliefs. Sarah expressed a willingness to reflect on the idea that persons from all faith perspectives face a challenge in being congruent with their beliefs and actions.

In a 2-week follow-up session, Sarah reported that she and her father were talking again, though she continued to feel somewhat bothered. She still had not discussed with her father how she really felt, but he had apologized for his angry outburst and she was ready to forgive him.

Upon reflection after meeting with Sarah, the counselor was concerned (a) that Sarah's need for approval from her father was great, but her relationship with him was still significantly strained; and (b) that the counselor's Christian values should not be introduced into the counseling process even subtly. He struggled with this nagging question: How could Sarah understand and experience authentic Christianity through her broken lens?

The counselor wanted Sarah to understand that it is commonplace for one's daily actions to differ from one's faith expressions and behavioral convictions. His rationale for pursuing this goal with Sarah was his belief that the patterns of unhealthy family communication and her father's mental health issues were largely the "cause" of the difficulties, not the religious system her parents espoused. The counselor hoped that in time Sarah would acknowledge these issues.

In short, the counselor wanted Sarah to be able to seek assistance when she recognized that harmful elements were occurring in her relationships. Ultimately, he hoped Sarah would develop and maintain healthy relationships as she transitioned into adulthood.

Questions

1. What are the potential legal and ethical issues related to this case study?
2. What counseling techniques are best suited to support Sarah with her negative personal and familial feelings and moral dilemma?
3. Is it really possible for counselors who are deeply spiritual or values driven to avoid influencing the counseling dynamic to some degree?
4. In what ways might family systems theory (Carr, 2013) better inform the counselor on how to support this adolescent and her family, and what could the counselor do to involve the father and mother more?

References

Carr, A. (2013). *The handbook of child and adolescent clinical psychology: A contextual approach.* New York, NY: Routledge.

Kendall, P. C. (Ed.). (2011). *Child and adolescent therapy: Cognitive–behavioral procedures.* New York, NY: Guilford Press.

Naar-King, S., & Suarez, M. (2011). *Motivational interviewing with adolescents and young adults.* New York, NY: Guilford Press.

 Response
Melissa Luke

The school counseling case of 16-year-old Sarah is complex, and regardless of how it is conceptualized, several potential legal and ethical issues need to be considered. In addition, the school counselor appears to recognize that his or her own Christian values may be interacting with Sarah's personal, familial, and cultural contexts (Bronfenbrenner, 2005). However, the counselor may not have used a systematic frame through which these issues can be identified, understood, and successfully negotiated.

Identifying Legal and Ethical Issues

To begin to answer Question 1 and identify the possible legal and ethical issues, I would recommend that the school counselor use the intercultural model of ethical decision making (IMED; Luke, Goodrich, & Gilbride, 2013a). The need for counselors to implement cultural, spiritual/religious worldview assessments in their work with clients has been established by counseling scholars (Ibrahim & Dykeman, 2011; Oakes & Raphel, 2008) and is embedded in the ethical standards of the field established by the American Counseling Association (ACA; see the *ACA Code of Ethics* [ACA, 2014]).

Until recently, however, there has not been any empirically tested school-counseling-specific framework through which counselors can be trained and supported in developing the skills and problem-solving strategies necessary in this work (Luke, Goodrich, & Gilbride, 2013b). The IMED (Luke et al., 2013a) offers school counselors a seven-step "flexible cognitive frame" (p. 181) to identify the counselor; client; and contextual attitudes, beliefs, and values embedded in a specific case. It also guides identification of relevant resources, information, and consultation.

In accordance with the IMED (Luke et al., 2013a), the school counselor first needs to recognize that various cultural, religious, and worldview (CRW) factors may be involved. In Sarah's case, it appears that the school counselor already understands that his or her Christian beliefs may be affecting the work with Sarah. However, additional CRW factors may be relevant, such as the counselor's or client's gender, age, sexual/affectual identity, and even the rural/regional aspect of the school context.

The second step of the IMED involves the school counselor's assessment of the CRW factors most relevant to the case. In Sarah's case, she has experienced conflict within and between her own and her parents' religious beliefs. In addition, the counselor's religious views may be influencing how the discrepancy between belief and behavior is understood and the treatment goals.

The third IMED step (Luke et al., 2013a) includes gathering information about the counselor's applicable legal and ethical responsibilities as well as the relevant institutional policies and procedures. In Sarah's case, I would advise the counselor to investigate the age of Sarah's boyfriend as well as the age of consent for sexual activity within the state, because both are relevant to how to proceed from a legal perspective. Exploration of how verbal/emotional abuse and parental endangerment or neglect is defined also seems prudent—Sarah's father's marijuana use and her mother's partying are placing Sarah and her underage sibling at risk.

This case poses additional ethical challenges. The school counselor also would be wise to explore more fully how to navigate his or her awareness of the father's mental health information because it may be relevant to the case.

The counselor needs to determine what, if any, school or district policies may relate to this case. For example, some school boards have clearly articulated policies related to the disclosure of information and the scope of school counseling session content. In this instance, the school and district's perspective on the role and responsibilities of the school counselor may influence how the counselor moves forward.

The fourth step (Luke et al., 2013a) suggests that, in accordance with the *ACA Code of Ethics* (ACA, 2014) and the American School Counselor Association's (ASCA's, 2010) *Ethical Standards for School Counselors*, the school counselor needs to consult with cultural experts to ensure that the applicable CRW factors have been illuminated. Within Sarah's case, this step might include consultation with other school counselors, mental health counselors in the community, and religious and family practitioners, as well as a review of the literature.

The fifth step (Luke et al., 2013a) asks the counselor to brainstorm all possible courses of action, including both the process aspects and the decisions. In this case, the counselor can begin with what has been done already, but he or she is strongly encouraged to expand the conceptualization to consider alternatives. Consultation across a variety of positions and viewpoints is thought to help in this regard.

Step 6 (Luke et al., 2013a) calls for an analysis of the relationship between each identified potential course of action and the relevant CRW factors. This examination needs to integrate the information gathered at the individual, family, school, and community levels, including the legal and ethical consultation. When practitioners believe they are "multicultural or ethical experts, they may take cognitive and practice-related short cuts" (Luke et al., 2013b, p. 233). I would strongly recommend that the counselor proactively guard against this possibility by intentionally seeking out multiple and divergent perspectives when determining the appropriate course of action.

The last IMED step (Luke et al., 2013a) calls for the counselor to select, document, and provide an ongoing evaluation of the course of action that best meets the student's needs. This counselor may want to check in with Sarah, her younger sister Suzy, and the family periodically even after the presenting issue appears to be resolved.

Counseling Techniques for Negative Feelings

Question 2 asks what counseling techniques are best suited to support Sarah with her presenting issue, currently defined as her negative personal and familial feelings and moral dilemma. Despite the rich case detail that has emerged through the counselor's work with Sarah up to this point, I am still unclear about the core issue (Halstead, Pehrsson, & Mullen, 2011) that resulted in Sarah's described experience. If I were the counselor, I would be unable to discern the root of her dilemma. Is it her sense of loss or dependence with respect to her family? Is it an inability or lack of modeling to directly express anger or fear? Is it a lack of clarity about the person she is or wants to become?

As such, the primary set of counseling techniques I would use coalesces around the goal of developing in Sarah a deeper understanding of self and others. Building off the already implemented cognitive–behavioral techniques (Kendall, 2011) designed to challenge Sarah's all-or-nothing thoughts and actions, I would incorporate values clarification, psychoeducation, and reframing within a system perspective. I might use a genogram to support Sarah's awareness of herself within a larger familial context. Over time, the basic genogram could be augmented to help Sarah see how her beliefs/thoughts, feelings, and behaviors are similar or connected to and unique from those of her family and community (Christian, rural, or otherwise).

Sarah also might benefit from group work with peers in which the focus is on developing intrapersonal and interpersonal awareness and skills (DeLucia-Waack, 2006). I would attempt to recognize the benefits and limitations of providing relatively brief services within a school context and prepare to provide referral for Sarah or, if warranted, any of her family members.

Counselor Beliefs and the Counseling Dynamic

The *ACA Code of Ethics* (ACA, 2014) and the ASCA's *Ethical Standards for School Counselors* (ASCA, 2010) make clear the responsibility of all counselors to bracket their own attitudes and beliefs, including CRW factors, and to work within the values and worldview of the client. Therefore, the answer to Question 3 about whether a counselor who is deeply spiritual or values driven can avoid influencing the counseling dynamic might more aptly be asked more concretely: What will the counselor do to prevent his or her own beliefs, values, and CRW factors from contaminating the work with the client? School counselors must be able to identify specific strategies they can use to guard against and continually assess for the possibility of their own attitudes, beliefs, and worldview interfering in an unethical manner.

Use of the IMED (Luke et al., 2013a, 2013b) is one strategy to provide a systematic framework through which the school counselor can conceptualize, consult, and intervene with the individual student directly. However, counselors also can intervene indirectly, with preventative efforts to increase their multicultural competence (Holcomb-McCoy & Chen-Hays, 2006), their multicultural self-efficacy (Holcomb-McCoy, Harris, Hines, & Johnston, 2008), and their school counselor leadership and multicultural advocacy (Evans, Zamrano, & Moyer, 2010). In addition, school counselors are encouraged to consider the role of broader interventions that target school climate as well as ongoing school–family–community partnerships. Both interventions involve a systemic approach that has been suggested as an effective means to limit the inappropriate influence of any individual counselor (Evans et al., 2010).

Family-Focused Interventions

In response to Question 4, it seems that family systems theory (FST; Carr, 2013) can be of assistance in this counselor's work with Sarah and her family. The use of FST might help shift the counselor's conceptualization about where and how to intervene. Up to this point, the counselor has used only an individual approach to his or her work with Sarah. The counselor attempted to contact the father by phone in the past, but additional efforts to involve both of the parents and sisters could include phone, email, postal letter, and even a home or community visit.

If I were the school counselor working with Sarah, I might implement the quick assessment of family functioning as described by Vernon (2004). Vernon illustrated how the assessment can be used to evaluate parental resources, the time frame of the issue, communication, hierarchy of authority, and rapport between helping adults—all of which appear pertinent in Sarah's case.

In addition to using this assessment to increase my professional awareness as a school counselor, I might modify the prescribed use of the tool with Sarah and have her complete it as grounding for further psychoeducational FST-focused intervention. Brief parent consultation (DeLucia-Waack, 2006) also may be effective in this case because the counselor focuses on family communication with a goal of behavioral change. Depending on school and community resources, family therapy or family group consultation (Carr, 2000) also could be used because it offers the school counselor an opportunity to facilitate and reinforce family-building relationships for mutual social support.

References

American Counseling Association. (2014). *ACA code of ethics.* Alexandria, VA: Author.

American School Counseling Association. (2010). *Ethical standards for school counselors.* Alexandria, VA: Author.

Bronfrenbrenner, U. (2005). *Making human beings human: Bioecological perspectives on human development.* Thousand Oaks, CA: Sage.

Carr, A. (2000). Evidence-based practice in family therapy and systemic consultation: Child focused problems. *Journal of Family Therapy, 22,* 29–60.

Carr, A. (2013). *The handbook of child and adolescent clinical psychology: A contextual approach.* New York, NY: Routledge.

DeLucia-Waack, J. L. (2006). *Leading psychoeducational groups for children and adolescents.* Thousand Oaks, CA: Sage.

Evans, M. P., Zamrano, E., & Moyer, M. (2010). Enhancing school counselor leadership and multicultural advocacy. *Journal of Professional Counseling: Theory, Practice, and Research, 2,* 62–67.

Halstead, R. W., Pehrsson, D., & Mullen, J. A. (2011). *Counseling children: A core issues approach.* Alexandria, VA: American Counseling Association.

Holcomb-McCoy, C., & Chen-Hays, S. (2006). Multiculturally competent school counselors: Affirming diversity by challenging oppression. In B. Erford (Ed.), *Transforming the school counseling profession* (pp. 98–120). New York, NY: Merrill/Prentice Hall.

Holcomb-McCoy, C., Harris, P., Hines, E. M., & Johnston, G. (2008). School counselors' multicultural self-efficacy: A preliminary investigation. *Professional School Counseling, 11,* 166–178.

Ibrahim, F. A., & Dykeman, C. (2011). Counseling Muslim Americans: Cultural and spiritual assessments. *Journal of Counseling & Development, 89,* 387–396.

Kendall, P. C. (2011). *Child and adolescent therapy: Cognitive–behavioral procedures.* New York, NY: Guilford Press.

Luke, M., Goodrich, K. M., & Gilbride, D. D. (2013a). Intercultural model of ethical decision making: Addressing worldview dilemmas in school counseling. *Counseling and Values, 58,* 177–194.

Luke, M., Goodrich, K. M., & Gilbride, D. D. (2013b). Testing the intercultural model of ethical decision making with counselor trainees. *Counselor Education and Supervision, 52,* 222–234.

Oakes, K. E., & Raphel, M. M. (2008). Spiritual assessment in counseling: Methods and practice. *Counseling and Values, 52,* 240–252.

Vernon, A. (2004). *Counseling children and adolescents.* Denver, CO: Love.

 ## Reflections
Tracey E. Robert and Virginia A. Kelly

Sarah sought the assistance of the school counselor in sorting out the inconsistencies she was experiencing at home. Her parents preached abstinence as a part of the family's overall religious values. Simultaneously, they indulged in partying, argued openly, slept in separate bedrooms, and ultimately divorced. However, even with the deterioration of the family structure, both parents continued to advocate for abstinence. Sarah is attempting to develop a unique identity and has sought help from the counselor in dealing with these family issues. We think that addressing spirituality in this case will be helpful in the following ways:

- The counselor can assist Sarah in detangling her sense of spirituality from the behavior she is witnessing.
- As Sarah continues to formulate a unique identity, she can benefit from considering if and how she wants to incorporate spirituality.

- Sarah may be able to use her own sense of spirituality to work through the guilt and shame she is carrying.

• • •

Chapter 4

Emerging Adulthood

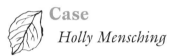

Case
Holly Mensching

Evelyn, a 19-year-old beginning her sophomore year at college, came to counseling reporting that "something was very wrong" with the way she was feeling since she came back to school. Unable to articulate what that "something" might be, she searched for a root cause of her unexpected disappointment and sadness. Evelyn had felt she had a successful freshman year and assumed she would continue to feel that way during her sophomore and subsequent years at college. She was deeply troubled and worried about what might have caused her feelings to change. Her feelings of emptiness, disappointment, and aloneness were so intense she sometimes felt as though she were outside of herself looking in.

Background

Evelyn grew up in a close-knit family and was the oldest of three daughters. Her youngest sister looked up to her as a model of ambition and excellence. Her father worked as a venture capitalist, and her mother owned an advertising agency. Evelyn described both parents as loving and supportive as well as successful and driven in their careers. She thought she would like to become a social worker, a departure from her parents' own areas of interest.

Evelyn reported that when she entered junior high school, she experienced a high level of anxiety accompanied by some repetitive behaviors, such as performing tasks and moving objects a specific number of times. She met with a school counselor once or twice, but no treatment was recommended or provided. Evelyn thought her anxiety lessened, and her repetitive behaviors abated as she matured and learned to better manage her stress and developed a highly disciplined schedule for schoolwork that allowed her to achieve the exceptional grades expected of her.

As Evelyn neared the end of her high school years, she became frightened about the prospect of going away to college. She had never been separated from her close-knit family, and while she was developing confidence that she could be independent, she feared that she "wouldn't make it" if she missed home life as much as she anticipated. She also feared that she would let her parents down if she failed.

Evelyn was pleasantly surprised when she arrived at college and found herself excited by the challenges that awaited her. She diligently planned her days to accomplish academic success, learned to make new friends, and tolerated a new roommate living in close quarters. Hearing stories of other students who did not thrive at college and had to return home early emboldened her to feel even more confident and successful on her own during her freshman year.

Evelyn finished her first year of college with pride and looked forward to her sophomore year. She knew she would be living in a dorm with friends and other like-minded students—everything she hoped and planned for.

Incident

Shortly after the start of her sophomore year, Evelyn came to counseling confused and anxious. She reported that she was crying all the time and could not determine any reason for it. She spoke to her parents about her feelings, but they reminded her that she had not been homesick the previous year, so it did not make sense that she would miss them so much during her second year. Evelyn thought that this must be true and looked elsewhere for the cause of her symptoms.

Most troubling to Evelyn were her strong feelings of emptiness, disappointment, and aloneness. She further reported panic symptoms that sometimes accompanied these strange, disconnected feelings. Worrying about when the next frightening episode of panic and detachment would strike prevented Evelyn from living what she thought was going to be a "perfect sophomore year."

Discussion

New college students often present with symptoms of homesickness at some point during their college years; in addition, they often experience anxiety about the challenging developmental hurdles they face during this period of emerging adulthood. Evelyn's symptoms seemed to be related to these experiences, but her symptoms of depersonalization required further observation and consultation.

As I was gathering information about Evelyn's symptoms during her sessions, I used a psychodynamic approach to encourage her to identify patterns of historical and current stressors that had occurred at times of high anxiety. She noted the pressure she always felt from her parents to perform well academically. Evelyn realized that she tended to feel positive about her life when things went as anticipated but often became anxious and overwhelmed when she was uncertain about how things would turn out.

Evelyn's ease in acclimating to college life during her freshman year came as somewhat of a surprise to her, and she gratefully accepted that she had made the transition "successfully." Her current symptoms of sadness and anxiety began when she started to feel disappointment that the second-year college experience she worked so hard to orchestrate was not turning out as she had hoped. The more Evelyn tried to deny her disappointment, the more it seemed that she felt disconnected from herself.

Psychiatric consultation and evaluation ruled out other physiological or psychological causes for Evelyn's symptoms of depersonalization. I held to my hypothesis that she was struggling with developmental anxiety about her increased autonomy and sense that she was becoming responsible for her own life as an emerging adult—something she felt was both exciting and terrifying.

After helping Evelyn understand her symptoms in light of her developmental process, I decided to focus on a cognitive–behavioral approach for developing new strategies for stress management (meditation and relaxation exercises). I also continued with psychodynamic counseling that would provide her with greater self-awareness.

As a result of our counseling work together, Evelyn developed a greater understanding of her personal response to the stressors. She learned to recognize states of increased anxiety and panic symptoms and to take steps toward remediating their negative effects by using the meditation and relaxation exercises, which I modified specifically for her.

Meditation may be contraindicated for patients who have feelings of depersonalization, which presented a challenge in working with Evelyn. The challenge was to find relaxation strategies that would ground her in her physical body while providing the opportunity to release tension.

Using the modifications, Evelyn learned to perform a body scan exercise at times of increased anxiety that focused on acknowledging her physical sensations as a reminder of her wholeness. In seated meditation, she used words that reminded her to accept her emerging self, allowing whatever feelings she was experiencing to be part of her here-and-now inventory. By Evelyn's last session, she welcomed finding herself on the path toward growth and change and looked forward to continued learning.

Questions

1. Evelyn seemed to resist knowing how she really felt about her college experience. How might a counselor help her explore increased self-awareness while maintaining focus on academic requirements?
2. How might a counselor help Evelyn explore ways in which she could continue to develop independence and autonomy despite feelings of insecurity and fear of failure?
3. What other strategies for stress management or spiritual interventions would you recommend to help ground Evelyn with a sense of connectedness with herself and with others?

Response
Ryan D. Foster

I would conceptualize Evelyn's case from a constructivist point of view. In reviewing her case, my initial reaction is to wonder what meaning her symptoms of dysfunction, areas for growth, and coping processes provide for her. Although there are a variety of constructivist interpretation systems (Fall, Holden, & Marquis, 2010), I tend to align with Michael Mahoney's (2003) constructivist school of thought because it merges cognitive–behavioral, existential–humanistic, psychoanalytic, and transpersonal perspectives. Not only does Mahoney's system of constructivist therapy provide professionals with a holistic way to conceptualize clients, his propositions also align with the counseling profession's global focus on working from a multicultural perspective (American Counseling Association, 2014).

However, little is known about Evelyn's cultural makeup. Therefore, before I can holistically answer the questions proposed regarding the intersection of Evelyn's self-awareness and academic requirements, further development of independence and autonomy, and intervention strategies, I would need to gather more information to better view Evelyn's world from her point of view. Whereas I do have some basic information about Evelyn in terms of her family constellation and parent subsystem, foremost on my mind to learn about her is her ethnic identity, spiritual or religious belief system, and how she believes she fits in with her family of origin and with her cultural value systems.

A Valuing Process

According to Mahoney (2003), persons innately engage in a process in which they value experiences that are satisfactory and devalue those that cause suffering. Our responses to new situations and experiences are then based on a meaning-making process. In other words, how we respond is, in large part, based on what we value. Initially, these values are based on what we have been taught. As we grow, we develop value systems that fit more satisfactorily into our picture of "the good life"—a system of meaning in which we pursue less suffering and more satisfaction.

One value that Evelyn appeared to indicate was a focus on career and, potentially, achievement. She described her parents as having strong dedication to their careers and expressed her own tentative desire to become a social worker. Alongside the importance she places on career, Evelyn appears to have great motivation to succeed academically. She also seems to value accomplishment in a number of domains, as evidenced by her report of feeling "pleasantly surprised" when she was able to overcome her fears early in her freshman year.

I would want to explore Evelyn's values in more depth. Which of these values fit for her at one time but no longer seem to bring her satisfaction? Which of these values seem to fit her now but are potentially contributing to her dissatisfaction? Which of these values fit her now and contribute to a sense of fulfillment? There are likely a myriad of other values that shape Evelyn's current style of life that are worth exploring.

Self-Awareness

Therefore, in response to Question 1, I would want to facilitate Evelyn's exploration of self as student. What parts of "student" does Evelyn value, and what parts does she devalue? What does it mean to her to be a sophomore in college, having "survived" the tumultuous potential of freshman year? There is no concrete threshold of what constitutes "healthy." Because indicators of the constructivist view of health(ier) include concepts such as hope, flexibility, active engagement in life, and holistic pursuit of life goals (Mahoney, 2003), I would want to explore with Evelyn how these constructs apply in her life. I would want to assist in Evelyn's concrete exposition of hope and active engagement. It is apparent to me that Evelyn values active engagement and thoughtful goal setting. How is she actively engaging in pursuit of her goals?

Exploration of these concepts of a healthier Evelyn supports, rather than contradicts, maintaining a focus on academic requirements. Because the case study did not provide data on how Evelyn's emotional state has affected her academic performance, I would need further information about any academic consequences she is experiencing. Primarily, I would be interested in Evelyn's self-reflection on how her academic work contributes to her sense of balanced fulfillment in terms of how she creates meaning through engagement in academics.

Search for Independence and Autonomy

Question 2 also calls for a constructivist approach to Evelyn's developmental dilemma. Her search for independence and autonomy is a natural indicator of her psychological and interpersonal development.

Her feelings of insecurity and fear of failure appear to represent a polarity: Evelyn is searching for increased autonomy but is scared to completely separate psychologically from her attachment figures—in this case, her parents. Her parents appear to operate in terms of linear processes: If you go to college and succeed, you will graduate and get a job and build a career and finally end up with a happy life. I might explore with Evelyn how much of this mantra she values and what she might fear the most if things don't actually turn out to be so stepwise and logical.

Moreover, because whole system disorganization often precedes personal growth and transformation (Mahoney, 2003), I would maintain an atmosphere of encouragement toward Evelyn that the disappointment and dissatisfaction she feels are a natural result of her normal developmental process. However, my sense is that because Evelyn feels such comfort in control, particularly when she can predict outcomes or when she has a major influence over a sequence of events, she responds with deep anxiety and terror to the unpredictable and nonlinear nature of growth and change.

I would encourage Evelyn to provide a narrative of what control and prediction mean to her and how she sees these conditions as both benefiting her and adding to her feelings of disappointment, anxiety, and depersonalization. In addition, I probably would explore what Evelyn might be able to learn from her fear and anxiety and how these feelings may be a signal to consider reorganizing meaning systems in her life.

To accomplish depth of self-reflection in these areas, I would propose journaling or other ways of creative expression. Expressive arts therapy is an established approach to counseling with emerging adults (Malchiodi, 2005). One expressive arts medium I have found successful in exploring developmental polarities surrounding the drive toward autonomy and yet being held back by fear of the unknown is sand tray, which is based on a humanistic approach (Armstrong, 2008). Using sand tray can engage clients in viewing their world from a meta-experiential perspective (Armstrong, 2008; Homeyer & Sweeney, 2011). During the processing phase, clients often discover polarities that cause them internal rifts. For Evelyn, using sand tray may help her explore her current polarity of autonomy versus fear of psychological separation.

Sense of Connectedness

Question 3 addresses therapeutic strategies in stress management and potential spiritual interventions to assist in developing Evelyn's increased sense of inner and outer connectedness. This is another area for which I would need more data about Evelyn's culture, particularly her spiritual and religious belief systems. According to the Spiritual Competencies of the Association for Spiritual, Ethical, and Religious Values in Counseling (2009), I would need to know more about Evelyn's current spiritual perspective so that I could be careful to avoid introducing a spiritual intervention that may violate her belief system.

In terms of spiritual development, emerging adults often are transitioning their basis of spiritual values from external authority figures to a self-defined belief system; they may try out new spiritual beliefs and practices but ultimately struggle with the notion that there is still a right or wrong spiritual point of view (Foster & Holden, 2011). Obtaining information about Evelyn's current systems of belief would help me better understand where she is along this developmental continuum. She may find that her sense of spirituality helps ground her to her increased sense of self.

One spiritual intervention that complements Evelyn's meditation practice is mindfulness. Although mindfulness is contemporarily associated with cognitive behavioral approaches, it originated in Buddhist thought (Greason, 2011). Because Evelyn has practiced a here-and-now orientation during meditation and body scan exercises, mindfulness would serve as a way to provide a foundation for her to nonjudgmentally observe her immediate experience.

I would encourage Evelyn to practice a "three-minute breathing space" (Segal, Williams, & Teasdale, 2002) in moments when she begins to feel disconnected from herself or when she finds herself withdrawing from others emotionally. This three-step exercise—becoming aware, shifting attention to the breath, and expanding awareness to the whole body—is a simple one that she could use to reconnect with her sense of self. Eventually, I would encourage her to use it as a daily practice even when she is in a healthier state of being.

Avenues in Counseling

Evelyn's presenting concerns, although painful and overwhelming for her, appear to be on the spectrum of normative reactions to turbulent developmental processes. Worthwhile avenues in counseling appear to include encouraging exploration of her depth-oriented value systems, facilitating an environment in which she can begin to authentically create her image of "the good life," and helping her practice strategies based in innerconnectedness and interconnectedness. Framing these approaches within constructivist theory (Mahoney, 2003) may ultimately help Evelyn move toward increased self-awareness of meaning, fulfillment, and connection.

References

American Counseling Association. (2014). *ACA code of ethics.* Alexandria, VA: Author.

Armstrong, S. A. (2008). *Sandtray therapy: A humanistic approach.* Dallas, TX: Ludic Press.

Association for Spiritual, Ethical, and Religious Values in Counseling. (2009). *Competencies for addressing spiritual and religious issues in counseling.* Retrieved from http:// www.aservic.org/resources/spiritual-competencies/

Fall, K. A., Holden, J. M., & Marquis, A. (2010). *Theoretical models of counseling and psychotherapy* (2nd ed.). New York, NY: Routledge.

Foster, R. D., & Holden, J. M. (2011). Human and spiritual development and transformation. In C. S. Cashwell & J. S. Young (Eds.), *Integrating spirituality and religion into counseling: A guide to competence practice* (2nd ed., pp. 97–118). Alexandria, VA: American Counseling Association.

Greason, D. P. B. (2011). *Mindfulness.* In C. S. Cashwell & J. S. Young (Eds.), *Integrating spirituality and religion into counseling: A guide to competence practice* (2nd ed., pp. 183–208). Alexandria, VA: American Counseling Association.

Homeyer, L. E., & Sweeney, D. S. (2011). *Sandtray therapy: A practical manual* (2nd ed.). New York, NY: Routledge.

Mahoney, M. J. (2003). *Constructivist psychotherapy: A practical guide.* New York, NY: Guilford Press.

Malchiodi, C. A. (2005). Art therapy. In C. A. Malchiodi (Ed.), *Expressive therapies.* New York, NY: Guilford Press.

Segal, Z. V., Williams, J. M. G., & Teasdale, J. D. (2002). *Mindfulness-based cognitive therapy for depression.* New York, NY: Guilford Press.

 ## Reflections

Tracey E. Robert and Virginia A. Kelly

Jeffrey Arnett introduced the term *emerging adulthood* around 2000 to propose a new concept of development for young persons in their late teens through their 20s. Erik Erikson's term *young adulthood* implied having reached an early stage of adulthood. Arnett noted that most persons in their 20s have not yet made the transitions associated with adult status. His term perhaps better captures the special challenges and concerns they have faced in recent years—limited job opportunities, financial pressures to live at home longer, a growing need for more education—in making important transitions in the midst of quickly changing economic and social factors.

Contrary to media characterizations of emerging adults as unmotivated and pessimistic, a 2012 Clark University survey of emerging adults indicated that this group is "striving and hopeful." However, emptiness, disappointment, and aloneness, as well as confusion about the intensity of these emotions, often serve as the triggers for emerging adults who are making transitions—leaving home, entering their first professional job, committing to relationships, changing cultures and friends. As Arnett pointed out, this is a time of anxiety and uncertainty for young people because their lives are unsettled and many "have no idea where their explorations will lead."

This case and response underline the importance of a holistic approach for counseling emerging adults and of recognizing the social, economic, and cultural pressures they experience. Counseling's focus on wellness and prevention can provide an effective foundation for working with them, and the optimism emerging adults expressed in the survey provides a positive environment in which to integrate personal, social, and career goals. Spiritually focused counseling can be beneficial to emerging adults in the following ways:

- Integrating spiritual interventions, such as meditation and the expressive arts, supports the meaning-making process.
- Connectedness and relationships benefit from exploration of values and goals in career and life planning.
- Tapping into the spiritual domain can reduce anxiety and depression and provide coping mechanisms to help in making stressful transitions and meeting life goals.

• • •

Chapter 5 Motherhood

Case
Michele L. Kielty

Carmella, a 35-year-old woman, came into counseling reporting a crisis about motherhood. She had been a stay-at-home mother for 9 years and had two children, ages 5 and 9. She recently divorced her husband because he had an addiction and was abusive. One result was a shift in Carmella's identity, from full-time stay-at-home mom to working single mother. Also, Carmella was attempting to adjust to a shared custody agreement with her now ex-husband.

Carmella noted that she felt a sense of relief in being free from her marriage and empowerment to work and provide for herself and her children. However, she was also experiencing feelings of profound loss, as well as an identity crisis, because her time with her children was now more defined by being "all on" or "all off" in her role as a mother.

Carmella felt she was swinging from one extreme to another, exhausted when she was with her children and grieving when she was not. Because her youngest child had had significant health problems resulting from a premature birth, she had dedicated several years of her life to him. Now she was having trouble sharing custody time with her ex-husband and his girlfriend, especially because he had not shown much interest in the children before the custody hearing.

Carmella wanted to rekindle some kind of faith life to help her manage the grief and stressors associated with her changing life and role as a single mother. She was not sure how to do this, given that she was feeling more and more disconnected from her concept of God as well as from those around her who had been a part of her faith community.

Background

Carmella was born in the northeastern United States to a large Italian Catholic family. She had five siblings and many aunts, uncles, and cousins. Carmella went to Catholic school as a child. Her main priority in life was to become a wife and mother.

Carmella met her husband while studying for her master's degree in teaching. He came from a fundamentalist Protestant background. After they got married, Carmella began teaching as a reading specialist. She and her husband practiced their faith in his childhood congregation.

Once they started having children, Carmella became a stay-at-home mother. Although she had been practicing faith in a fundamentalist church, she was beginning to wonder whether the teachings really matched what she believed. She felt like many of the answers she was hearing from her church friends were too simple for her and could not explain the suffering she had endured—her husband's addiction and subsequent emotional abuses had been escalating. Carmella found herself doubting the existence of God, especially a benevolent God that her Catholic roots and current religious community claimed there to be.

Carmella began to wonder whether the male leaders in her current church and childhood congregation could possibly understand the pressures and grief she was feeling as her roles as a woman and mother were drastically changing. She felt anger at their pious messages of love, forgiveness, and hope emanating from a loving Father God. She began to resent the idea that God could love her because her experiences had been so hurtful and she had suffered at the hands of her husband, who had promised to love and cherish her at their church wedding.

Since her divorce, Carmella was feeling looked down upon by her current church family for being a working mother. It seemed to her that she had often been invited to events and outings when she was a married stay-at-home mother but was now regularly excluded. She felt that her identity as a single working mom made those around her uncomfortable.

Incident

Carmella came to counseling because she couldn't understand why she was having so much trouble being without her children on the off weekends—she really needed the break but missed them terribly. She was overwhelmed with her grief about her changing roles in life. She was no longer a wife, which was painful for her, even though she felt a sense of relief in no longer living with an addict.

Carmella also felt that social and religious perceptions of her were changing and that she was constrained by expectations that were no longer relevant for her. She wanted to feel a spiritual connection but was experiencing a sense of numbness with regard to her faith life.

Discussion

In working with Carmella, I wanted her to feel accepted and heard for who she was and I wanted to validate her experiences. In addition, I wanted to make sure not to reopen the wounds she had suffered from her husband as well as from her faith community and society. It was important to allow her to fully express and explore her experience as well as her hopes and dreams. She needed to be heard, without judgment, before moving forward with any goal-setting endeavors.

Carmella needed to tell her story about the painful decision she had had to make to leave her marriage. She needed to process the trauma that resulted from living with an addict.

Carmella also needed to explore the loss associated with making major life and family changes, especially as her identity had shifted from full-time stay-at-home mother to working single mother. She needed to sit with the depth of the grief she was feeling as she processed the changes in her relationships with her children and with the construct of motherhood.

In addition, Carmella needed the freedom to explore her spiritual questions and to express feelings toward her God that she had found unacceptable. Her fears of expressing her anger, disappointment, and confusion toward her God seemed to be shutting down any expression of faith, which had previously been foundational to her life.

Carmella needed to sit with the full scope of the events, emotions, changes, and challenges she had experienced. It was only then that I felt it was appropriate to move forward with encouraging action in the areas of her life she had expressed dissatisfaction with.

Throughout the process of working together, Carmella began to nurture herself more fully, especially on the weekends when she did not have her children. She engaged in her old passions of painting and horseback riding and took the time to journal about what she had been through and where she was hoping to go with her life.

Carmella allowed herself to reflect on her questions of faith. She began attending a women's spiritual exploration group at a nondenominational church. She also meditated once a week during lunch at the local Catholic chapel, where she felt a sense of peace and calm reconnecting with her roots.

Carmella began connecting with new people who could honor her role as both a single mother and a single woman. Making new friends and connecting with open-minded people in her community took some time, but she took small steps to meet others. Carmella also learned to nurture her body and spirit during the off times so that she could be replenished and present for her children. She began to feel more complete, yet she had not anticipated how painful and slow the process would be.

Questions

1. Carmella experienced much loss with the demise of her marriage and her changing life roles with regard to motherhood. How can the counselor balance the exploration of these issues alongside her faith crisis?
2. How can the counselor honor Carmella's faith journey while helping her find a healthier and more supportive connection with the divine?
3. How can Carmella's role as a mother inform counseling goals, including spiritually based interventions?

 Response
Leila F. Roach

Carmella's struggles with integrating her spiritual and religious beliefs into the challenges she faces as a divorced and single mother are not uncommon. What makes her case especially difficult is that the religious messages that have become a part of her identity conflict with her current circumstances. Thus, she faces a crisis that hits at the very core of her long-held beliefs. The feelings of shame that emerge are exacerbated by disapproval from her once-supportive church family.

The counselor's nonjudgmental approach to hearing Carmella's story and allowing her to process the trauma resulting from her losses helps build a strong therapeutic relationship in which she can feel safe and accepted. By being authentically present with her and conveying unconditional positive regard and empathic understanding, the counselor meets Carmella in the depths of her pain and confusion. Rogers (1980) conceptualized this sacred space as a touching of inner spirits that allows two persons to connect on the deepest level. This foundation is essential in allowing Carmella to feel the magnitude of her losses deeply and to explore her faith more fully. The counselor provides a bridge of support so that Carmella can begin to reach out for others who are more open and accepting.

Religious Coping

The counselor asks how Carmella can explore the demise of her marriage and her changing life roles with regard to motherhood alongside her faith crisis. Krumrei, Mahoney, and Pargament (2011) pointed out an important link between spiritual stress and coping and adjustment to divorce. Their research suggests that counselors are in a unique position to assess a client's response to divorce and his or her religious interpretations.

The counselor can explore whether Carmella's distress is exacerbated by various forms of negative religious coping, such as feeling angry with God or experiencing conflict with her religious community regarding the divorce, that may inhibit her role as a mother. The counselor also can help Carmella explore and access positive religious coping methods that could be sources of support, such as praying and meditating, seeking guidance from God, and making connections with other believers who are more open-minded. The counselor can work within Carmella's belief system to facilitate positive religious coping methods that enhance her well-being and help her develop a deeper and richer understanding of what it means to be a single mother.

Faith Journey

The counselor wonders how to honor Carmella's faith journey while helping her find a healthier and more supportive connection with the divine. This is an important question, considering some clients' tendency to engage in the spiritual bypass (Cashwell, Bentley, & Yarborough, 2007) that occurs when they use spiritual or religious practices to avoid psychological wounds and other personal emotional unfinished business. A personal crisis presents Carmella with an opportunity for growth and development, although too much contradiction and a lack of support could cause her to reach back to the familiarity of her long-held religious beliefs to avoid the psychological pain of her current circumstances.

Fowler (1981) posited that spiritual and religious beliefs and practices that form the foundation for one's faith are often fundamental to developing a coherent sense of values and identity. Currently, Carmella sees the world through the lens of Fowler's third stage, synthetic–conventional faith. She is acutely tuned to the expectations and judgments of significant others and does not yet have a sure enough grasp on her own identity and autonomous judgment to construct and maintain an independent perspective. She finds it difficult to step outside of her beliefs at this stage and reflect on or examine them explicitly or systematically. She runs the risk of jeopardizing her own autonomy because the evaluations and expectations of others can become powerfully internalized, thus limiting her ability to develop both her own identity as a single mother and a supportive connection with the divine.

Therefore, it is important for the counselor to help Carmella develop critical awareness (Brown, 2007) so that she can understand her experiences with motherhood in the context of the larger social systems, in particular, religion and community. The counselor can explore how Carmella's changing role as a single mother conflicts with who, what, and how she believes she is supposed to be and thus creates deep feelings of shame and fear. She may begin to believe that she is weak or flawed and therefore unworthy of God's acceptance or belonging to her religious community. Because Carmella has given great credibility to her religious leaders, she feels misunderstood and isolated when they tell her that she should not have gotten divorced or that she is not a good mother because she is working.

Carmella could benefit from exploring the social and community expectations that fuel her shame and inhibit her identity development. She should recognize that it is these expectations that put pressure on her to be a stay-at-home mom and give her feelings of inadequacy as a mother that are reinforced in her religious environment. Once Carmella understands these forces, she can begin to develop the courage to make meaningful changes in her life, show compassion for herself and others, and make a stronger connection with the divine. Carmella can begin to build a community of faith that affirms and accepts her while supporting and strengthening her relationship with others, including her children.

Counseling Goals

The counselor asks how Carmella's role as a mother informs counseling goals, including spiritually based interventions. Once Carmella has identified her concerns about what others (her religious community) think (what it means if they no longer see her as a good mother), she can begin to reflect on her identity and on her spiritual and religious beliefs critically. She can examine and let go of the layers of internalized and competing expectations of self and begin to truly understand the reality and the context of her life as a single mother and what that means for her. She can reach out for connection rather than allow her fear to insulate her from others.

The counselor and Carmella can coconstruct goals that are meaningful and encourage her resilience. She can be encouraged to develop positive religious coping methods that focus on integrating spiritual needs with personal and social needs. For example, a counseling goal for Carmella might include increasing positive spiritual and religious coping methods to reduce symptoms of depression (depressed mood; feelings of hopelessness, worthlessness, and guilt; diminished interest in activities; and fatigue). Interventions that could be used to help Carmella address her changing role as a mother, while honoring her spiritual and religious traditions, include prayer, meditation, journaling, and bibliotherapy.

Another counseling goal for Carmella might be to nurture her self-awareness and connection with the divine and reduce her sense of loss and isolation. The counselor recommended that she attend a women's spirituality group where she could connect with others who share her desire to deepen their faith and who would be accepting and supportive of her as a mother. The counselor might also recommend that Carmella read books, such as *Motherhood: A Spiritual Journey* by Ellyn Sanna (1997), so that she can further integrate her changing roles alongside her developing faith.

Pargament (1997) pointed out the importance of fostering balance so clients do not develop one-sided solutions to their problems. Including goals and interventions that address and encourage spiritual, personal, and social needs can help Carmella contextualize her concerns so she sees the big picture and realizes she is not the only one who faces such challenges.

Taking a Holistic View

Carmella's struggle to integrate her spiritual and religious beliefs with her new role as a single working mother provides challenges to the counseling professional. The counselor might be tempted to ignore Carmella's spiritual and religious concerns and focus on her grief, the trauma of living with an addict, and her changing role as a single mother. However, spirituality and religion provide a meaningful context through which to view the full range of conflicting and competing expectations that have presented Carmella with a series of impossible choices as she navigates this difficult life transition. Only by taking a holistic view and contextualizing her struggles within her spiritual and religious framework can we fully understand the complexities of her story and help her develop the resilience needed to meet life's challenges.

References

Brown, B. (2007). *I thought it was just me (but it isn't): Women reclaiming power and courage in a culture of shame.* New York, NY: Gotham Books.

Cashwell, C. S., Bentley, P. B., & Yarborough, J. P. (2007). The only way out is through: The peril of spiritual bypass. *Counseling and Values, 51,* 139–148.

Fowler, J. W. (1981). *Stages of faith: The psychology of human development and the quest for meaning.* San Francisco, CA: Harper & Row.

Krumrei, E. J., Mahoney A., & Pargament, K. I. (2011). Spiritual stress and coping model of divorce: A longitudinal study. *Journal of Family Psychology, 25,* 973–985. doi:10.1037/a0025879

Pargament, K. I. (1997). *The psychology of religion and coping: Theory, research, practice.* New York, NY: Guilford Press

Rogers, C. R. (1980). *A way of being.* Boston, MA: Houghton Mifflin.

Sanna, E. (1997). *Motherhood: A spiritual journey.* New York, NY: Paulist Press.

Reflections

Tracey E. Robert and Virginia A. Kelly

Addressing conflicts between strongly held beliefs and life crises can present counselors with difficult challenges. Social and faith belief systems may fail to support clients as they move through various life events and transitions. Counselors must provide a safe and nurturing environment where clients can explore their confusion and the painful loss of what comfort they had received from their past beliefs. In Carmella's case, she was feeling judged and not supported by her church community, which left her isolated and disconnected.

Faith communities can be helpful or harmful. Discerning how clients perceive their situation and helping them identify what is missing for them within their belief system is important. In this case and response, two counselors are following the client's lead and helping her process her trauma and reflect on her religious coping methods, both positive and negative. A spiritual focus for addressing motherhood in counseling can be helpful in the following ways:

- It can enrich understanding of the impact of motherhood on a woman's physical, mental, social, and emotional life and bring deeper meaning to the experience.
- It can strengthen and enhance coping skills to reduce stress and anxiety.
- It offers an opportunity to engage in wellness activities for self-care, such as meditation, exercise, and contemplation, to reduce loneliness and depression.

● ● ●

Chapter 6 Couples

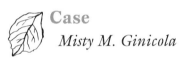

Case

Misty M. Ginicola

Upon Michael's request, his partner, Ethan, agreed to enter couples counseling for what they identified as communication issues. It became apparent very quickly, however, that issues surrounding religion were at the forefront of their very complex case. Michael reported that they argued frequently, particularly about Ethan's very religious parents. Ethan responded that he felt pulled in three directions—his love for God, his love for his parents, and his love for Michael.

Background

Michael, a 37-year-old White male, was born into a nonreligious family in New Jersey. He identified as being from a middle-class family with two older siblings. He paid his own way through college, earning a business degree and ultimately working in advertising. Michael reported coming out to his parents as gay when he was 22 years old. Although they did not react well at first, they soon warmed up and accepted him with open arms. When Michael was 31 years old, he met Ethan through a mutual friend.

Ethan, a 36-year-old White male, was born to a conservative Baptist family in upstate New York. He had one older brother and one younger sister. Ethan reported coming from meager financial beginnings. He earned an associate's degree after high school and currently worked with persons with disabilities. Ethan reported that he knew he was gay when he was very young but used faith-based and psychotherapeutic approaches to "change" his sexual orientation. He married a woman when he was 19 but got divorced when he was 26. Although he had been dating men since that time, he had not come out to his family or his church. Ethan attended church every week with his family; Michael did not share his religious beliefs and did not attend.

Although Michael and Ethan had been together for more than 5 years, Ethan had not told his family or religious friends that they were a couple. They kept two bedrooms fully furnished so that when Ethan's family visited, Michael was described as his friend and roommate. Michael's family knew Ethan as his partner and fully embraced him as family.

Michael and Ethan recently had begun talking about getting married in a state where same-sex marriage was legal, because New York, where they resided, now recognized all other states' marriage licenses. Although Ethan wanted to get married, he told Michael that he still was not comfortable sharing this information with his family or his church.

Incident

Michael and Ethan came to counseling because they felt their relationship was close to being over. Michael stated, "I have worked so hard to accept my sexual orientation. I feel proud to be who I am and comfortable with my identity. I love Ethan, but I am no longer willing to be a second-class citizen in this relationship." To Ethan, he said, "I am more than your roommate."

Michael reported that the last straw for him happened after they had discussed getting married. Ethan told him that he was finally willing to come out to his family. After much practice, discussions, and anxiety, Ethan went to meet his mother for lunch. He came home an hour later and informed Michael that he was unable to follow through with his plans to come out. Michael reported feeling devastated.

Although Ethan was reluctant to participate in counseling at first, he reported that he was desperate to keep Michael in his life because he loved him intensely and Michael was the only "real" thing in his life. Ethan reported that he was a devout believer in the Bible, and although now he did not take all the scriptural passages regarding homosexuality literally, his parents and his church absolutely did. He felt it was a very real possibility that, after coming out, he would lose the support of his entire family and his church. When asked what his church meant to him, he responded, "Everything. They helped me when I was a teenager and suicidal. They loved me, have been part of my life for as long as I can remember."

Discussion

In working with Michael and Ethan, my primary goal was to help each become empathic and to understand the other's position on coming out and being a *public* couple. A secondary goal was to increase their communication in articulating their feelings surrounding coming out officially. Working from an existential approach, I encouraged them both to explore their meanings associated with religion, their families, and each other.

In conceptualizing Michael and Ethan's case, I found they faced the following issues together: being part of an interfaith relationship, experiencing both internal and external pressures and negative associations with their sexual orientation, being at uneven sexual orientation identity stages, and being at an impasse about whose feelings were more important to recognize and honor. Ethan faced the following additional issues: the real possibility he would lose everything except Michael and his job, a potential crisis of faith, and a feeling he might be forced to come out rather than do so of his own volition.

As part of our work together, we explored both Michael's and Ethan's meanings and hope for their relationship. They clearly loved one another very much and wanted to continue their partnership and get married. Building on a strength-based model, we identified positive assets that each brought to the relationship individually and in a partnership.

Both Michael and Ethan felt more comfortable negotiating with each other after exploring the viewpoint of the other, using positive communication strategies, giving voice to their fears and anxieties, and role playing the opposite partner. Having a solid motivation and dedication for working on the relationship, each was willing to develop a plan that represented a middle ground between their two positions.

Questions

1. What are the issues involved in being in an interfaith relationship? How can a counselor help each client communicate the importance or unimportance of religion and still respect each other's position equally?

2. The main issue for Ethan as a person and as a partner was his ability to negotiate his sexual orientation identity and his religious identity. How can a counselor help a client integrate these two identities?

3. Although Ethan and Michael's case had similarities to those of many interfaith couples, the impact that oppression, prejudice, and discrimination may have on lesbian, gay, bisexual, and transgender relationships can add complexity to a client's presenting issues. How does this make the counselor's work more challenging? What should a counselor do to help prepare clients for these experiences and teach them how to combat the impact of discrimination on their personal lives and relationships?

4. How might spiritual interventions enhance the counseling process for couples?

Response
J. Scott Young

It appears that Ethan and Michael are in a relationship crisis, one triggered by the new possibility of becoming legally married. It also appears that they were able to function comfortably in the relationship for 5 or 6 years; only recently had the issue of their differing religious values begun to create a division that seriously jeopardized the stability of their partnership. From the beginning, each partner was aware of the other's stance regarding traditional religion and its practice and was willing to accept these differences in the other, at least until now.

Emotionally Focused Couples Therapy (EFCT)

In conceptualizing the case, I would use the EFCT approach because the model has been well researched (Johnson, 2004) and research results have consistently indicated that the vast majority of couples who participate in this approach report improvements in their relationship (Jacobson, Follette, & Pagel, 1986). I view this as a case in which the couple became embroiled in a dissatisfying pattern of relating in which it sounds as though Michael is the pursuer and Ethan the withdrawer—Michael reaches out, complains, pushes, and feels anger, and Ethan withdraws and feels hurt, misunderstood, and unable to "get it right" for Michael.

The current issues of religious beliefs and the decision to marry are likely symptomatic of Ethan and Michael's struggles as a couple generally and recently have become the concern around which their struggles are playing out. Therefore, I would begin by helping them recognize their interaction patterns in which Michael pressures Ethan and Ethan collapses in the face of that pressure. As both begin to own their part of the dynamic, by labeling it and recognizing when it plays out in their day-to-day interactions, they likely would begin to feel some relief from the immediate crisis.

As part of this early EFCT work, I would gently help each explore his underlying feeling or primary attachment emotions that are being activated in the relationship. These are the tender emotions that persons are generally hesitant to articulate because of the vulnerability they bring with them. For Michael, it may include feelings of "I'm not important to you" and "My needs don't matter," and for Ethan, "I am never enough" and "I can't do it right." As these deeper, more tender emotions are explored, a new level of understanding of, and affection for, the partner could be enjoyed.

My hypothesis is that the current relational struggles relate to the religious mismatch in the relationship. For Michael, Ethan's reluctance to come out to his church and family and to marry has become symbolic of Michael's feelings that other relationships (parents, church, church friends) are more important to Ethan than their partnership. As a result, Michael is pushing harder for the marriage. This push unwittingly serves to increase Ethan's withdrawal, anxiety, and feelings of helplessness in the face of his religious beliefs and his relational stance of never being enough or getting it right. I can imagine that in Ethan's mind he feels that no matter what he decides, "someone is going to be very disappointed." From Michael's perspective, there is likely a strong feeling that "I am far less important to Ethan than his need to maintain the appearance of a good Christian."

As with all issues around which couples develop power struggles, the counselor's work is to listen deeply for the underlying feelings, beliefs, and experiences and to bring these to the surface to help each partner hear the other's concerns in more nuanced and therefore new ways. In this case, I would help Michael hear how trapped and stuck Ethan feels—between his background and beliefs, which he deeply values, and his current relationship with Michael, which he also holds as central to his life. In a similar manner, I would work to help Ethan understand Michael's feeling that he is not truly the most important person in Ethan's life, which leaves him afraid and questioning his value as a person.

My intention over time would be to have each member of the partnership gain new perspectives on his partner's struggles by using the EFCT approach of empathic attunement to both of their concerns. I would highlight the nature of their dynamic and help them recognize that the pattern they are caught in, not their partner, is the problem. When enough safety has been reestablished, I would work to help Ethan reach for Michael with new vulnerability to let him know that Michael is *the* most important person in his life and that he is terrified of getting it wrong with Michael and being rejected.

Interfaith Relationships

Question 1 asked what issues are involved in an interfaith relationship and how can a counselor help each client communicate the importance or unimportance of religion. Any interfaith relationship has the potential complication that partners hold core values that differ from one another's. This is a concern in that many of the beliefs inherent in religious commitment are, as James Fowler (1991) indicated, beyond mere belief. Fowler suggested that belief is a cognitive process in which one accepts something as true that cannot literally be proven (e.g., the Christian trinity). However, according to Fowler, faith is a meaning-making process that everyone engages in, regardless of religious commitments, such that faith structures are formed over time. They are built from experiences, churches, developmental processes, stories, and many other events that make sense only from within the personal context of the individual. Therefore, a highly religious Christian and a highly religious Jew might understand one another better than would a highly religious Christian and a minimally religious Christian.

The work of the counselor with an interfaith couple, or a couple in which one does not come from a religious background, is to move the conversation to the level of values and meaning making and away from belief and theology. Everyone must make meaning of their lives. So, if the counselor focuses on the value statements "Here is how I make sense of the big questions in life" and "Here is how that guides me day to day," a couple has greater hope of empathic understanding of one another.

Integrating Identities

Question 2 asked how a counselor can help a client integrate sexual orientation and religious identities. For Ethan, reconciliation of his sexual identity and his religious identity indeed seems to be a critical issue in his development as a person. He probably has made internal compromises in which he maintains the beliefs of his youth (except for the prohibition against homosexuality) and continues to live out his religious beliefs not unlike he did when he was younger.

To help Ethan integrate these two identities, a counselor can explore his faith development processes with him to determine when he began to make bargains and compromises that required him to compartmentalize his sexuality to maintain acceptance by his parents and church. If it becomes clear that Ethan is ready to move beyond his current position to a more integrated stance, the counselor could use any number of spiritual/faith models to help him explore and challenge his current stance to do so, likely with much fear and uncertainty (Fowler, 1981; Genia, 1990, 1995; Oser & Gmünder, 1981; Pargament, 2006; Washburn, 1995; Wilber, 2000). This process would be appropriate and prove beneficial only if Ethan wants to do this work. It should not be imposed on him.

Dealing With Discrimination

Question 3 asked about how the impact that oppression, prejudice, and discrimination may have on lesbian, gay, bisexual, and transgender relationships can add complexity to a client's presenting issues, how this makes the counselor's work more challenging, and what a counselor should do to help prepare clients for these experiences. Michael and Ethan being nearly 40 years old, educated, and stable in their work and personal lives indicates that they probably are used to dealing with the discrimination that same-sex couples face. In this case, however, because Ethan participates in a community that is prejudicial against their relationship, Michael likely feels particularly sensitive to religious groups that judge homosexuality negatively. In some sense he may feel that Ethan's religious participation is a betrayal of their relationship. This sense of betrayal would need to be explored in couples counseling to gain clarity about each partner's stance and to determine how each conceptualizes the discrimination he perceives.

I can imagine that some of the couples work would flow from Michael's questioning, "How can you say you love me and be a part of that judgmental small-minded group?" An approach that a counselor could take to help this sexual minority couple prepare for experiences of discrimination would be to assist them in talking about their own perspectives—Ethan's closely held conservative beliefs and Michael's distrust of these beliefs.

More broadly, a counselor should develop an understanding of Cass's stage model of gay and lesbian identity development: (a) confusion, (b) comparison, (c) tolerance, (d) acceptance, (e) pride, and (f) synthesis (Ritter & Terndrup, 2002). The mismatch of stage development among members of a partnership likely would create relational dissonance and suggest differing strategies and levels of reactivity toward discrimination.

Interventions

Question 4 asked how spiritual interventions might enhance the counseling process for couples. Spiritual interventions can be used with couples in a variety of ways, assuming the couple is open to their use. In the case of Ethan and Michael, I imagine that much of the spiritual intervention would center around guiding each through carefully communicating his own spiritual perspectives and explaining the unique values and beliefs—and, for Ethan, his faith—that guide his life. Helping each share aspects of his spiritual life that he perhaps never has shared before with a counselor present to guide the process may foster new understanding and appreciation. The counselor could use spiritual genograms (Wiggins-Frame, 2003) or autobiographies (Staude, 2005) completed by each partner to stimulate the exploration.

Exploring models of faith development (Fowler, 1981; Genia, 1990, 1995; Wilber, 2000) could help Michael understand the ways in which Ethan's religious life guides, supports, and creates meaning for his existence. Michael might develop the capacity to separate the "religion" (which he likely views as a negative) from the "spirituality" (the lived level of religion done right) as it applies to Ethan. For Michael to share in depth how he creates meaning without a religious background or commitment, including the ethical, moral, philosophical, and other belief structures he uses to move through his life, could strengthen

Ethan's respect for his partner's experiences. Other interventions might include forgiveness work, if there are past hurts in the relationship that need addressing (Luskin, 2003); formal or informal spiritual/religious assessment; and appropriate use of prayer or mindfulness practices.

References

Fowler, J. W. (1981). *Stages of faith: The psychology of human development and the quest for meaning.* San Francisco, CA: Harper & Row.

Fowler, J. W. (1991). Stages in faith consciousness. *New Directions for Child and Adolescent Development, 52,* 27–45.

Genia, V. (1990). Religious development: A synthesis and reformulation. *Journal of Religion and Health, 29,* 85–99.

Genia, V. (1995). *Counseling and psychotherapy for religious clients.* Westport, CT: Prager.

Jacobson, N. S., Follette, W. C., & Pagel, M. (1986). Predicting who will benefit from behavioral marital therapy. *Journal of Consulting and Counseling Psychology, 54,* 518–522.

Johnson, S. (2004). *The practice of emotionally focused couples therapy: Creating connection.* (2nd ed.). New York, NY: Brunner-Routledge.

Luskin. F. (2003). *Forgive for good.* New York, NY: HarperCollins.

Oser, F. K., & Gmünder, P. (1991). *Religious judgment: A developmental perspective.* Birmingham, AL: Religious Education.

Pargament, K. I. (2006). The meaning of spiritual transformation. In J. D. Koss-Chiono & P. Hefner (Eds.), *Spiritual transformation and healing: Anthropological, theological and neuroscientific, and clinical perspectives* (pp. 10–24). New York, NY: Altamira.

Ritter, K. Y., & Terndrup, A. I. (2002). *Handbook of affirmative psychotherapy with lesbians and gay men.* New York, NY: Guilford Press.

Staude, J. (2005). Autobiography as a spiritual practice. *Journal of Gerontological Social Work, 43,* 249–226.doi:10.1300/JO83v45n03_01

Washburn, M. (1995). *The ego and the dynamic ground: A transpersonal theory of human development* (2nd ed.). Albany, NY: State University of New York.

Wiggins-Frame, M. (2003). *Integrating religion and spirituality into counseling: A comprehensive approach.* Pacific Grove, CA: Thompson.

Wilber, K. (2000). *Integral psychology: Consciousness, spirit, psychology, therapy.* Boston, MA: Shambhala.

 ## Reflections
Tracey E. Robert and Virginia A. Kelly

Interfaith marriages have been on the rise. As in this case, a couple's discussion of religious differences often lacks depth and is put off until a serious life decision about parenting, illness, or death needs to be made—when the differences are likely to cause conflict.

A theme apparent throughout this case is one of meaning making and relationships. The couple faced several challenges to a healthy relationship. For one, they appear to be at different developmental stages in regard to sexual identity and religious orientation. However, the interfaith component and the difference in depth of belief between partners can present more difficult barriers. Working competently on a couple's differing values and beliefs can enhance repair and healing of the relationship conflict. Helping them understand the developmental process in many aspects of their lives, not just the physical, can form a bridge for them to pursue meaning and purpose in life. Discussion of spirituality and religion can improve couples counseling in the following ways:

- It can reduce anxiety about differences to introduce a comforting way to explore different beliefs and discover the possibility of acceptance.
- It can identify resources to increase forgiveness or tolerance for differences.
- It can open up new avenues to explore possible activities to share that are sensitive to the partners' differing beliefs and respectful of each.

• • •

Chapter 7

Women in Midlife Transition

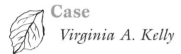

Case

Virginia A. Kelly

Juanita, a 47-year-old Latina woman, came to counseling for the first time. She reported feeling lost and bored and could not identify the cause of her lack of energy and zest for life. Juanita spoke openly about the spiritual void she was experiencing, stating, "Something is missing."

Background

Born in Puerto Rico, Juanita immigrated to the United States with her family at the age of 3. She described herself as "American" but felt her Hispanic roots had a significant influence on who she had become.

Juanita married Greg at the age of 21. They met in college, a large state university close to her home. Greg lived in a dorm on campus, and Juanita was a commuter student. He was one year ahead of her in school. Juanita and Greg decided to marry upon his graduation—before Juanita would have graduated—thinking that she could finish school whenever she wanted to. Both were interested in getting married and starting a family.

Juanita and Greg had been married for 26 years when she came to counseling, and they had three children: Dennis, 25; Kim, 22; and Stuart, 20. Dennis was a graduate student, and Kim and Stuart were undergrads.

Juanita described her marriage as "good." She reported that both she and Greg had been focused on the children throughout their marriage and that they had maintained fairly conventional roles. Greg was an engineer and had been the family's wage earner, and Juanita always had been a stay-at-home mom. She claimed that she loved this role and was grateful to be in a position to have it.

Juanita shared that religion had been a significant part of her childhood. She remembered her family being active in a local Catholic church that had a predominantly Hispanic congregation. She described this part of her life as comforting and meaningful.

Juanita had begun to pull away from churchgoing as an adolescent, and by the time she went to college, she was attending mass only on holidays. Greg had been raised as a Protestant, but his family did not attend church on a regular basis. Without directly addressing the issue of religion in their own family, Juanita and Greg fell into a pattern of attending a local Presbyterian church on major religious holidays.

Incident

Juanita came to me for counseling because she had feelings of low-level depression. The feelings had begun when Stuart left the house. Juanita had been aware of women experiencing empty nest syndrome and attributed her initial symptoms to this. She felt that a phase in her life had ended, and she was unsure of what purpose she might find now that her children were reaching the age of independence. Because Juanita assumed that these feelings were "normal," she did not address them immediately.

Juanita had expected that the symptoms she was experiencing would decrease as she adjusted to her new life without children to care for on a daily basis. However, she began to notice that her initial sadness and sense of loss did not diminish. In fact, they seemed to increase with time. Juanita reported that, in addition to feeling lost and sometimes "useless," she was having difficulty motivating herself to accomplish even simple everyday tasks.

Discussion

My primary goal was to help Juanita identify the root of her low-level depressive symptoms. Working from an empowerment model, I encouraged her to share her story in the hope that she might begin to rediscover a sense of self that seemed to have become dormant.

I hypothesized that Juanita "abandoned" herself when she got married and became a mother and put all her energy and purpose into raising her children and maintaining her family. Although she reported that this role was gratifying and that she was "happy" with her life, this purpose had come to its natural ending.

Juanita needed to make a midlife transition, which required her to reevaluate her life and perhaps identify a new sense of purpose or meaning. Using transition theory, we reviewed her life with a lifeline activity.

Because the process was difficult for Juanita—she reported feeling overwhelmed with the prospect of "starting over"—I introduced an action model that encourages taking small steps and uses cognitive–behavioral therapy interventions to deal with anxiety and the feeling of being overwhelmed.

As a result of our work together, Juanita has discussed the possibility of returning to school, although she finds this idea extremely frightening. She also has shared her desire to reclaim a part of her religious roots and has been seeking out a Catholic church where she feels at home. This step has given her some sense of purpose and awakened a desire to continue to explore her feelings and her options.

Questions

1. Juanita seems to have become disconnected with herself. As a busy full-time mother, she did not attend to her sense of self. How might a counselor continue to address this exploration of sense of self?
2. The primary issue for Juanita seems to involve finding meaning in this new phase of her life. How might a counselor help her explore this issue more deeply?
3. How does religion play into this case, and how might a counselor help Juanita explore this aspect of her life?

 ## Response
Tracey E. Robert

Conceptualizing this case from the viewpoint of wellness, one of the founding constructs of professional counseling, I would recommend integrating spirituality and Juanita's belief system to provide a comprehensive, holistic approach to addressing all the areas of concern during this midlife transition period.

The wellness model provides a strong foundation for exploration and self-discovery that allows for integrating religion and spirituality into the counseling process (Witmer & Sweeney, 1992). Using a wellness framework, which has spirituality at its core, the counselor can address the whole client (Cashwell, 2005). The wellness model also supports the need to be culturally sensitive to clients' beliefs and how they might influence the counseling process, as outlined in the *ACA Code of Ethics* (American Counseling Association [ACA], 2014, Standards C.5 and E.8).

Juanita appears to be dealing with many midlife transitions, including spiritual well-being, career, and family relationships. The counselor should be commended for using a relevant model that tapped into Juanita's strengths and identified finding a new sense of self as the key to dealing with these transitions. Working from an empowerment and feminist approach, she helped Juanita address her lack of energy and motivation and rediscover her sense of self. Using transition theory with a lifeline activity, she helped Juanita explore her sense of purpose and meaning in life. She also used cognitive–behavioral strategies to address Juanita's anxiety and feeling of being overwhelmed.

In reviewing the case with the referring counselor, I would address how the wellness model may be used to more deeply explore Juanita's options in working toward a successful midlife transition.

Exploring Sense of Self

The first question asked is how a counselor might further facilitate Juanita's exploration of sense of self. The counselor stated that Juanita feels "lost" and may not know who she is at this point in her life. Her roles in life have changed and are changing. It also has been noted that a person's spiritual beliefs change over time (Cashwell, 2005; Comas-Diaz, 2012).

A holistic approach to the loss of identity, again incorporating the wellness model, might help address the client's depression and search for meaning. The wellness model "provides strength-based strategies for assessing clients, conceptualizing issues developmentally, and planning interventions to remediate dysfunction and optimize growth" (Myers & Sweeney, 2008, p. 482). By using the narrative and allowing Juanita to tell her story, the counselor has worked well within this model.

I would administer the WEL (the Wellness Evaluation of Lifestyle; Myers, Sweeney, & Witmer, 1998). This assessment tool, grounded in the Adlerian concept of the indivisible self, incorporates life span development and spirituality in the model.

The Wheel of Wellness, part of the WEL assessment tool, allows the counselor to address the whole person—mind, body, and spirit—and to work on multiple domains of the person's life. The model includes five major life tasks—spirituality, self-direction, work and leisure, friendship, and love—and 12 subtasks of self-direction—sense of worth, sense of control, realistic beliefs, emotional awareness and coping, problem solving and creativity, sense of humor, exercise, nutrition, self-care, stress management, gender identity, and cultural identity.

In Juanita's case, the counselor is addressing the spirituality, work and leisure, sense of worth, and emotional awareness and coping areas, as follows:

- Spirituality is a person's personal, private belief system.
- The area of work and leisure includes job satisfaction and contributes to overall well-being.
- Sense of worth refers to the client's self-esteem and self-acceptance.
- The area of emotional awareness and coping refers to the ability to cope with positive and negative emotions as well as being aware of sense of energy and response to life events.

In addition, the wellness model allows for assessment of the client's health and self-care behaviors. In Juanita's case, this assessment would help the counselor eliminate any physical or medical reasons for her anxiety and depression.

Spirituality lies at the core of the model. Research has shown that a strong sense of spiritual well-being can be an indicator of a strong sense of purpose and meaning in life and lead to a lessening of depression or anxiety (Paloutzian & Ellison, 1982; Robert, Young, & Kelly, 2006).

Exploration of Juanita's spiritual well-being could provide her with a stronger sense of self and lessen her feelings of being overwhelmed and depressed. She indicated that her areas of concern were work, religion, and spiritual well-being and reported strengths and assets in her life, including friendships, intact family relationships, and religious beliefs. Knowing a client's concerns and strengths, the counselor can identify areas for development, create a treatment plan, and provide positive feedback and encouragement to help find a stronger sense of self.

Finding Meaning

The second question asked how the counselor can help Juanita further explore the issue of finding meaning in her life. In the descriptions of the symptoms and the demographic information, Juanita has posed an existential question about the meaning and purpose of her life. Persons in midlife often recognize a "spiritual void," as Juanita has reported, and a spiritual awakening may occur, particularly in women (Howell, 2001).

The WEL assessment would provide the counselor and Juanita with key areas to focus on that might contribute to meaning and purpose in life. I would administer the Spiritual Well-Being Scale, an instrument that assesses overall spiritual well-being with the use of Existential Well-Being and Religious Well-Being subscales (Ellison & Paloutzian, 1982). This tool has helped clients identify areas of strength and support in their life.

The work domain often provides a sense of meaning and purpose in life. Working adults who have found job satisfaction have expressed a high sense of existential well-being, defined as meaning and purpose in life (Degges-White & Shurts, 2005; Robert et al., 2006). To explore work satisfaction, the counselor could provide career assessment with a focus on values and interests, which would allow Juanita to form a picture of where she is now and relate that to where she wants to be. This career exploration in midlife provides a rich opportunity for clients to identify strengths and areas to develop.

Juanita mentioned that she is interested in going back to school, although she is frightened. Career assessment has helped clients gain motivation to return to school or to try out volunteer/work opportunities in gathering information about the world of work and the client's place in that world. The connections between work and spirituality have produced research studies showing a strong correlation between job satisfaction and spiritual well-being (Robert et al., 2006). This exploration also can be linked to Juanita's renewed interest in religion.

The Role of Religion

Question 3 asked how the counselor can help Juanita explore the role that religion plays in her life. The wellness model again would give the counselor a starting point to review the importance of religion in her life and culture. As Comas-Diaz (2012) stated, spirituality has been found to enhance women's psychological well-being and health by addressing "self-esteem, resilience, and empowerment" (p. 160). Comas-Diaz (2012) reported on a revival of interest in women's spirituality and the inclusion of minorities and indigenous belief systems. Juanita's earlier religious beliefs and practices anchored in her cultural heritage can offer a path for strengthening identity and self-worth. Tisdell (2002) stated that development of a woman's spirituality can contribute to development of her personal identity.

Integrating the spiritual domain with Juanita's exploration of self can enhance the outcome with a stronger commitment and purpose in pursuing a new course or activity in work, life, or leisure. As I mentioned, research has shown that midlife can be a time for powerful spiritual explorations (Geertsma & Cummings, 2004). Often, midlife transitions cause a feeling of imbalance and sense of something missing, as reported by Juanita. Addressing the life span issues for women at midlife can help Juanita recognize that her feelings of low-level depression might be a natural expression of loss of her role and purpose in her family and life.

Turning to something that had provided meaning in the past— Juanita's nuclear family's participation in a Catholic church that served the Hispanic community—might be a way to address her lack of motivation and purpose. She stated that she would like to reclaim her religious roots. The WEL assessment tool would support that as an area of strength, and integrating that information into goals and objectives for treatment would enhance the counseling process.

Referral to a women's spirituality group might be helpful. Juanita's local church might have a women's group, and there may be spiritually theme-based women's groups that are not affiliated with a church. Research on women in midlife has shown these groups to be therapeutic and meaningful for participants (Geertsma & Cummings, 2004).

An approach based on spirituality and wellness provides the counselor with a case conceptualization that is broad and deep. Exploring

Juanita's definition of spirituality and her religious beliefs could foster a sense of comfort to overcome her anxiety and depression and could provide her with the structure to find new life roles.

References

American Counseling Association. (2014). *ACA code of ethics*. Alexandria, VA: Author.

Cashwell, C. S. (2005). Spirituality and wellness. In J. E. Myers & T. J. Sweeney (Eds.), *Counseling for wellness: Theory, research, and practice* (pp. 197–205). Alexandria, VA: American Counseling Association.

Comas-Diaz, L. (2012). Sophia's dream: The awakening of women's spirituality. In P. K. Lundberg-Love, K. L. Nadal, & M. A. Paludi (Eds.), *Women and mental disorders: Vol. 1. Understanding women's unique life experiences* (pp. 153–165). Santa Barbara, CA: Praeger/ABC-CLIO.

Degges-White, S. E., & Shurts, W. M. (2005). Research on adult wellness. In J. E. Myers & T. J. Sweeney (Eds.), *Counseling for wellness: Theory, research, and practice* (pp. 89–98). Alexandria, VA: American Counseling Association.

Ellison, C. W., & Paloutzian, R. F. (1982). *Spiritual well-being scale*. Nyack, NY: Life Advance.

Geertsma, E. J., & Cummings, A. L. (2004). Midlife transition and women's spirituality groups: A preliminary investigation. *Counseling and Values, 49,* 27–38.

Howell, L. C. (2001). Spirituality and women's midlife development. *Adultspan Journal, 3,* 51–61.

Myers, J. E., & Sweeney, T. J. (2008). Wellness counseling: The evidence base for practice. *Journal of Counseling & Development, 86,* 482–493.

Myers, J. E., Sweeney, T. J., & Witmer, J. M. (1998). *The wellness evaluation of lifestyle*. Palo Alto, CA: Mindgarden.

Paloutzian, R. F., & Ellison, C. W. (1982). Loneliness, spiritual well-being and the quality of life. In L. A. Peplau & D. Pearlman (Eds.), *Loneliness: A sourcebook of current theory, research and therapy* (pp. 224–237). New York, NY: Wiley.

Robert, T. E., Young, J. S., & Kelly, V. A. (2006). The relationship between adult workers' spiritual well-being and job satisfaction: A preliminary study. *Counseling and Values, 50,* 165–175.

Tisdell, E. (2002). Spiritual development and cultural context in the lives of women adult educators for social change. *Journal of Adult Development, 9,* 127–140.

Witmer, J. M., & Sweeney, T. J. (1992). A holistic model for wellness and prevention over the life span. *Journal of Counseling & Development, 71,* 140–148.

Reflections
Tracey E. Robert and Virginia A. Kelly

The population of persons in midlife is growing. Juanita's case demonstrates the plight of many because they often struggle with their life direction during that period. Midlife is when they are most affected by change, with frequent shifts in life roles and multiple roles to fill.

Some persons cope with change, some cannot, some lose their way. They often are seeking balance, direction, and connection. Persons who enter counseling often do so at midlife rather than earlier because that's when many life challenges arise.

Women in particular have difficulty in making midlife transitions because of their multiple life roles and caregiver responsibilities. Women's identity development during midlife often is a focus of spiritual exploration.

Traditional counseling focuses on the physical and psychological domains. Counseling for persons in midlife transition that does not include a spiritual focus might miss career and "aging well" issues and the need to assess the whole person.

Midlife is an important stage that presents counselors with multiple challenges and calls for a comprehensive approach to the counseling process. Because the spiritual domain is very active during midlife, integrating the components of spirituality during assessment, diagnosis, and treatment is essential for effective practice. Counseling for persons in midlife transition that has a spiritual focus improves the counseling process in the following ways:

- Connection, enhancement of self-esteem, and an improved sense of overall well-being cannot be attained without integrating the spiritual side of the client.
- To cope with change that occurs during midlife transitions, clients would benefit from the mind–body–spirit connection, according to the World Health Organization definition of wellness.
- Our experience in practice has shown that if a person gains a high sense of spiritual well-being, then life satisfaction, job satisfaction, and self-esteem improve.

• • •

Chapter 8 Older Adults

Case

Summer M. Reiner

Al, a 65-year-old White male, reluctantly came to counseling for the first time in his life. He reported that his significant other of 20 years pushed him to come to counseling. She threatened to leave him if he did not "work out his problems with dying."

Background

Born in New York City, Al lived with his loving parents until his mother died when he was 8 years old. Shortly after his mother's death, Al's father placed him and his six younger siblings in an orphanage. Al resented his father for leaving him with the cruel nuns and never visiting.

Al left the orphanage when he joined the military at age 18 during the Vietnam War. His job was to collect dead soldiers and their body parts. He often felt ill by the gruesomeness of the bodies and saddened that some soldiers could never be pieced back together.

Once the war ended, Al found a great-paying job as an artist for product promotion. He also met Mary, whom he married at age 25. Eleven years and three children later, Mary decided she was in love with someone else and divorced Al. He tried to maintain a relationship with his children, but Mary made it challenging. He resented paying child support to a woman who kept him from his children.

As a single man, Al tried to find new interests to fill his time. He began spending time with his friend Jack and Jack's wife, Dolores.

Over the years, the three became very close. Nearly 10 years into the friendship, Jack became ill. As Jack was dying, he told Al, "Take good care of my wife when I am gone." Al comforted his friend and told him that he would take very good care of Dolores.

When Jack died, he left Dolores with a heap of bills, Social Security income, and a child who was in high school. She knew she could not maintain their home of 20 years financially. Dolores was devastated that her son would lose his father and home in the same year. Seeing her burden, Al suggested that he help Dolores with her finances by becoming her housemate.

Al and Dolores were extremely compatible housemates and spent nearly all their time together. Al, however, did not accompany Dolores to church. Al was not religious and really questioned the existence of God. Although Dolores and Al had been able to overcome their religious and spiritual differences in the past, it was becoming an issue.

Incident

Al had diabetes, and after years of poor disease management, he started to have serious complications and was facing leg amputation. Dolores was struggling with "watching another man die." She insisted that they begin planning for their deaths. She wanted to know how he wanted his body prepared, the types of ceremonies he would want, what his obituary should read, and how he expected her to pay for it all. She was insistent that she not have to "bury another man" without his help in planning. Finally, Dolores wanted Al to make amends with God so that he would be in heaven with her rather than in hell.

Al could not face his own mortality. He would break into a cold sweat thinking about ceremonies, burial options, or seeing his name in an obituary. He believed that if he thought about his death, he would die. He was terrified to die. He also did not want to think about God.

Discussion

In working with Al, I found that he displayed an unconditional love for those in his life (Dolores, her adult children, and her grandchildren). His father and previous wife, however, were spoken of with great resentment. I noted a similar resentment when he spoke of "a possible God."

I hypothesized that Al was experiencing some attachment issues (Bowlby, 1969), which may have been affecting his spiritual attachment (Reinert, Edwards, & Hendrix, 2009). I suspected that his sense of abandonment affected his sense of self, so I conducted a lifestyle interview and asked him to complete adult attachment and lifestyle inventories (Peluso, Peluso, White, & Kern, 2004), the Wellness Evaluation of Lifestyle (Myers, Sweeney, & Witmer, 1998), and the Experiences in Close Relationships—Revised (Fraley, Waller, & Brennan, 2000).

As a therapist who draws from Adlerian principles, I thought it would be helpful to encourage Al to look at his sense of purpose and belonging. He acknowledged that he struggled with both. He identified his purpose as making others happy, which also helped him belong. He expressed great fear about losing Dolores—the only person who had not left him *yet*.

I also encouraged Al to discuss his fear of death. He shared that he was afraid to die because he "would rot in the ground" or "go to hell." He felt challenged to believe in a God who would have abandoned him and allowed so many bad things to happen to him.

Questions

1. How do I get Al to explore his eventual death without traumatizing him?
2. How do I help Al address his sense of abandonment from his parents, his God, and his possible abandonment by Dolores?
3. How do I help Al find more meaning and purpose in this late stage of his life?

References

Bowlby, J. (1969). *Attachment and loss: Vol. 1. Attachment.* London, UK: Hogarth Press.

Fraley, R. C., Waller, N. G., & Brennan, K. A. (2000). An item-response theory analysis of self report measures of adult attachment. *Journal of Personality and Social Psychology, 78,* 350–365.

Myers, J. E., Sweeney, T. J., & Witmer, J. M. (1998). *The wellness evaluation of lifestyle.* Palo Alto, CA: Mindgarden.

Peluso, P. R., Peluso, J. P., White, J. F., & Kern, R. M. (2004). A comparison of attachment theory and individual psychology: A review of the literature. *Journal of Counseling & Development, 82,* 139–145.

Reinert, D. F., Edwards, C. E., & Hendrix, R. R. (2009). Attachment theory and religiosity: A summary of empirical research with implications for counseling Christian clients. *Counseling and Values, 53,* 112–125.

Response
E. Christine Moll

Bartlett (1919) credited Benjamin Franklin for the adage, "in this world nothing is certain except death and taxes." However, death can present a "mortality crisis," as Sheehy (1995) suggested, which appears to be the case with the client, Al, and his partner, Dolores.

Significant losses have occurred within both of their lives. In addition, each appears to be dealing with grief. Kübler-Ross and Kessler (2005) proposed the following:

> Grief is an emotional, spiritual, and psychological journey to healing . . . we don't appreciate its healing powers, yet they are extraordinary and wondrous . . . many problems in our lives stem from grief unresolved and unhealed. When we do not work through our grief, we lose an opportunity to heal our soul, psyche and heart. (p. 190)

Underlying Al's feelings of abandonment, his anger with his father (perhaps his mother as well), his former wife, and God, in addition to his fear of death, all seem to stem from his unresolved grief. It does not surprise me that the assessment instruments used by the counselor confirmed his or her hypothesis that Al displays attachment-related stresses. The narrative of the trauma he experienced throughout his life span presents a heartbreaking story of a life lived in grief. I concur with the counselor's wellness perspective and pursuit of an Adlerian-based "sense of purpose and belonging" with Al.

Before consulting with Al's counselor, I reflected on the benefits of using Frankl's logotherapy (Viktor Frankl Institute of Logotherapy, n.d.), which stemmed from his experience in concentration camps during the Holocaust. Frankl believed that persons are motivated by a "'will to meaning,' an inner pull to find a meaning in life." He proposed that everyone has the freedom or choice to find "meaning," even in life's most devastating moments. Persons can discover this meaning in three ways: (a) create a work or do a deed, (b) experience something or encounter someone, and (c) choose how to deal with unavoidable suffering (Viktor Frankl Institute of Logotherapy, n.d.).

Ramsey (2012) cited a Frankl student, Kimble, who wrote extensively regarding a person's later life and the critical need to make sense and meaning of life, including bewildering losses throughout life and changes that occur in later life. Ramsey suggested, "Resiliency is enhanced when elders find the strength to rearrange the events of the past, present, and future, so that what is ultimately important can be placed at the forefront of one's life stage and what is penultimate can recede into the background" (p. 133). Al may need some assistance to gain a dose of resiliency and find meaning or purpose in his life.

However, meaning making and resiliency do not occur naturally. Suggestions toward meaning making may be met with resistance, fear, and anger—feelings similar to Al's. Parsons and Peluso (2012, p. 92) recommended that "reframing can help to shift the focus to more on how one lives and quality of life, especially one's physical health"—today versus throughout the person's life span. Supporting Al's counselor's wellness perspective, Parsons and Peluso (2012, p. 92) stated, "To underscore the importance of health and active living, many studies are now pointing to the fact that a decline in physical health may lead to co-morbid conditions of decreased mental health." Al's issues with diabetes and perhaps other health issues may not mix well with his anger and sense of abandonment.

Dolores insisted Al seek counseling after years of his poor health choices, particularly with his diabetes. She did not want to "bury another man." Al may fear Dolores abandoning him, but it appears that she worries that, with his choices, Al will abandon her first.

Combining the counselor's Adlerian-based "sense of purpose and belonging" with some narrative therapy, Beck's cognitive restructuring or shifting, and couples counseling, I look to the counselor's questions. I have reordered them to provide a progression for the therapeutic journey.

Reframing Abandonment

Question 2 asked how I might help Al address his sense of abandonment from his parents and his God and his possible abandonment by Dolores. Al carved out a life, seemingly well lived and enjoyed, with Dolores, her children, and her grandchildren. However, he did not arrive at this moment in life without time spent as a youth or young adult—Al reflected on his youth and young adulthood, as well as his dad and first wife, with harsh feelings.

In helping Al retell his life story, the counselor could use difficult events as metaphors for lessons learned and suggest a revised midlife and older adulthood through those metaphors. "Through narrative methods in both clinical practice and empirical research, the spiritual dimension of particular life events can be discerned within the telling of daily life experiences, or through deeper reflecting on those events" (Ramsey, 2012, p. 35). As they age, clients may not so much care about the "what" that occurred years earlier, but they may now place significance on the "why" and how difficult events played a role in the bigger picture of their life span (Ramsey, 2012).

The events in Al's childhood, adolescence, and young adulthood contributed to what Beck (1995) called "core beliefs." Beck (1995) stated that these all-encompassing thoughts about oneself and one's world are formed early in one's life and are unyielding and tough to change. Jameson and Cully (2011) suggested that completely removing dysfunctional thinking may not be possible with older adults, but "targeting more surface-level automatic thoughts and possibly intermediate beliefs may serve as viable and meaningful goals" (p. 307).

Thus, Al's mother's death and his eventual placement in an orphanage were most unfortunate and sad. It is certainly understandable how an 8-year-old boy might feel abandoned. However, I wonder if he would want his mother to continue life unable to mother him and his siblings because she had a chronic, debilitating illness. In hindsight, as awful as the orphanage might seem, I wonder what life might have been if Al's dad needed to work two jobs and depend on Al to parent his siblings. In addition, though Al knows the pain of abandonment, I wonder if his lack of self-care and his diabetes possibly leading to a premature death might be considered as abandoning Dolores.

Finding Meaning and Purpose

Question 3 asked how I might help Al find more meaning and purpose in this late stage of his life. Kelly (1995) delineated how religion contributes to a person's development in the following positive ways: reinforcing a youngster's appreciation for trust and hope, providing a framework for developing identity with values during adolescence, challenging/inviting the need to contribute to the community through generativity, and helping the youngster reflect on life with a sense of meaning. However, it might be argued that, for Al, religion contributed to the negative, or dystonic, elements of Erikson's life-cycle stages. Scholars (Erikson, 1997) often present the syntonic qualities of the life stages first (e.g., trust, autonomy). Sometimes life confronts a person first with the dystonic characteristics (e.g., mistrust, shame/doubt), with challenges he or she might not overcome, especially someone like Al who has little support to handle the life tasks presented. Erik Erikson's wife, Joan, in writing the extended version of *The Life Cycle Completed*, suggested that he might remind us, "Despair expresses the feeling that the time is now short, too short for the attempt to start another life and to try out alternate roads" (Erikson, 1997, p. 113).

Erik Erikson's eighth stage invites a personal ownership of one's life to date. Al appears to regret missed opportunities rather than welcome or accept those moments well lived (e.g., honoring slain veterans and their families with appropriate care in the field-morgues; honoring his friends Jack and Dolores with his continuing friendship, care, and concern). With little time to begin a whole life anew, Al can obtain some cognitive shifts and find meaning in his current life, from this moment forward.

Weber and Orsborn (2012) suggested that fear to confront the important, meaning-making questions of life may be common. "We want clarity and certainty, and in wanting these, we are sometimes willing to settle for lies and illusions that mask as truth, rather than face the following deeper existential and spiritual questions" (p. 12). They offered questions for honest reflection. For Al, these questions might look like the following:

1. Have your diabetes and health concerns stirred up some "life dust" that might give you pause to consider the realities of life?
2. How might your past beliefs (about yourself, your family, and even God) perhaps have been partially illusions and your way of protecting yourself from more pain?

3. Through the years, especially recently, might you allow your sense of self and self-worth to increase as a result of your relationship with Dolores and her family, even with the limitations of your diabetes, profound lifelong losses, and your sense of isolation in the past?

In helping Al come to terms with the dystonic elements of his life, the counselor could work with him to find meaning across his life experience, perhaps to take responsibility for his health concerns, and to begin to grieve appropriately for his life losses. This work would lead him to the ninth stage of the life cycle, Gerotranscendence. Joan Erikson (Erikson, 1997) defined this stage in the following way:

> I have found that "transcendence" becomes very much alive if it is activated into "transcen*dance*," which speaks to soul and body and challenges it to rise above the dystonic, clinging aspects of our worldly existence that burden and distract us from true growth and aspiration. (p. 127)

Erikson (1997) stated that transcen*dance* moves persons to retry skills left by the wayside years ago. These might include play, music, and hobbies, "and above all, a major leap above and beyond the fear of death. It provides an opening forward into the unknown with a trusting leap . . . [that] demands an honest and steadfast humility" (p. 127).

Discussions About Death

Question 1 asked how I might get Al to explore his eventual death without traumatizing him. As the counselor and Al make progress toward shifting former core beliefs and finding meaning in a life he previously viewed negatively, I suggest the counselor invite Dolores to join with Al in the counseling process. In a conversation recorded in Carlson, Peluso, Figenbaum, and Oles (2012), Carlson well summed up my attempt to respond to the counselor's questions:

> Therapists need to be able to have a way to talk about the reality of death. Only death and taxes are sure things. However, we act like death won't happen to us. I have my own beliefs and I'm going to share them with people if asked but I think it's more important to talk about and discuss what it means to them.
>
> And, all sorts of people want to find meaning in their life and a lot of people are trying to avoid death and yet getting older. We talk about death directly and indirectly, for example, "what do you want to do before you die" or "what's your bucket list?" There is [sic] all sorts of ways to talk about the reality of death. Everyone has his or her own views. (p. 238)

The counselor could invite Al to share a summary of their therapeutic conversations with Dolores and explain why he invited her to join the counseling process. The reasons could include to share and discuss each of their views of death, their fears, their beliefs, and their anticipatory grief regarding the loss of each other and their own deaths. Eventually the conversations could address Dolores and Al's preferences for their "final arrangements."

Kübler-Ross and Kessler's stages of grief (2005) are similar to Kübler-Ross's stages of death and dying (1969). A person may experience some or all of the stages (denial, anger, bargaining, depression, and acceptance) before a loved one dies and experience the stages again after the loved one's death. Sharing the stages of grieving with Dolores and Al could lead to an interesting conversation about whether one or the other is "stuck" at any given stage when considering the death of loved ones. The conversation might include questions about what support the couple needs and suggestions they have to move forward.

Kübler-Ross and Kessler (2005) stated, "The loss happens in time, in fact in a moment, but its aftermath lasts a lifetime" (p. 168). Thus, grief is something persons learn to either tolerate or deny. In fact, grief is a journey that has the potential to bring with it some healing. "That pain and our love are forever connected. To avoid the pain of loss would be to avoid the love and life we share ... to deny that loss is to deny the love" (p. 168). Such ideas could present Al and Dolores with additional cognitive shifts and help each move forward with previous losses as well as anticipate the eventual loss of one another.

Combining Principles and Spirituality

The use of principles from Adler, Beck, and narrative therapy and the infusion of spirituality into the counseling process could empower Al to reach these goals: revisit the losses he experienced throughout his life, find meaning amidst the trauma, perhaps reframe his core beliefs, and move through the stages of grieving toward acceptance. The process could help him gain a more positive view of God. Inviting Dolores into the conversations might help the couple navigate their fear of abandonment and discuss their anticipatory grief and anxiety together.

Kessler reflected on his own grief after the death of Kübler-Ross, his friend and writing partner:

> When we first lose a loved one, our lives feel meaningless. As we experience the five stages of grief, we are returned to a life with the possibility of meaningfulness that was unimaginable when we first dealt with the loss. I believe that grief and its unique healing powers take us from meaninglessness to meaningfulness again. If there is a sixth stage, I would call it "meaningfulness," or "renewed meaning." We do not get over our loss, we don't find recovery; we may find renewed meaning and enrichment for having known our loved one. (Kübler-Ross & Kessler, 2005, p. 189)

Dolores and Al have loved, lost, and survived together. With the counselor's assistance, they can help each other move through their life until death separates them.

References

Bartlett, J. (1919). *Familiar quotations* (10th ed., no. 3952). Retrieved from http://www.bartleby.com/100/245.24.html

Beck, J. S. (1995). *Cognitive therapy: Basics and beyond.* New York, NY: Guilford Press.

Carlson, J., Peluso, P. R., Figenbaum, N., & Oles, K. (2012). An interview with Jon Carlson. In P. R. Peluso, R. E. Watts, & M. Parson (Eds.), *Changing aging, changing family therapy: Practicing with 21st century realities* (pp. 229–246). New York, NY: Routledge.

Erikson, J. (1997). Extended version with new chapters on the ninth stage of development. In E. H. Erikson, *The life cycle completed* (pp. 105–129). New York, NY: Norton.

Jameson, J. P., & Cully, J. A., (2011). Cognitive behavioral therapy for older adults in the primary care setting. In K. H. Sorocco & S. Lauderdale (Eds.), *Cognitive behavior therapy with older adults* (pp. 291–316). New York, NY: Springer.

Kelly, E. W. (1995). *Spirituality and religion in counseling and psychotherapy: Diversity in theory and practice.* Alexandria, VA: American Counseling Association.

Kübler-Ross, E. (1969). *On death and dying: What the dying have to teach doctors, nurses, clergy, and their own families.* New York, NY: MacMillan.

Kübler-Ross, E., & Kessler, D. (2005). *On grief and grieving: Finding the meaning of grief through the five stages of loss.* New York, NY: Scribner.

Parsons, M., & Peluso, P. R. (2012). Physical health in the elderly. In P. R. Peluso, R. E. Watts, & M. Parson (Eds.), *Changing aging, changing family therapy: Practicing with 21st century realities* (pp. 79–95). New York, NY: Routledge.

Ramsey, J. (2012). Spirituality and aging: Cognitive, affective and relational pathways to resiliency. *Annual Review of Gerontology & Geriatrics, 32,* 131–152.

Sheehy, G. (1995). Mortality crisis. In *New passages: Mapping your life across time* (pp. 159–175). New York, NY: Ballantine Books.

Viktor Frankl Institute of Logotherapy. (n.d.). *About logotherapy.* Retrieved from http://www.logotherapyinstitute.org/About_Logotherapy.html

Weber, R. L., & Orsborn, C. (2013). The question(s) of age: Calling for a new vision of spiritual aging. *Aging Today, 34,* 11–12.

 ## Reflections

Tracey E. Robert and Virginia A. Kelly

In 2012, the Substance Abuse and Mental Health Services Administration and the National Council on Aging issued briefs on behavioral health issues for older adults—including anxiety, depression, and an increase in substance abuse—that support an integrated approach to promoting physical and behavioral health. A wellness/prevention model that integrates spirituality into the care and treatment of older adults is recommended.

Older adults often reflect on their lives and review life events through a critical lens. The lessons learned and resulting self-understanding are gifts that can enhance the ability to change and heal at this later stage of life. Al has harbored anger, loss, abandonment, and fear for many years. What has worked in the past for him—denial and detachment—is not working now. When used to address the developmental task of integrity versus despair, spirituality can provide hope and healing as well as coping mechanisms. Using a spiritual focus for counseling older adults can improve the process in these ways:

- A spiritual assessment can identify attachment and loss issues and create opportunities to conduct a comprehensive life review.
- Spiritual interventions, such as journaling, spiritual bibliotherapy, and meditation, can enhance access to early trauma and anger issues.
- Discussion of spiritual virtues, such as compassion, forgiveness, gratitude, and hope, can provide healing and increased coping strategies for this stage of life.

* * *

Chapter 9 End of Life

Case

Eileen R. O'Shea

Laura, an 18-year-old patient, recently had been diagnosed with Ewing sarcoma, a malignant tumor in her tibia. The tumor was small and had not metastasized to any organs, but with treatment, the best prognosis was a 75% chance of cure (Arndt, 2007). A bedside nurse was perplexed at how best to support Laura as her life was changing suddenly and drastically, and Laura was grappling with some overwhelming questions about the meaning of her life. She asked, "Why me? What have I done to deserve this?"

Background

Laura was the older of two children in her family, the only daughter. Her family was fairly religious, attending a Protestant church on a regular basis.

Laura was a senior in high school who had achieved high honors. Her dream was to become a graphic arts designer. During the previous summer, she had toured several colleges and ranked her top three favorites. She was elated to be accepted to her first choice. Things were coming together—the time and effort she had dedicated to her studies had resulted in the promise of a bright new future.

Laura also was looking forward to her senior prom and spending time with her friends to celebrate their last semester of high school together. Each friend had personal struggles because each was focused on making career choices and planning his or her next steps after high school. This final semester was to be an exciting time of connection, transition, and celebration for all.

Then Laura received her cancer diagnosis and learned that her college plans needed to be postponed so that she could receive urgent treatment. Also, attending the senior prom with her friends would not be an option.

Incident

Two days before her hospital admission, Laura had presented to her pediatrician complaining of right lower leg pain and calf tenderness. She also had a low-grade fever and was limping as a result of the pain. Laura stated that she hurt her leg while playing soccer with her friends a few weeks earlier. Her pediatrician ordered X-ray films and an MRI of her right lower leg. The images revealed a small tumor on the right tibia.

After delivering this unexpected diagnosis to Laura and her family, the pediatrician referred Laura to a nearby children's hospital that specialized in pediatric cancer care. Upon admittance, Laura met a team of medical health professionals. Laura did not have much time to process all the information provided to her and her family. Further tests, including a bone marrow biopsy, were needed to determine the type of tumor. Treatment most likely would include chemotherapy and radiation or surgery. Laura could not comprehend all of this. All she could think about was the "big C" word. She had been diagnosed with cancer.

The bedside nurse was spending time in Laura's hospital room to prepare her for the chemotherapy that would begin once the cell type of the tumor was determined. Laura was extremely quiet and distant, and her family and the oncology team were quite concerned at the change in her behavior. Laura was typically a vibrant and outgoing person. She loved to laugh and enjoyed talking with her friends about high school life. For the previous 48 hours, Laura had not wanted to talk to her parents or to her friends. She refused phone calls and visitors. As a result, the oncology team ordered a psychiatric evaluation.

The psychiatric evaluation revealed that Laura was depressed, and antidepressant medication was prescribed to assist her during her cancer journey. However, the bedside nurse perceived that some greater emotions were gnawing away at Laura. Rather than discuss the new treatment regimen, the nurse asked Laura how she was managing all of the information that the varied physicians and specialists were providing. Laura said that she was "devastated" and that all her dreams had been shattered.

Laura asked her nurse, "What has been the purpose of my life? Why did I work so hard to achieve the milestone of receiving a high school diploma with honors? Will I have cancer forever? Will my cancer respond to treatment? What if it does not? And what does this all mean for my future? Do I have a future, or *am I going to die?*"

Discussion

Holistic nursing care includes addressing the spiritual domain. As a nurse and an educator, I suggested that the bedside nurse consider discussing Laura's spirituality. Patients often pose questions of a spiritual nature to their nurses because a special bond is formed between them. However, nurses sometimes overlook providing spiritual care because there is confusion about who is best prepared to make this assessment (Hart & Schneider, 1997).

Like other health care professionals, nurses question whether spiritual discussions fall solely under the practice of pastoral care. Because nurses often establish trusting relationships with their patients, they are entrusted with private conversations and challenging questions. Not knowing how to address these intense questions may entice a health care provider to change the subject rather than be present and confront spiritual issues directly. In this case study, the nurse realized that addressing Laura's spiritual needs was a vital part of her care. She was committed to supporting Laura throughout the cancer journey.

Together, the nurse and I discussed developing a spiritual plan of care that would include collaboration with the pastoral care department. The initial step was to conduct a spiritual screening by using the Faith and Belief, Importance, Community, and Address in Care questionnaire (Brooks & Ennis-Durstine, 2011). Then, the results would serve to identify Laura's spiritual needs and to describe her relationship with her faith community. In addition, the screening would provide important information for the support structures and personnel that could be added to Laura's health care team.

It takes a multidisciplinary team to fully address all the needs that arise when a child or adolescent battles a life-threatening illness. Few teenagers ever experience a cancer diagnosis or contemplate what it means to die. Using a spiritual plan of care and seeking counseling from pastoral care aided Laura's recovery. The cancer responded to medical treatment, and after Laura's spiritual needs were addressed, her personality returned to baseline. She learned to trust her friends and family to support her through the cancer journey. One year later, she was able to pursue her college dreams.

Questions

1. How can spiritual counseling support Laura during this time of shock, anger, and disbelief?
2. How do the roles of pastoral care differ or align with those of a spiritual counselor?
3. How can the roles of pastoral care and/or counseling services support staff nurses (care for caregivers) during times of personal spiritual distress or emotional burdens, such as a patient's suffering and/or death?

References

Arndt, C. A. S. (2007). Malignant tumors of bone. In R. M. Kleigman, R. E. Behrman, H. B. Jenson, & B. F. Stanton (Eds.), *Nelson textbook of pediatrics* (pp. 2146–2151). Philadelphia, PA: Elsevier.

Brooks, J., & Ennis-Durstine, K. (2011). Faith, hope, and love: An interdisciplinary approach to providing spiritual care. In J. Wolfe, P. Hinds, & B. Sourkes (Eds.), *Textbook of interdisciplinary pediatric palliative care* (pp. 111–118). Philadelphia, PA: Elsevier.

Hart, D., & Schneider, D. (1997). Spiritual care for children with cancer. *Seminars in Oncology Nursing, 13,* 263–270.

Response
Janice Miner Holden

From the perspective of my guiding meta-theory of counseling, Ken Wilber's (1999, 2000a, 2000b) integral theory, I endorse many aspects of the health care services described in the case of Laura. Indeed, even the seminal 19th-century figure in the history of modern nursing, Florence Nightingale, included in her view of patient care a nurse's attention to the patient's spiritual needs. Numerous contemporary nursing organizations have affirmed such attention through their ethical and other guiding documents (Mandalise, 2013). Thus, a nurse who perceives that a patient may be in spiritual distress is functioning within his or her scope of practice to attend to the matter through discourse with the patient, assessment of the patient's needs, and development of a treatment plan based on the assessment.

The Faith and Belief, Importance and Influence, Community, and Address in Care (FICA) instrument, or FICA Spirituality History Tool, that Christina Puchalski (2000, 2010; Puchalski & Romer, 2000) developed seems fitting because she considered it a spiritual tool appropriate for any clinician to use (Puchalski, 2010, p. 54). The multidisciplinary team approach also seems ideal to ensure that all interrelated aspects of Laura's needs and wishes—biological, psychological, social, and spiritual—are addressed.

Applying Integral Theory

As I read the case, I also had some thoughts and questions, many arising from my theoretical orientation. From an integral perspective, persons are conceptualized primarily in terms of developmental level and the four-quadrant model (Fall, Holden, & Marquis, 2010). Clues about Laura's developmental level are her age as a late teen and her presumed intelligence as evidenced by her academic success; she likely is predominantly functioning at Level 4, Rules and Roles—identifying and fulfilling the rules and roles of society—with some emergence into Level 5, Formal Reflexive—transcending conformity through independent reflection. Because encounters with existential issues characterize Level 6, it begins to become clear how diagnosis with a potentially terminal illness could thrust Laura into a developmental crisis in which she is confronted with issues beyond her prevailing developmental level—a phenomenon addressed in the case description with the assertion "Few teenagers . . . contemplate what it means to die."

The case description also reveals some information relevant to each of the quadrants. The lower right and lower left quadrants represent the person's sociocultural context. Socially—referring to the externally observable systems of which a person is a member—Laura is a 21st-century (presumably) U.S. citizen, probably from the middle to upper class, presumably active in public school and a Protestant church, and currently involved deeply in the allopathic medical establishment. She is the older of two children in a nuclear family presumably, intact with her biological parents. She has a network of friends. Culturally—referring to the internally subjective shared meanings and values of the groups to which a person belongs—Laura seems to have values and goals characteristic of Western culture. Although her ethnicity was not specified in the case, values in her cultural world appear to include education and professional preparation.

The upper right behavioral quadrant addresses the person's exterior, observable phenomena. Included in this quadrant are Laura's cancer diagnosis, depression diagnosis, and medicines and treatments that address both diagnoses. The upper left experiential quadrant addresses the person's interior, subjective world of feelings, thoughts, and beliefs. Laura's planfulness about college and her career indicates that she is future focused with assumptions about how life would unfold and how to achieve security and fulfillment in life; in that context, again, it is understandable that diagnosis with a potentially terminal illness would provoke an existential crisis involving both an encounter with existential vulnerability and death and accompanying existential questions about causality in and meaning of life. Her feeling of devastation that "all her dreams had been shattered" represents a very strong reaction, even in the face of the circumstances, suggesting possible cognitive distortions known to characterize depression (Beck, 2011).

Spiritual Worldview

What is not clear from the case description is Laura's spiritual/religious worldview. Having attended Protestant church throughout her upbringing, she probably held a Protestant worldview, but that should be hypothesized and not assumed. Other possibilities include that she participated in church only superficially for its social benefits or to appease her parents, had long or recently questioned the Protestant faith deeply and may not have shared this doubt with others, or recently had decided to leave the Protestant church without as yet having disclosed the decision to anyone.

I also noted that Laura's questions were exclusively existential; that is, they did not include explicit spiritual or religious references. Thus, although confrontation with existential dilemmas often progresses to spiritual unfolding (Assagioli, 1971), it is not clear from the case description whether Laura had, as yet, connected the existential crisis she faced with spirituality—her personal sense of meaning about and connectedness to something greater than herself—or religion—the social institution addressing the spiritual domain in earthly life.

For these reasons, from an integral perspective, the initial decision to collaborate with the pastoral care department before administering the FICA would be considered premature. Rather, the nurse, under the supervision of the case author, would do well to first administer the FICA to learn from Laura about her spiritual or religious affiliation and/or belief system; the importance of faith in her life; her own perception of her membership in a spiritual, religious, or secular support community; and what referral options from the many listed in the FICA she would prefer. Examples in FICA include "referral to chaplains, pastoral counselors, spiritual directors, journaling, and music or art therapy . . . sometimes . . . simply [for the healthcare provider oneself] to listen and support the person" (Puchalski, 2010, p. 55).

Having acquired this information, the nurse and supervisor could discuss how to connect Laura to the sources of support she preferred, if any, which may not include involvement of the pastoral care department. So, for example, Laura might have an established relationship with a secular counselor with whom she wanted to resume counseling, and her mother could make the arrangements, obviating the need for the pastoral care department to be involved. Although many options would include the department's involvement, not all would, so consultation with them is better not assumed but rather held as a possible aspect of the treatment plan.

In a similar manner, the case description includes that antidepressant medication was prescribed upon Laura's diagnosis with depression. In light of the actual and potential losses Laura was confronting, her depression is understandable, and in light of an apparent absence of a history of depression, it may be reactive rather than endogenous. Although medication is a viable option—and assuming that, as the case description implies, she is not suicidal—other options may be equally quick and effective at alleviating her depressive symptoms, such as counseling with or without a pastoral or spiritual component. In addition to their standard psychiatric assessment, psychiatric health care team members likely would serve Laura best by administering the FICA themselves and providing Laura with the full range of options to address her depression. These options might include immediate medication or medication as an alternative after nonmedical interventions had been attempted.

Answering Spiritual Questions

With these ideas in mind, I respond to the three questions. The first is how spiritual counseling might be a source of support for Laura as she grieves the actual and potential losses she faces, and the second is how the roles of pastoral care compare with those of spiritual counseling. From an integral perspective, answers to these questions would be good to include when discussing Laura's options with her.

I might say, for example, that in the process of facing losses both immediate and potentially long-term—depending on Laura's spiritual and religious beliefs and affiliations—she might find it helpful to talk with a spiritual or religious counselor. Among other things, the counselor could help her make meaning of her unexpected situation and find unique sources of support in coping with and possibly overcoming it. Options include a spiritual counselor, someone who focuses on the spiritual aspect of clients in a way that may or may not include reference to a specific religion, and a pastoral counselor, someone whose practice is based in the Judeo-Christian tradition and is most likely to be Christian (Clinebell, 2011; Doehring, 2006; Townsend, 2009). Both professionals' purpose is to help clients find spiritual and/or religious resources to manage life challenges.

The third question addresses pastoral care and spiritual counseling services for support staff nurses during times of personal spiritual distress or emotional burdens. Indeed, the same principles apply for them as for their medical patients. Witnessing the suffering and death of patients, especially those with whom caregivers have become emotionally attached, can contribute to the development of problematic conditions, including depression, posttraumatic stress disorder, and burnout.

Options include making use of pastoral counseling (for nurses who affiliate with the Christian religion), counseling associated with another faith (for nurses who affiliate with a religion other than Christianity), and spiritual counseling (for nurses who prefer a more ecumenically spiritual perspective, regardless of whether they are affiliated with a particular religion). Nurses seeking referrals might consult with leaders of their religious communities or hospital chaplains trained to accommodate both spiritual and a variety of religious perspectives.

Meeting Psychospiritual Challenges

Serious medical conditions can provoke psychospiritual challenges for both patients and their caregivers. Members of health care teams do well to monitor the apparent spiritual well-being of their patients, themselves, and each other. They need to stand ready with assessment and treatment options that can help in coping with medical crises—some of the greatest existential challenges that life presents.

References

Assagioli, R. (1971). *Psychosynthesis: A collection of basic writings.* New York, NY: Penguin.

Beck, J. S. (2011). *Cognitive behavior therapy: Basics and beyond* (2nd ed.). New York, NY: Guilford Press.

Clinebell, H. J. (2011). *Basic types of pastoral care & counseling: Resources for the ministry of healing and growth.* Nashville, TN: Abingdon Press.

Doehring, C. (2006). *The practice of pastoral care.* Louisville, KY: Westminster John Knox Press.

Fall, K. A., Holden, J. M., & Marquis, A. (2010). *Theoretical models of counseling and psychotherapy* (2nd ed.). New York, NY: Routledge.

Mandalise, J. (2013). The nursing profession and near-death experiences: A personal and professional update. *Journal of Near-Death Studies, 32,* 59–79.

Puchalski, C. M. (2000). Spiritual assessment tool. *Journal of Palliative Medicine, 3,* 131.

Puchalski, C. M. (2010). Formal and informal spiritual assessment. *Asian Pacific Journal of Cancer Prevention, 11*(MECC Supplement), 51–57.

Puchalski, C. M., & Romer, A. L. (2000). Taking a spiritual history allows clinicians to understand patients more fully. *Journal of Palliative Medicine, 3,* 129–137.

Townsend, L. (2009). *Introduction to pastoral counseling.* Nashville, TN: Abingdon Press.

Wilber, K. (1999). *The collected works of Ken Wilber* (Vols. 1–4). Boston, MA: Shambhala.

Wilber, K. (2000a). *The collected works of Ken Wilber* (Vols. 5–8). Boston, MA: Shambhala.

Wilber, K. (2000b). *Integral psychology: Consciousness, spirit, psychology, therapy.* Boston, MA: Shambhala.

 Reflections

Tracey E. Robert and Virginia A. Kelly

As stated in the case and response, many health care providers believe that spiritual discussions and care lie solely within the scope of practice of pastoral care. The responder made the good point that one cannot assume that Laura's existential questions include spiritual or religious ones. Careful assessment and clarification of Laura's needs is important.

Integration of spirituality into nursing care, particularly end-of-life care, has been a strong focus in nursing education at both the undergraduate and graduate levels. Nursing students have identified strengthening understanding of the role of palliative care as a major need. Working with a patient in spiritual distress is functioning within one's scope of practice. Feeling comfortable in that role requires training and support for the caregiver. Nursing with a spiritual focus can improve counseling during the end-of-life process in the following ways:

- Bedside nurses can serve as a companion and guide for patients struggling with end-of-life issues.
- Discussion of spiritual values and beliefs can strengthen the bond between the nurse and the patient.
- Our experience in practice has shown that psychoeducation for nursing students that has a spiritual focus can alleviate caregiver stress and improve care.

• • •

Section II

Spirituality and Wellness

Chapter 10 Grief and Loss

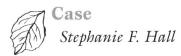 Case
Stephanie F. Hall

Barbara, a 36-year-old White woman, came to counseling for the first time reporting feelings of persistent anxiety and sadness. She had experienced many losses in the previous few years and, as a result, had begun to question even her most firmly held religious beliefs. She stated that what she had been through shouldn't happen to anyone.

Background

Barbara was born in a small southern town in the United States and raised as a Baptist. She was one of three children, the youngest and the only girl. Barbara married John at age 19. They had lived down the street from one another and met because their sisters were friends. Both wanted to start a family immediately but were delayed because John served in the military.

When Barbara came for counseling, she and John had been married for 17 years and had two children, Elizabeth, 12, and Carolyn, 8. Barbara stated that John was a good provider for their family. He wasn't affectionate, but their children respected him.

Barbara was raised in a religious home and for much of her life felt a strong connection to her Baptist roots. Many of her memories involved being at church or participating in activities that occurred after coming home from church on Sundays. Barbara, John, and the whole family were involved in their church. John was a deacon, and she sang in the church choir. She was happy her children were being raised as she had been, in a religious home with strong moral values.

Barbara reported that, from a very young age, she knew she wanted to be just like her mother. She was elated to become a mother herself and described her children as her "most important accomplishment."

Barbara was 21 when her mother was diagnosed with cancer. She stated that her world was "turned upside down." Her mother died, and that was when the problems began for her. She relied heavily on her spirituality at that time and through the years had been telling herself that it was her mother's time to go and that it was what was supposed to happen, though she experienced frequent doubts. Barbara reported having a significant grief reaction every year around the time of her mother's death.

Barbara stated that she felt disconnected from John and he showed a lack of sensitivity about her loss but that divorce wasn't an option. She sometimes felt like a fraud because of her unhappy marriage and because she was attending church and talking to others about their faith when she had begun to question her own religious beliefs.

Incident

Barbara came to me for counseling because she described feeling "empty" when she thought about her life. She indicated that the past year had been much more difficult for her because her best friend Theresa had been diagnosed with cancer and then had died a few months later. Since Theresa died, Barbara had felt anxious almost constantly and had become preoccupied with her children's safety. She had become even more dissatisfied with her marriage and John's lack of support and more concerned about her questioning of her religious beliefs.

Discussion

In working with Barbara, my primary goal was to establish a supportive and nurturing environment in which she could begin to untangle the threads of loss she was experiencing. The recent loss of Theresa coupled with the loss of her mother and the loss in her marriage had laid the foundation for problematic grieving. From a wellness model perspective, some existential anxiety is expected at Barbara's stage of life. However, her anxiety had been exacerbated by the losses she had experienced.

From the beginning, Barbara and I focused on ways to manage her anxiety as we moved through the process of therapy. She responded particularly well to relaxation techniques, such as guided imagery, progressive muscle relaxation, and meditation. She reported that, while meditating, she felt close to her mother and more connected spiritually.

Early on when working with Barbara, I introduced a "safe place" activity in which she developed a visualization that included a place she could go to quickly when her anxiety felt overwhelming. She reported feeling the safest as a child when she was next to her mother. Barbara recalled a memory in which she was out shopping with her mother after a rough day in school. Her mother stopped and sat down with her, taking off her own sweater to wrap around Barbara's shoulders. She recalled that, since her mother's death, she was missing two major things: someone listening to her and someone providing comfort.

It became apparent to me that Barbara had been experiencing complicated grief since the death of her mother. This unresolved grief had an impact on every part of Barbara's life: her spirituality, her marriage, her friendships and, most recently, the way she had begun to grieve the loss of her friend Theresa.

With Barbara's permission, we began the work of actualizing the loss of her mother and working toward resolution of her grief. The main goal was to make meaning of the loss Barbara had experienced at such a young age.

To move toward making meaning of Barbara's loss, we first focused on accepting the reality of the loss (Worden, 2008), including how she had dealt with her mother's death (or not) over the years and how that loss affected her identity as a woman, daughter, and mother. Next, we began processing the pain of her grief, focusing on the pain rather than trying to avoid it as many people tend to do.

During this time, an intervention that seemed particularly powerful for Barbara was bringing in photographs of her mother. I asked her to look at her favorite photograph, which happened to be her mother staring into the camera during one of Barbara's birthday celebrations, and share with her what it had been like to live life without her.

At this stage, Barbara was able to connect pain that she had felt in many situations over the years to the loss of her mother. She described that, for many years, she felt like she had a hole in her chest that couldn't be filled. She recounted many instances of being angry and feeling inconsolable and directing those feelings at others in her life—most often toward her husband.

The final steps for Barbara were to adjust to the world without her mother and find an enduring connection with her as she moved on. She identified several ways that she already maintained a connection to her mother. Now she would be more intentional about including her in rituals and celebrations because it seemed to bring Barbara comfort. As a result of working through the grief about her mother, Barbara also was able to process feelings about the loss of Theresa and to begin communicating her needs more effectively to John.

Questions

1. Barbara presented with several concerns to work on in counseling: grief related to the loss of her mother and Theresa, anxiety, an unhappy marriage, and questioning of her religious beliefs. How would you approach working with her around these issues? How is your conceptualization of this case related to your theoretical orientation?

2. One of Barbara's presenting concerns was that she felt disconnected spiritually, apparently stemming from her mother's death. How would you work with a client who begins to question her spiritual beliefs after a death?
3. What further information do you need to know to work with Barbara?
4. Do you see any potential areas for countertransference in working with Barbara? Why or why not?

References

Worden, J. W. (2008). *Grief counseling and grief therapy: A handbook for the mental health practitioner* (4th ed.). New York, NY: Springer.

 Response

Catherine B. Roland and Richard G. Deaner

Our theoretical lens in reviewing this case was influenced by both Alfred Adler and Viktor Frankl. However, a more recent approach, relational–cultural theory (Jordan, 2012), may provide a strong avenue toward making the counseling process more effective.

Adler and Frankl formed the theoretical foundation of our conceptualization of Barbara's case. Adler was among the first theorists to dispute Freud's view of religion/spirituality—Freud viewed religion/spirituality as a form of neurosis (Freud, 1939), but Adler suggested that religion/spirituality (finding meaning in one's life) is an essential component within a person's life (Mosak & Dreikurs, 2000). Mosak and Dreikurs (2000) asserted that religion/spirituality should be considered as one of Adler's life tasks, which also include love (family), friendship, self-acceptance, and work (contribution to society). According to Adler, people approach life tasks with adaptive or maladaptive patterns of behavior that are based on how they perceive the world, and that behavior is purposeful and goal directed (Ansbacher & Ansbacher, 1964).

Frankl, a former student of Adler's school of individual psychology, expanded on Adler's insight regarding finding meaning in one's life. Within an existential view, finding meaning in life is essential. Frankl asserted that finding meaning is a discovery process that can be illuminated during adverse experiences and that persons find meaning in their experiences with love, work, suffering, and creation (Frankl, 2006). He stated that people must seek and create meaning in their own mortal lives to find purpose and that personal experience often is defined as providing spiritual or existential meaning.

Adler focused on *how* a person approaches life. Frankl explained *why* a person approaches life. In this case, we examine *how and why* Barbara navigates her life.

In a postmodern view, a relational approach that has at its core the tenants of mutuality, empowerment, egalitarian regard, and holistic connection would provide a workable counseling process (Jordan, Kaplan, Baker Miller, Stiver, & Surrey, 1997). Relational–cultural theory may not have an obvious direct link to the existential point of view of Frankl, but it could be gleaned from this approach that the existential embrace of meaning in life and all relationships in some ways has deserted Barbara. With the death of her mother—the closest person in her life—and then the death of her friend—with whom she shared her innermost thoughts and feelings—Barbara was bereft of support and love. The absence of the safety and joy of her religion and sense of spirituality left Barbara with no avenue of support other than her husband, John, who seemingly had been absent emotionally for some time.

Barbara no longer had a mutuality of feeling, a balance to her life, or a system of support and empowerment. Her relationships had become skewed and, according to Adler's social interest construct—how persons view themselves in relation to the external world—there may be little hope for connection in a meaningful way. A relational way of learning to connect and gain back interest in Barbara's self, others, and religion/spirituality would allow her to examine all the relationships in her life, especially those with her husband, her friend, and her mother.

Questioning Spiritual Beliefs

Barbara is questioning her Baptist upbringing and experiencing feelings of confusion, guilt, anger, and anxiety because of the loss of her mother and her friend. Her feelings probably are affecting her relationships with self, others, and religion/spirituality, but these issues may be worked on successfully in counseling. The notion of social interest, one of Adler's most distinctive concepts that affects Barbara's case, is related to systemic relationships with self, others, and spiritual meaning (Watts, 2000). According to Watts, the relational notion of social interest fits well with Christianity. He stated, "The Bible affirms that humans have a three-fold relational responsibility: to God, to others, and to themselves" (Watts, 2000, p. 320).

Barbara's social interest probably has been compromised. The counselor should explore how to help her enhance her social interest and should develop an egalitarian relationship in which social interest can be fostered in an adaptive manner. For Barbara, social interest may be the catalyst for change and adaptation. Her social interest will affect *how* she will function in the world in a holistic context.

To develop a more balanced relationship with Barbara, the counselor may need to create a safe and open environment in which she can examine her relationships with self, others, and her religion/spirituality. These three areas can be addressed in any order. Because Barbara's relationships with self, others, and religion/spirituality are intertwined and interrelated, we first address her relationship with her husband.

Spousal Relationship

Barbara stated that she wanted her husband to listen to her. The divide between Barbara and her husband probably is a manifestation of a need for couples counseling. The dynamics of the relationship that we understand thus far are seen from Barbara's point of view. Gaining insight into the actual dynamics would be helpful both to the couple and to Barbara individually.

Barbara's mother likely provided unconditional love and nurturance through nonjudgmental listening. After her death, Barbara's need to be nurtured may have transferred to her friend Theresa until her recent death. Unable to find an ear, she turned to her husband, who may not have displayed the same skills of active listening. Essentially, Barbara displayed purposeful behavior within a very different relationship while expecting the same results.

The counselor could engage Barbara in Socratic dialogue to produce insight regarding her purposeful behavior. Barbara eventually may understand the consequences of her perceptions and maladaptive patterns of behavior. The counselor could assist her in reorienting her behaviors, goals, and expectations in an adaptive manner.

A truncated life review might yield interesting insights from Barbara, including the level of attachment she had with her mother, both in her developmental years and in her adult years. Some questions might address differentiation and how Barbara saw it in relation to her mother and then her husband. She could engage in writing or drawing, particularly around issues of power and empowerment in regard to her relationship with her mother, and look at that developmentally. She would do this by segmenting her life as a child, an adolescent, and, finally, as an adult and explore how each segment has affected her personal growth and development.

Inviting Barbara's husband to attend one of her counseling sessions would be a strategy to observe the dynamics of the couple, which would lead to a referral for couples counseling. Even this early on, it appears that ongoing couples counseling, with an unbiased counselor, could be a helpful course of action. Even the one session with Barbara and her therapist would need to be discussed with her, and guidelines and boundaries would need to be established. Before any sessions with her husband, Barbara would need to gain insight related to her need for nurturance by discussing her needs and exploring realistic options for achieving them.

If Barbara and her husband agree to regular couples counseling with an outside therapist, the counselor should provide a comfortable and accepting environment for them, just as was done in individual counseling for Barbara, while modeling appropriate communication skills. Barbara would need to express her fears, sadness, anger, needs, and goals in an adaptive manner and learn to seek nurturance and attention appropriately. Her husband should learn the skills needed to attend to his wife in a nurturing, responsive, and nonjudgmental manner without trying to fix or dismiss the situation. A goal of the couples counseling would be to enhance their relationship as they learn to express their needs in adaptive ways and, in turn, positively affect their relationships with self, others, and religion/spirituality.

A blended model of family and couples therapy could include an existential concept of continuing bonds and a cognitive–behavior therapy—rational emotive–behavior therapy (CBT-REBT) model that focuses on adapting to death in a healthy manner (Malkinson, 2010). This blended model would make the distinction between irrational and rational processes of grief. Conducting an inventory of Barbara's thoughts about her mother's death (and perhaps her friend's death) would allow her some needed release. The strategy to combine a CBT-REBT model and a more existential view also would help Barbara accept the common bonds aspect of always having her mother in some sense throughout her life and reframe her grief within a rational construct.

Barbara's relationships with her mother and friend require further attention. She will still have relationships with them in the form of memories. The counselor can elicit memories and process feelings of guilt, sadness, fear, anger, happiness, and love.

Attending to feelings of sadness, guilt, and anger will be a primary concern. All too often, persons are not given permission to communicate sorrow and anger without others attempting to rescue them from misery. The grieving person is denied the opportunity to process these feelings in an adaptive way. As a result, they often are overlooked, minimized, and denied. The counselor should validate the feelings in a supportive environment.

To illustrate how cognitions and memory can influence perception and feelings, the counselor can use the "push-button technique," an Adlerian intervention to help persons who think they do not have control of their emotions (Mosak, 1985). This process could help Barbara freely experience memory and feelings and learn to sustain relationships and memories in adaptive ways. The counselor might recommend that Barbara gather photographs of family celebrations or functions held to honor their memory. She might light a candle in memory of these occasions. In concert with the counselor, she might determine which practices or rituals could sustain these relationships in the most meaningful way.

Relationships With Spirituality/Religion

Through these interventions, Barbara may discover a newly constructed sense of spirituality. Choosing favorite or meaningful passages from the

Bible might be a good way to process her grief while developing a personalized sense of spirituality (Watts, 2000). This is where Barbara's "will to meaning" can grow and flourish from an existential perspective (Frankl, 2006) and where the *how* she navigates her life will transform into the *why*. Barbara's personal journey to wellness also may involve feelings of anxiety and fear related to her own mortality. If these feelings are detected, the counselor should attend to them while Barbara explores meaning.

Throughout the counseling process, the counselor needs to be keenly aware of her or his own issues related to grief, religion/spirituality, transition, and death. Many counselors have experienced the loss of a parental figure or close friend. During these difficult times, they may have used strategies that were effective for them in dealing with loss. These same strategies may not be effective for everyone. If the counseling relationship is contaminated with countertransference issues related to the counselor's unfinished business or grief, the counseling relationship will not function properly. Because grief is a deeply personal and intimate form of expression, the discussion should be related solely to Barbara's journey to wellness.

References

Ansbacher, H. L., & Ansbacher, R. R. (Eds.). (1964). *Alfred Adler: Superiority and social interest.* New York, NY: Horton.

Frankl, V. (2006). *Man's search for meaning.* Boston, MA: Beacon Press.

Freud, S. (1939). *Moses and monotheism.* New York, NY: Alfred A. Knopf.

Jordan, J. (2012). *Relational–cultural therapy.* Washington, DC: American Psychological Association.

Jordan, J., Kaplan, A., Baker Miller, J., Stiver, I., & Surrey, J. (Eds.). (1991). *Women's growth in connection: Writings from the Stone Center.* New York, NY: Guilford Press.

Malkinson, R. (2010). Cognitive–behavioral grief therapy: The ABC model of rational–emotive behavior therapy. *Psychological Topics, 19,* 289–305.

Mosak, H. H. (1985). Interrupting a depression: The push-button technique. *The Journal of Individual Psychology, 41,* 210–214.

Mosak, H. H., & Dreikurs, R. (2000). Spirituality: The fifth life task. *The Journal of Individual Psychology, 56,* 155–171.

Watts, R. E. (2000). Biblically-based Christian spirituality and Adlerian psychotherapy. *Journal of Individual Psychology, 66,* 316–328.

 ## Reflections
Tracey E. Robert and Virginia A. Kelly

Complicated grief can be devastating and disrupt clients' lives for years after the loss. Getting them to understand that grief is not a problem to "fix" but instead involves a healing process unique to each client can help them come to accept the loss. In this case and response, we see the application of many theories. Each theory allows for integration of the spiritual issues that the client has brought to the counseling process, and the models of grief and loss offer the counselor useful strategies and interventions to address the client's needs.

Support systems are critical for clients suffering from grief and loss. However, many clients isolate and withdraw from social contact. Help and comfort provided through counseling often is ignored or pushed away. The pain can be intense, so clients do not want to deal with it. We think that a spiritual approach to counseling for grief and loss is beneficial because it can do the following:

- offer interventions that address anxiety, depression, and comfort while improving communication and self-awareness;
- provide a forum for open discussion of topics that often are not supported or communicated, especially after a certain length of time; and
- allow for exploration of meaning and purpose in life and address the existential issues that often arise from grief and loss.

· · ·

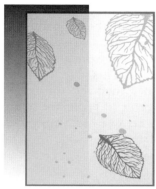

Chapter 11

Family Sexual Abuse

Case
Joyce Shea

Peggy and Bob, both 35 years old, arrived at the outpatient clinic with their 7-year-old son, Sam. They were referred to me for evaluation and therapy by the psychiatric crisis team at the local hospital after Sam allegedly had been molested by his 15-year-old brother, Justin. Bob appeared angry while Peggy tearfully explained the situation and Sam sat quietly playing video games. Peggy concluded her summary by stating, "I really can't believe this has happened. Everything is just falling apart."

Background

Peggy and Bob both were of White, working class, Italian and Irish heritage. Bob, an electrician, owned his business; Peggy was a stay-at-home mom. The couple had met in high school and dated on and off and then became more involved after graduating. Peggy found out she was pregnant with Justin, and they decided to get married. Although they struggled financially for several years, Peggy convinced Bob that they should have another child. She described herself as "ecstatic" when Sam arrived and reported having felt that her life was complete.

Peggy described Justin as a highly energetic child who had some difficulty in following directions but functioned reasonably well until his younger brother was born. From age 8 onward, Justin repeatedly got into trouble at school and at home. By the time he was in middle school, he was smoking cigarettes and experimenting with alcohol and drugs. As a sophomore in high school, Justin recently had been arrested for vandalism and petty theft. His parents also discovered that he had been sexually active with a 21-year-old woman.

Sam, the quieter of the two boys, always adored his older brother. In spite of their age difference, Peggy described their relationship as "very close," with Justin often taking on the role of protector of his younger brother. Until the events of a few weeks earlier, Peggy and Bob often had trusted Justin to babysit his brother.

Incident

Late one morning, 2 weeks before the family came to see me, Peggy received a phone call from the principal at Sam's school asking her to come in for a meeting. Upon her arrival, she found Sam's teacher, the school psychologist, and a case worker from the state's Department of Children and Families waiting to speak with her. They explained that Sam's behavior had changed recently and that he had shared with his teacher that day that Justin had been doing "things" to him over the previous month that were upsetting him. Upon preliminary investigation, they believed that Sam had been sexually molested by Justin on at least three occasions and stated that a full investigation would be launched.

The police had been sent to pick up Justin and bring him to the hospital for an evaluation. Bob met Peggy at the hospital after arranging for his sister to stay with Sam. The evaluation determined that Justin did not meet the criteria for hospitalization, and the police did not intend to put him in jail for that night. Justin would be staying with his grandparents on an interim basis, and Bob and Peggy were directed to bring Sam to the clinic for further evaluation.

Discussion

As Peggy shared her story, her extreme anguish became evident. She described being horrified by the details of the alleged abuse, feeling devastated for Sam, and simultaneously being furious with and frightened for Justin. Peggy had been a practicing Roman Catholic since childhood, and as such she saw Justin's actions as a mortal sin. As a mother, she was torn between her great concern for Sam and her extreme feelings of anger, revulsion, and fear for Justin. Peggy questioned how she, as the mom, could have missed the signs that the abuse was occurring.

In contrast, Bob sat in stony silence for most of the session. When questioned directly, he indicated that he had no conflict in terms of his feelings. He was disgusted by Justin's alleged actions and somewhat annoyed that Sam hadn't spoken to him instead of the teacher. He stated that he fully intended to cut off his relationship with Justin: "No son of mine will be a pervert."

Speaking separately with Sam, I found him to be resistive to sharing details about the incident. He appeared to be most sensitive about the fact that sharing the story with his teacher had resulted in his immediate loss of contact with his brother and in his parents' obvious distress. Sam also was at a loss about how to deal with his father's intense anger and his mother's sense of desperation. He had not returned to school since the day of the incident. In short, Sam's decision to share his story that day had changed his world forever.

My immediate response was to assess Peggy, Bob, and Sam for safety. Decisions had to be made quickly as to the priority of needs to be addressed and approaches to be used for the most effective treatment. Incorporating a tool designed to measure suicide risk (Cutliffe & Barker, 2004), I determined that none of the persons involved had active thoughts of self-harm, a plan to carry out the thoughts, actual intent to do so, or a past history of self-harmful behaviors.

My next response was to address the complex interweave of physical, cognitive, emotional, and spiritual issues raised in this case for both the individuals and the family unit. The approach I used was based on the integrative treatment model, which incorporates a person-centered, holistic approach to planning treatment and interventions that are based on multiple perspectives (e.g., conventional as well as complementary and alternative therapies) and that focus on maximizing health (Tusaie, 2013). The initial treatment plan addressed primarily the physical, emotional, and spiritual needs of the son and the emotional and spiritual needs of the parents. Each family member needed guidance in putting the pieces of his or her world back together.

Questions

1. Where does spiritual distress fall in terms of the priorities the counselor needs to address with this family?
2. How might the counselor assist the individual family members in finding meaning in the events that unfolded?
3. What strategies would be most effective for the counselor to use if and when reintegrating the older brother into the family became necessary?
4. How can the counselor best deal with his or her own emotions brought out by this case?

References

Cutcliffe, J. R., & Barker, P. (2004). The Nurses' Global Assessment of Suicide Risk (NGASR): Developing a tool for clinical practice. *Journal of Psychiatric and Mental Health Nursing*, *11*, 393–400.

Tusaie, K. R. (2013). Synergy of integrative treatment. In K. R. Tusaie & J. J. Fitzpatrick (Eds.), *Advanced practice psychiatric nursing: Integrating psychotherapy, psychopharmacology, and complementary and alternative approaches* (pp. 26–35). New York, NY: Springer.

Response
Mark E. Young

The case of Justin, Sam, Peggy, and Bob perfectly demonstrates that couples and family treatment often has two distinct phases, a crisis intervention stage and a longer-term stage in which the underlying issues must be addressed (Long & Young, 2007). The first three questions the counselor posed—dealing with spiritual distress, finding meaning, and reintegrating a family member when that member has fallen from grace—fall into the longer-term scenario (Stathopoulos, 2012). Dealing with these issues typically takes place at least 3 months after the initial crisis when family members' emotions have been reduced and a new daily routine established. In this case, crisis intervention has already begun with placement of the offending brother, Justin, with his grandparents. Both Sam and his parents need the support of a counselor during this initial period, and, if there are to be visits with Justin, a safety plan must be developed.

Although many therapists may be tempted to treat the perpetrator at this point, in my experience, adolescents who have committed family sexual abuse have been more than reluctant to talk about the issue and can offer no useful explanations for their behavior. Counselors who expect such clients to open up in these circumstances usually are disappointed because the shame and public humiliation are so severe that the adolescent may be unable to speak at all (Calder, 2006). However, the same counselor who will work with the family later can begin by developing a trusting relationship with the offending client, which will help in reintegrating the outcast. From the beginning, the counselor is performing a delicate balancing act between helping the perpetrator and helping the victims (Keane, Guest, & Padbury, 2013).

Prioritizing Spiritual Distress

Thus, my answer to the first question, "Where does spiritual distress fall in terms of the priorities the counselor needs to address with this family?" is that spiritual distress is not an immediate priority. The first priority is stabilizing the family members, especially the children, so that the family can be rebuilt. For example, although no danger of self-harm has been identified, the adolescent perpetrator is still at risk for suicide (D. H. Granello & Granello, 2007), and that must be monitored carefully. The counselor or counselors involved also must move quickly to help the victim, Sam, get back into a normal schedule, deal with issues of guilt, and help his parents deal with their own sense of responsibility.

So, when should spiritual distress be addressed? From the case we see that Peggy's religion came into play as she considered her elder son to be a sinner. At the same time, Bob began to see their child as a "pervert." Consequently, Phase 2 of the treatment probably should focus on the executive branch of the family, Peggy and Bob. Referral to a couples counselor might provide them with a safe place to think about their joint response to the situation. When seeing them together, a couples counselor could allow them to express their spiritual and moral outrage as well as their sense of failure without exposing the children to these reactions. Crises such as this can divide couples, and an early session with Peggy and Bob could help get them on the same page and address the tendency to blame each other (Levinson & Morin, 2001).

In the couples sessions, the counselor also should assess both members of the couple's religious and spiritual background guided by the Association for Spiritual, Ethical, and Religious Values in Counseling's (ASERVIC's; 2009) spiritual competencies. The purpose would be to evaluate the impact of the event on their sense of spiritual or religious stability and the degree to which they might be able to use their beliefs and experiences to cope with the crisis and forge a longer-term plan.

The counselor should try to determine whether the spiritual distress is caused by feelings of anger toward God for letting this happen or feeling that God is not there when strength is needed. Spiritually competent counselors can honor clients' spiritual background and encourage them to use the salutary aspects of their beliefs to achieve their goals (Cashwell & Young, 2011). A spiritual competency every counselor should possess is the knowledge and willingness to refer to appropriate clergy when clients are seeking the position of scripture or the church on their situation. A referral to Roman Catholic clergy could provide support for the couple in this crisis.

Meaning Making

The second question posed in this case is, "How might the counselor assist the individual family members in finding meaning in the events that unfolded?" Helping clients find meaning in traumatic events perhaps is the most important step after crisis stabilization (Altmaier & Prieto, 2012). In this case, the parents, victim, and perpetrator all must find ways to put the event in context. The counselor's task is not so much to help clients find meaning but to transform the meanings that they have already made.

For each of the subsystems in the family, the counselor or counselors must assess the current attributions of meaning for the event. Do the parents believe that they neglected their children and this was the cause of the abuse? Does Justin see himself as a sexual predator, or "pervert," as his father says? The process of finding meaning in these cases is a slow and methodical shift from the immediate attributions of guilt, permanent damage, and moral depravity and a reframing to seeing the event as capable of resolution, forgiveness, and a changing of one's self-image (cf. Cooney, Allan, Allan, McKillop, & Drake, 2011). These goals are not likely to be accomplished early in therapy or quickly but rather in a longer-term or periodic use of counseling and perhaps in support groups or group therapy (Wade & Meyer, 2009).

As the survivor of sexual abuse, 7-year-old Sam may be the last one to find meaning because of his developmental stage. Although the meaning for him may center around betrayal by a brother, he may be unable to make sense of what has happened cognitively. In this case, the counselor must coach the parents to help him feel safe and to develop a narrative about the situation that empowers him and excludes him from blame. In cases of divorce, parents try to emphasize that the problem is between them and is not the child's fault. Until children really accept this story, they harbor guilt for the parents' breakup. In a similar manner, for Sam, the story the parents tell him about this event is crucial and should be developed with the counselor. The message can be reinforced through bibliotherapy, play therapy, and counseling.

Reintegrating the Offender

The third question asked, "What strategies would be most effective for the counselor to use if and when reintegrating the older brother into the family became necessary?" The wording suggests that reintegrating the older brother into the family may be a necessary evil. Certainly there are family situations in which the sexual abuse was not the only problem, and addiction, neglect, or other kinds of abuse are prevalent. Thus, reunification does not fit all scenarios.

The reunification process can be difficult, and it may involve legal issues (U.S. Department of Health & Human Services, Administration for Children & Families, Child Welfare Information Gateway, n.d.). If professionals determine that the abused child is still at risk, a plan should be formulated to protect the child. Factors to consider include the type of sexual abuse, the relationship between the victim and the offender, and reactions and functioning of the nonoffending parent. The choices may be to remove the offender or to remove the victim. Removing the offender often is considered preferable because it sends the message to all involved that he or she has done something wrong. Practices differ from state to state.

Research in this area, particularly research focused on sibling abuse, has been minimal (Harper, 2012). Family courts, which have local authority, are responsible for risk assessment and decide whether reunification is granted. Nonreunification could result in long-term disruption of the family. If the relationship between the offender and the victim is close or they live together, the risk for future emotional abuse is higher. Therefore, reunification decisions are based on the safety of the victim.

If safety can be ensured, there is reason to think that reunification of the family may be therapeutic (Levinson & Morin, 2001; Schladale, 2007). Through reunification, the perpetrator can reestablish relationships and atone for his actions. The parents can regain a sense of family unity, and the victim can find a way to develop a new relationship with the sibling perpetrator and let go of some of the guilt associated with kicking the perpetrator out of the family.

Techniques for reunification are described in Budrionis and Jongsma (2003). Family therapy probably is the treatment of choice, although there is not much research to guide us on the best methods. Clinical experience suggests that family sessions should precede unification. They should focus on the future rules and roles in the family, safety of the victim, communication, and establishment of periodic family therapy and family meetings to assess progress (Cherry & O'Shea, 2006).

Counselor Self-Care

The fourth question is, "How can the counselor best deal with his or her own emotions brought out by this case?" Counselors can be traumatized by their clients' experiences, and supervision and self-care are the obvious weapons against the resulting burnout (Azar, 2000; Figley, 2002). The counselor in this case certainly identified with the "anguish" of the parents. Thus, leaving the parents' couples counseling to another therapist might be a good idea. Another possible aspect of the counselor's emotional reaction in this case is little mention of Justin's emotional state. This omission may be because of a lack of information, or it may be the result of anger or disgust that the counselor feels toward him. It would be the counselor's supervisor's job to point out that Justin is a child too and needs compassion and help.

Besides supervision, the counselor needs to increase self-care when dealing with clients' traumatic experiences. Part of self-care is nurturing one's relationships and body, mind, and spirit wellness (P. F. Granello, 2013). Keeping fit is something one does for clients. They deserve someone who can look directly at the wound and not flinch and who can be present and optimistic week after week. The counselor needs to deal with negative emotions of anger and helplessness and convey the powerful weapons of hope and faith in the family's resilience (Larson, 2013).

References

Altmaier, E. M., & Prieto, L. R. (2012). Through a glass darkly: Meaning-making, spiritual transformation and posttraumatic growth. *Counseling Psychology Quarterly, 4,* 345.

Association for Spiritual, Ethical and Religious Values in Counseling. (2009). *Spiritual competencies.* Retrieved from: http://aservic.org

Azar, S. T. (2000). Preventing burnout in professionals and paraprofessionals who work with child abuse and neglect cases: A cognitive behavioral approach to supervision. *Journal of Clinical Psychology, 56,* 643–663.

Budrionis, R., & Jongsma, A. R. (2003). *The sexual abuse victim and sexual offender treatment planner.* Hoboken, NJ: Wiley.

Calder, M. (Ed.). (2006). *Children and young people who sexually abuse: New theory, research and practice developments.* Lyme Regis, Dorset, United Kingdom: Russell House.

Cashwell, C., & Young, J. S. (2011). *Integrating spirituality and religion into counseling* (2nd ed.). Alexandria, VA: American Counseling Association.

Cherry C., & O'Shea, D. (2006). Therapeutic work with families of young people who sexually abuse. In M. Erooga & H. Masson (Eds.), *Children and young people who sexually abuse others* (pp. 200–214). London, United Kingdom: Routledge.

Cooney, A., Allan, A., Allan, M. M., McKillop, D., & Drake, D. G. (2011). The forgiveness process in primary and secondary victims of violent and sexual offences. *Australian Journal of Psychology, 63,* 107–118. doi:10.1111/j.1742-9536.2011.00012.x

Figley, C. R. (2002). Compassion fatigue and the psychotherapist's chronic lack of self-care. *Journal of Clinical Psychology, 58,* 1433–1441.

Granello, D. H., & Granello P. F. (2007). *Suicide: An essential guide for helping professionals and educators.* Upper Saddle River, NJ: Pearson.

Granello, P. F. (2013). *Wellness counseling.* Upper Saddle River, NJ: Pearson.

Harper, B. M. (2012). Moving families to future health: Reunification experiences after sibling incest. *Doctorate in Social Work (DSW) Dissertations, Paper 26.* Retrieved from http://repository.upenn.edu/cgi/viewcontent.cgi?article=1027&context=edissertations_sp2

Keane, M., Guest, A., & Padbury, J. (2013). A balancing act: A family perspective to sibling sexual abuse. *Child Abuse Review, 22,* 246–254.

Larson, S. (2013). The power of hope. *Reclaiming Children & Youth, 21,* 44–46.

Levinson, J. S., & Morin, J. W. (2001). *Treating nonoffending parents in child sexual abuse cases: Connections for family safety.* Thousand Oaks, CA: Sage.

Long, L. L., & Young, M. E. (2007). *Counseling and therapy for couples.* Pacific Grove, CA: Brooks/Cole.

Schladale, J. (2007). A collaborative approach for family reconciliation and reunification with youth who have caused sexual harm. In D. S. Prescott (Ed.), *Knowledge and practice: Challenges in the treatment and supervision of sexual abusers* (pp. 239–279). Oklahoma City, OK: Wood and Barnes.

Stathopoulos, M. (2012). Sibling sexual abuse. In *Australian Centre for the Study of Sexual Assault (ACSSA) research summaries* (pp. 1–18). Melbourne, Australia: Australian Institute of Family Studies.

U.S. Department of Health & Human Services, Administration for Children & Families. Child Welfare Information Gateway. (n.d.). *Investigation of child sexual abuse*. Retrieved from https://www.childwelfare.gov/pubs/usermanuals/sexabuse/sexabused.cfm

Wade, N. G., & Meyer, J. E. (2009). Comparison of brief group interventions to promote forgiveness: A pilot outcome study. *International Journal of Group Psychotherapy, 59,* 199–220. doi:10.1521/ijgp.2009.59.2

 ## Reflections

Tracey E. Robert and Virginia A. Kelly

This case highlights a form of family violence, sibling abuse, that is underreported and not widely researched. The family response to this type of abuse often determines the type of care and treatment offered to the victim as well as to the perpetrator. Sibling abuse is the most prevalent form of incest, which might come as a surprise to many therapists because most of the research focuses on father–daughter incest. When siblings are involved, the parents often do not reach out for help or recognize the behavior as a serious concern.

As the responder mentioned, the parents need to provide a context for Sam so that he can start to heal from the abuse. They may need help in working through a story where they are consistent and on the same page. This can be difficult if they have different parenting styles. Counseling support from the couples' counselor, the school counselor, and any individual therapists working with family members separately needs to be coordinated and integrated. Throughout this case, the need for hope and forgiveness—spiritual virtues—is apparent. A spiritual focus for working with family sexual abuse would be beneficial in the following ways:

- Use of the parents' faith system may provide comfort and solace during a time of crisis.
- Introducing expressive arts—writing, art, music, and, movement—into the counseling process could provide tools for soothing family members and healing.
- Interventions that support self-care, such as meditation, relaxation, and journaling, can enhance coping skills and resiliency.

• • •

Chapter 12

Healing
and Trauma

Case

Mary Jo Mason and Joel Clark Mason

Susan, a single 26-year-old White female, was living with her parents after being discharged from the mental health unit in the local hospital. This hospitalization, her first, was for a dissociative episode. She had seen a counselor for depression as a teenager. Susan was referred upon discharge. During her first session, she stated, "I don't know who I am."

Background

Susan, the oldest of three siblings, had lived all her life in a small upscale town near a large northeastern city. Her parents held professional positions; her father, a financial analyst and her mother, an attorney. Susan had completed 14 years of school. She worked as a personal trainer in a local gym and had private clients.

Susan had been in an 8-year relationship with Jim, whom she had known since third grade. During the course of their relationship, she began abusing alcohol. Jim, who ran his own landscaping company, did not drink.

Susan's parents were members of the Lutheran church all her life. Their primary reason for going to church was that her father enjoyed singing in the choir. Susan was not encouraged to go to church and did not attend any Christian education or youth programs in the church. While she lived with Jim, they did not attend church. She described herself as not having any religious beliefs but reported a recent desire to grow more spiritually.

Incident

Susan was taken to the emergency department of the hospital after Jim discovered her in her car one night in an alcoholic blackout. Psychiatric examination determined that, in addition to the alcohol abuse, she had been experiencing dissociative states, even when sober. She was admitted to the psychiatric unit, where she received intensive one-on-one and group therapy. After 2 weeks, she was discharged.

The dissociative episodes were determined to have been precipitated by an enmeshed relationship with Jim that mirrored the relationship she had with her mother in her family of origin. Jim, along with her mother, became powerful negative maternal objects.

Susan's discharge plan required her to attend an intensive outpatient alcohol rehabilitation program, to attend 12-step meetings, and to participate in individual counseling.

Discussion

During Susan's first session, it became clear that the primary focus, starting out, would be the developmental work of building stronger boundaries to help her form a sense of self. For her to begin the work of knowing herself, spiritual direction was indicated. The power of the negative objects in her life (Jim and her mother), which she had internalized, would have to be reclaimed. The issues concerning alcohol would, for the purposes of our meetings, be secondary. In the course of counseling, Susan revealed that she had been raped 10 years earlier. We then began working on issues resulting from post-traumatic stress symptoms.

It became evident that Susan's development of self was stunted by three things: her family of origin (negative maternal object), her relationship pattern with Jim, and the exacerbation of symptoms caused by the rape that resulted in posttraumatic stress disorder (PTSD). For Susan to have healthy relationships going forward in her life, the primary relationship she needed to work on was with herself. She really didn't know who she was.

To do this work, we embarked on a three-level plan that has its basis in the spiritual program of Tilden Edwards (1977). The plan included the following:

1. Commitment—a stated agreement to work on discovering the person she truly is.
2. Acceptance—of the good, the bad, the ugly, and the beautiful aspects of who she is without moralization or judgment.
3. Confidence—which flows naturally from the work accomplished on the first two.

A genogram of Susan's extended family was valuable in helping her see, graphically, the patterns that flowed through the generations.

Through counseling, she was able to understand how Jim was, in terms of personality and character, very similar to her mother. With this knowledge, she became more attentive to the familial patterns she encountered in her private and professional life and how they produced emotional reactions within her.

In the short term, we focused on a technique to help Susan differentiate from her mother. This strategy involved taking the following five steps when she felt conflict:

1. When you feel an emotional response, hold the emotion and go into your head.
2. Ask yourself, "What did she *say*?"
3. Ask yourself, "What did she *really* say?" (What is the subtext?)
4. Ask yourself, "Do I want to *react*?"
5. Ask yourself, "Do I want to *act*?"

Practice and referral to a spiritual advisor helped Susan sort through religious confusion by providing her a narrative framework based on wisdom from various traditions. Susan's personal boundaries began to take shape as she reconstructed her own unique personality. Along with the insights from systemic patterns, Susan feels more confident now with her relationships at home and with the possibility of dating.

Questions

1. Spiritual direction flows from a centuries-old tradition. How is spiritual direction different from counseling? How can you integrate spiritual direction into a counseling setting?
2. Most counselors have many resources at hand, such as group settings, in-house treatment centers, drug and alcohol counselors/centers, and psychiatrists. What guidelines and resources are there for identifying good spiritual directors?
3. Spiritual development and religious upbringing are very personal. Is it possible to offer spiritual wisdom without personal bias in the context of a counseling situation?

References

Edwards, T. (1977). *Living simply through the day: Spiritual survival in a complex age.* Mahwah, NJ: Paulist Press.

Response
Geri Miller

I conceptualize this case from the viewpoint of spirituality in relation to addiction and trauma. I recommend integration of these three contexts into the counseling approach, with spirituality as the central focus.

In working with Susan, if a counselor is acting *strictly* as a counselor, without an explicit role or the credentials of a spiritual or religious counselor, he or she needs to develop a careful and thoughtful approach before integrating exploration of the client's spiritual side into the counseling process. The counselor needs to be cautious about claiming this area as one of expertise unless he or she has received appropriate and adequate training.

However, the counselor can legitimately explore Susan's spirituality from a holistic perspective because this aspect often has been added to the biopsychosocial model of treatment (G. A. Miller, in press). Thus, counselors can separately examine and conjointly explore and address clients' biological, psychological, social, and spiritual (biopsychosocialspiritual) aspects.

In this case, Susan's recent desire to grow spiritually is an invitation to the counselor to explore her spiritual aspect of self while still practicing within the counselor's area of competence. Spirituality is part of a holistic approach; the counselor is acting in the best interests of the client who has expressed such an interest. The answers to the three questions posed are integrated throughout this response.

Defining Spiritual Direction

Regarding the overall spiritual focus, the counselor could serve as the client's spiritual director or refer the client to a spiritual director, depending on the definitions of *spirituality*, *spiritual direction*, and *spiritual director* as outlined in the following paragraphs. In addition, the counselor's comfort level and a healthy match with the client's welfare are paramount to the client's recovery. Before responding specifically to Susan's case, it is necessary to explore the definitions of spirituality, spiritual direction, and spiritual director relative to her situation.

Spirituality has been described as a "nonsensical word" because of its various meanings (Ault, 2013). The concept of spirituality I have used is embedded in the question, "What keeps your spirit alive?" (G. A. Miller, 2003). Because Susan's addiction recovery process has a spiritual aspect (treatment and Alcoholics Anonymous [AA]) and the general approach to spirituality has been a core component of addiction recovery (Kurtz, 1987), exploring spirituality with Susan is a legitimate counseling avenue.

Spiritual direction, an ancient practice that has become increasingly popular in the past 20 years, is a process of assisting a person in developing his or her spiritual aspect of self (Frykholm, 2011). Spiritual direction typically focuses on the individual person but also occurs in group and community settings (Ault, 2013). This practice involves connection and community because it strengthens the person's commitment to spirituality and to deeper community (Frykholm, 2011).

Spiritual direction is associated with psychology and therapy because it helps clients grow spiritually by discussing issues or sharing stories with a spiritual director. Although they do not draw directly on psychology and therapy, spiritual direction and counseling can be readily integrated, and they all complement one another (Frykholm, 2011).

The *spiritual director* has been described as a "companion, guide, midwife and host or hostess" (Ault, 2013, p. 83) who helps the client grow spiritually. The relationship is one of trust in which the presence of the divine is explored (Frykholm, 2011). Although there is a lack of agreement on the definition of a spiritual director and who can earn that designation, one example follows: "The [spiritual] director is someone who aids in the process of holy listening" (Frykholm, 2011, p. 28). The director is basically a listener.

In the field of addiction counseling, spiritual directors need not be religious clergy (W. R. Miller, Forcehimes, O'Leary, & LaNoue, 2008). Thus, the counselor has room to act as a spiritual director in exploring spirituality with clients who are addicted.

With Susan, the counselor can explore the spiritual dimension and legitimately act as her spiritual director. He or she can use a holistic view that incorporates the biopsychosocialspiritual model in the context of her addiction and her issues, which are common for women who are addicted (e.g., boundary issues and PTSD). However, the counselor may be more comfortable making a referral to a spiritual director who fits better with Susan's cultural framework.

Integrating Spirituality Into the Treatment Plan

If the counselor decides to assist Susan in exploring her spiritual component, the counselor can readily match it to her treatment goals in these areas: addiction, development of self (boundaries, sense of self) as affected by trauma (PTSD), and increased self-awareness. Assuming that Susan is maintaining abstinence throughout the counseling process, augmenting her addiction recovery with a spiritual focus through exploration of her addiction-related issues is legitimate.

Spiritual direction and various spiritual direction techniques can be incorporated into this process. However, the counselor needs to assess Susan's addiction recovery on an ongoing basis to ensure that she is remaining sober and her issues are stable. The baseline of stability is required to appropriately explore the spiritual aspects of her recovery. There is no strict definition of a stable recovery, but at its core, the counselor and the client determine that the client can remain abstinent while exploring different dimensions of self, such as spirituality. Such exploration does not destabilize her recovery program. With the assurance of a stable recovery, spiritual direction and techniques can be integrated to enhance her addiction recovery.

Addiction treatment often occurs in groups, and recovery typically includes involvement in group/community settings, such as AA (G. A. Miller, in press). Numerous possible spiritual guidance techniques include spiritual disciplines, such as "acceptance, celebration, fasting, gratitude, guidance, meditation, prayer, reconciliation, reflection, service to others, solitude, & worship" (W. R. Miller et al., 2008, pp. 435–436). The practices associated with these disciplines, along with self-care, can be integrated effectively into addiction treatment (W. R. Miller et al., 2008). For example, Susan may find it helps her addiction recovery to begin her day meditating out of a daily reading text that focuses on addiction recovery.

A counselor then can explore and incorporate these techniques or practices into the counseling process as they appeal to the client and contribute to his or her welfare. These practices, as well as retreats, can be incorporated into Susan's counseling process, depending on what is comfortable and appropriate for her. The counselor has, at least, the following three options for including spirituality in the process of counseling Susan:

1. Set up specific counseling sessions that focus on exploration of spirituality.
2. Refer her to a specific spiritual director (paid or unpaid) to augment counseling.
3. Assist her in attending retreats that enhance her recovery process.

Identifying Spiritual Resources

Counselors may not have specific guidelines or resources at hand for identifying effective spiritual directors. However, one resource is Spiritual Directors International, a global learning community that consists of persons from numerous faiths and nations. This group focuses on spiritual companionship and offers information regarding spiritual directors and spiritual direction. At their website (www.sdiworld.org), a counselor can access a guide for finding a spiritual director, a definition of spiritual direction, and a list of questions to ask.

Some guidelines specific to certain areas of spiritual direction, such as those that are religiously affiliated, are available (Frykholm, 2011). Resources in this area are best explored on a case-by-case basis in collaboration with the client. For example, if the client has extremely limited finances, the counselor may help in examining his or her community of support for natural healers (e.g., sponsors in the AA community).

In Susan's case, it is critical to explore her resources with her, especially resources that encourage empowerment so that she can learn to listen for and express her own voice. Susan may need assistance from her counselor in "trying on these resources" by experiencing an activity once (e.g., a retreat) and then having the opportunity to process her experience with her counselor. The counselor needs to be careful of countertransference issues related to spirituality and provide spiritual wisdom by using Susan's welfare as the guiding principle in exploring this area with her.

In choosing a spiritual director, Susan needs to find someone she trusts who will assist her in finding and expressing her voice to enhance her sense of empowerment. Such a strengthening of her core sense of self will further her recovery from addiction and help her address developmental issues connected to being female and her PTSD.

References

Ault, N. (2013). Theological reflection and spiritual direction. *Australian Catholic Record, 90*, 81–91.

Frykholm, A. (2011). Holy listening: The spiritual direction movement. *Christian Century, 26*, 26–29.

Kurtz, E. (1987). *Not God: A history of Alcoholics Anonymous.* Center City, MN: Hazelden.

Miller, G. A. (2003). *Incorporating spirituality in counseling and psychotherapy.* Hoboken, NJ: Wiley.

Miller, G. A. (in press). *Learning the language of addiction counseling* (4th ed.). Hoboken, NJ: Wiley.

Miller, W. R., Forcehimes, A., O'Leary, M. J., & LaNoue, M. D. (2008). Spiritual direction in addiction treatment: Two clinical trials. *Journal of Substance Abuse Treatment, 35*, 435–442. doi:10.1016/j.jsat.2008.02.004

 Reflections

Tracey E. Robert and Virginia A. Kelly

Counselors often use trauma-focused and spiritually focused therapy successfully when encountering natural disasters, terrorism, unexpected violent events, and tragedies. There are many faith-based and religious beliefs in North America; clients often use religious beliefs as coping mechanisms during times of trauma. Donald Meichenbaum developed a spiritually integrated model for treating trauma and recovery that acknowledged this social context as an aid to counselors.

Spiritual interventions, such as mindfulness meditation, have been adapted by the Veterans' Administration to treat PTSD in returning vets. Understanding how spirituality can enhance the treatment of trauma and provide the counselor with tools for healing and recovery can contribute to more effective outcomes. A spiritual focus in treating trauma can benefit the counseling process in the following ways:

- Client welfare is at the core of the process, and clients' beliefs are central to achieving treatment goals, including exploration of spirituality and its place in the client's life.
- Spiritual interventions that increase self-awareness, such as mindfulness meditation, contemplative prayer, and journaling, can support the addiction recovery process.
- Integration of spiritually focused activities, such as spiritual direction, retreats, and recovery groups, can support hope, forgiveness, and self-compassion and help clients achieve movement toward wellness.

• • •

Chapter 13
Disaster Mental Health

Case
Stephanie Dailey

Amanda, a 34-year-old married White female from a town on the Jersey Shore, talked gloomily as I handed her a cup of coffee and care packages for her two small children. I identified myself as a volunteer with the American Red Cross's (ARC's) Emotional Care team for the Hurricane Sandy recovery effort. Amanda looked at me with tired eyes and told me she had lost her home and most of the family's belongings. Having just arrived at the ARC relief center, she reported,

> We spent 4 days in a church shelter. We do not know what to do or where to go. We have lost everything—even our dog is missing. I keep asking, "Why God, why? Are we being punished?" I completely ignored the clergy at the church shelter—I just could not look them in the eye. I can't even pray anymore. I desperately want to, but I just can't.

Background

Amanda grew up in a small town in southwestern Virginia. She was raised in a conservative Southern Baptist home by her biological parents and was the fourth of seven children. Amanda described her childhood as "sheltered," saying she spent a great deal of time at school and church. Because her mom was busy raising seven children, Amanda made sure she wasn't a "troublemaker" and performed well academically. Amanda remembered her father as loving and attentive but often busy with work.

After Amanda attended a local college and married her high school sweetheart, also a Southern Baptist, her husband received a job transfer and they moved to the Jersey Shore. Her parents strongly discouraged her moving away from home but felt better about the move after she joined a local Southern Baptist church and took a position at the church as a preschool teacher. After a few years, Amanda and her husband started a family. Their two children are Peter, 8, and Liam, 4.

When asked to recall what happened, Amanda remembered news reports of the storm approaching but stated that she and her husband did not recognize the severity of the storm until it was too late. She described the last few minutes she spent in her home as "terrifying," as emergency response personnel evacuated her entire family. Having less than 10 minutes to gather their belongings, they were able to grab only a few clothes and absolute necessities. Unable to find their dog, Lucky, in the storm, they presumed he was dead.

Although the details were "fuzzy," Amanda reported that she heard that their house, only blocks from the shoreline, was destroyed. When she found out their church was also destroyed, she stated, "I can't cry anymore. I just feel numb and angry. Why us? I keep asking. Why us? We are good people."

It should be noted that background information often is not available in disaster response. The counselor has to work in the here and now. However, there are times when the counselor might be able to spend more time with a disaster client.

Incident

Amanda and her family needed many things right away—temporary housing, clothing, food and water, and case management to help them rebuild their lives. As I led Amanda to the client casework line, I recognized some factors that might place her at risk. First, she had lost her home and her belongings, as well as a pet. Second, she and her family had been exposed to a life-threatening event and might be at risk for an adjustment or acute stress disorder.

However, because my work with Amanda was extremely short term, I recognized that traditional therapy protocols were not appropriate. My role was to help Amanda access her own support network and identify coping strategies as she rebuilt her life. As we walked, Amanda continued to talk about her loss of faith and how she "desperately wants to know why she was being punished by God."

Discussion

A licensed clinical mental health counselor, I worked as a disaster mental health (DMH) volunteer for the ARC Hurricane Sandy recovery effort. Before volunteering with my local ARC chapter, I completed the required courses: ARC Foundations of Disaster Mental Health and Psychological First Aid (PFA). I was deployed outside of my local chapter for the first time.

As a DMH worker, I understood that my role was to work alongside others on the Disaster Relief Operation team. In addition, I was to provide competent and compassionate mental health support to both survivors and relief workers. My primary goals were to identify any mental health needs that survivors might have and recognize those in need of secondary assessment and referrals. I realized that DMH support is not therapy and that I was not to use any therapeutic interventions aside from those prescribed for DMH work (PFA).

I proceeded by asking open-ended questions, such as "How are you doing?" and "How are things going?" In working with survivors, I had to remember that the goal was not to treat them and assess the crisis or trauma but to listen and mitigate stress (Roberts & Ashley, 2008). Drawing largely on the work of Abraham Maslow, Victor Frankl, and Carl Rogers, my work with Amanda was guided by the belief that persons have internal means for interpersonal growth and healing (Halpern & Tramontin, 2007). After attending to her basic needs (food, water, shelter, and medical care), I could help Amanda find a spiritual care worker who could help her assess any spiritual resources that were available to her or, if given the opportunity, work with her to tap into some of her strengths, such as prayer, to augment coping and aid resilience.

If I had been able to spend some time with Amanda (even just for one long discussion), I would have helped her identify her spiritual strengths. I would have listened to her story of grief and loss, communicated care through presence (the "ministry of presence"), and helped her identify areas of spiritual and religious coping that had been helpful to her in the past (Halpern & Tramontin, 2007; Roberts & Ashley, 2008). I had to remember to take a pragmatic approach that was grounded in empathy, genuine respect, calmness, and flexibility (Halpern & Tramontin, 2007). Work within the spiritual dimension in a disaster scenario can best be characterized by the use of appropriate acts of care and comfort that validate survivors' experiences and assist, if appropriate, in identifying adaptive coping skills based on their spiritual and religious perspectives. Consistent with the American Counseling Association's (ACA's) *Code of Ethics* (ACA, 2014), DMH workers must never impose their own values or beliefs on to any survivor.

Regardless of type, all disasters have an emotional impact on those they touch (Myers & Wee, 2005). Disaster exposure can have significant effects on emotional and spiritual functions (Halpern & Tramontin, 2007; Norris, Phifer, & Kaniasty, 1994; Webber, Mascari, Dubi, & Gentry, 2006). Initial spiritual responses to disaster include feelings of guilt and shame; anger at God (but also wanting assurance that God's presence is available); reconsideration of beliefs, values, and the power of spiritual tools (e.g., "Why me?" Why would God?" "Does prayer really work?"); feelings of hopelessness and punishment; a desire to be purified; and significant questions about reality, meaning, justice, and the afterlife (Roberts & Ashley, 2008).

People often find themselves having difficulty adhering to regular religious practices, such as prayer and meditation. Some may even disengage from religious practices and avoid interaction with faith leaders and faith communities (Harding, 2007). Although not everyone who is affected by a disaster faces a spiritual crisis, research illustrates a marked increase in spiritual and religious introspection after a disaster (Adams, Anderson, Turner, & Armstrong, 2011; Bjorck & Thurman, 2007; Pargament, Smith, Koenig, & Perez, 1998). For example, studies revealed that after the terrorist attacks of September 11, 2001, there was a considerable increase in attendance at religious services (Meisenhelder, 2002). People were more likely (60%) to seek emotional support from spiritual care workers (e.g., clergy, religious leaders, spiritual counselors) than mental health workers who did not address the spiritual domain (ARC, 2002).

First responders also lean toward spiritual practices for coping with disaster. One study reported that 26% of first responders used prayer as a coping resource during Hurricane Katrina (Adams et al., 2011). In a similar manner, 5.3% of them indicated that their spiritual beliefs served as a vital coping resource during disaster response.

Questions

1. Amanda was having problems accessing her spiritual resources, such as prayer, and expressed a desire to pray again. How could a counselor help her access these resources?
2. The primary spiritual question Amanda faced was why she and her family were "being punished." How might a counselor help Amanda explore this issue within the confines of a disaster mental health setting?
3. What are some critical ethical issues DMH workers might want to consider when working with Amanda?

References

Adams, T., Anderson, L., Turner, M., & Armstrong, J. (2011). Coping through a disaster: Lessons from Hurricane Katrina. *Journal of Homeland Security and Emergency Management, 8*(1). Article 19. Retrieved from http://www.bepress.com/jhsem/vol8/iss1/19. doi:10.2202/1547-7355.1836

American Counseling Association. (2014). *ACA code of ethics.* Alexandria, VA: Author.

American Red Cross. (2002). *Disaster mental health services: An overview, instructor's manual* (ARC Publication No. 3077-2). Washington, DC: Author.

Bjorck, J. P., & Thurman, J. W. (2007). Negative life events, patterns of positive and negative religious coping, and psychological functioning. *Journal for the Scientific Study of Religion, 46,* 159–167.

Halpern, J., & Tramontin, M. (2007). *Disaster mental health: Theory and practice.* Belmont, CA: Thompson Brooks/Cole.

Harding, S. (2007). Spiritual care and mental health for disaster response and recovery. New York, NY: New York Disaster Interfaith Services.

Meisenhelder, J. B. (2002). Terrorism, posttraumatic stress, and religious coping. *Issues in Mental Health Nursing, 23,* 771–782.

Myers, D., & Wee, D. F. (2005). *Disaster mental health services: A primer for practitioners.* New York, NY: Routledge.

Norris, F. H., Phifer, J. F., & Kaniasty, K. (1994). Individual and community reactions to the Kentucky floods: Findings from a longitudinal study of older adults. In R. J. Ursano, B. G. McCaughey, C. S. Fullerton, & B. Raphael (Eds.), *Individual and community response to disaster: The structure of human chaos* (pp. 378–400). Cambridge, England: Cambridge University Press.

Pargament, K. I., Smith, B. W., Koenig, H. G., & Perez, L. (1998). Patterns of positive and negative religious coping with major life stressors. *Journal for the Scientific Study of Religion, 37,* 710–724.

Roberts, S. B., & Ashley, W. W. C. (Eds.). (2008). *Disaster spiritual care: Practical clergy responses to community, regional and national tragedy.* Woodstock, VT: Longhill Partners.

Webber, J. M., Mascari, B., Dubi, M., & Gentry, J. E. (2006). Moving forward: Issues in trauma response and treatment. In G. R. Walz & R. Yep (Eds.), *VISTAS: Perspectives on counseling 2006* (pp. 17–21). Alexandria, VA: American Counseling Association.

 ## Response
Lisa R. Jackson-Cherry

My first self-check as a DMH worker with the ARC is to have a clear understanding of the following: my scope of practice as a DMH support worker, my role in the unit I am assigned to, and how this role may differ from my traditional mental health counseling approach in working with clients in my private practice. Although the same counseling skills are used in both settings, the prioritization of Amanda's presenting issues must be dealt with methodically and in compliance with her needs as a survivor of a disaster situation. This prioritization is imperative to the overall objective for the team to function effectively and to address the survivor's needs.

Assessing, Supporting, Connecting

In most disaster interventions and during the initial stages of a disaster, DMH workers most frequently focus on (a) assessing the needs of the survivors, (b) offering support to the survivors, and (c) connecting and referring the survivors to resources. Assessing basic needs, such as food, shelter, and safety, is of high priority. The most important issues that DMH workers address in the immediate aftermath of a disaster include reconnecting survivors with loved ones, providing shelter, helping with relocation and adjustments in transitional shelter settings, providing food and water, helping connect survivors with resources, aiding survivors in accessing financial and government support, and addressing safety concerns (McGlothlin, 2013).

An essential but often overlooked component of the healing process is instilling some sense of control through the DMH worker's role in retrieving information, making appropriate connections, and following up on unresolved questions. Offering some control of these items, which survivors may perceive as uncontrollable, may actually restore some sense of mastery, power, and hope for them. In most circumstances, the shock and denial experienced during the initial stages of the disaster do not provide an appropriate forum for mental health counseling. As a self-check, I need to ask myself, "Have I made the situation better right now, in the present?" "Have I decreased any emotional suffering related to the crisis?" and "Have I connected Amanda to appropriate referrals and resources needed to address her unique issues related to the disaster?"

Even with a good understanding of their role in a crisis situation, DMH workers should stay on high alert and keep as a high priority any indication or sign of persons who present as a harm to self or others. DMH workers should remain cognizant that they do not actually know anything about the survivors in emergency situations in which they are deployed. They do not know survivors' background, past coping skills, personal hardships, prior crises and responses, and complicated losses that may lead them to harm themselves or others.

Obtaining a valid assessment may be difficult because in the initial stages of a disaster people may not demonstrate signs of harm to self or others. A survivor's affect, behaviors, and cognitions may be exaggerated or blunted during the initial crisis. Because people react differently, risk identification may be difficult. Hence, the DMH workers should remain on alert, know the protocol set forth by the agency in these situations, and, if necessary, refer to the unit that is addressing risk. I would keep all of this in mind in working with Amanda.

Normalizing Thoughts and Feelings

It may seem simplistic, but DMH workers should remember that normalizing disaster survivors' thoughts and feelings may be helpful.

I would not say to Amanda, "I know how you are feeling." I might say, "Many people who experience such disasters often report a sense of hopelessness and numbness or may feel out of control, especially in the initial onset of a disaster."

At some point, DMH workers also may integrate psychoeducational components to evaluate and activate coping mechanisms and skills. Although the DMH worker's role is focused on "assessing, supporting, and connecting," he or she should always look out for people who may be struggling more than they are coping and explore how this may be affecting them right now. Again, DMH workers may not be the ones addressing the issues, but they can refer to the team member who is assigned.

With most survivors, exploring too far into the future during the initial stages of a disaster may be of no use because most survivors may be fixated on the present, and rightly so. However, underlying issues that may affect a survivor's adjustment and coping—such as expressed guilt and blame for not preparing properly or loss of a family member or pet, as was reported by Amanda—should not be ignored. Such issues should be addressed for further assessment as to how they are currently affecting her and her family.

Emergency disasters of any kind can affect survivors' spiritual and religious faith and connections. A survivor may experience an increased reliance on his or her faith or spirituality or may start to blame or withdraw from faith or spiritual connections. Having an awareness of the Association for Spiritual, Ethical, and Religious Values in Counseling's (ASERVIC's) spiritual and religious competencies (ASERVIC, 2009) and how they can be used in crisis situations can be very helpful. However, the spiritual competencies were developed primarily for professional counselors and may not be the focus of DMH support workers.

Still, some spiritual competencies are very relevant to crisis settings. For example, the ASERVIC competency focused on not imposing personal faith/spiritual practices but being open to exploring the survivor's faith and practices is essential to implement in Amanda's situation. I would not assume that I know what she means by prayer, so I would ask her to share with me from her practice and framework her struggles with not praying. Just as I should not impose my own religious values, I also must be comfortable asking about her religious and spiritual values. If I do not inquire, I am not serving in a supportive and compassionate role and may be ineffective because Amanda reported this as a presenting concern.

Spiritual Resources

Regarding Question 1, Amanda appears to be experiencing some spiritual and religious turmoil that may be affected by reported separation from spiritual resources, such as prayer. As a DMH worker, I would first affirm her need for her spiritual resources because she stated that prayer had been valuable to her in the past. I might even inquire into other situations in which she relied on her religious or spiritual practices/faith and the outcomes.

I would first take an inventory of what Amanda defines as resources. Resources may be anything from religious or spiritual leaders and places of worship to persons of the same faith and practices. In particular, Amanda mentioned the need for prayer. I would need to understand whether there is a blockage to her continuing need to pray because of blame or shame or whether she simply needs a quiet place or religious items that the crisis team may have available to assist her.

Taking an assessment of these resource needs is important in determining what resources might be available onsite. There might be religious or spiritual leaders working in the setting, counselors working with the ARC to whom Amanda can be referred, other survivors expressing similar needs, places that can be assigned to serve as resources for prayer, or religious articles that may help meet her needs. Also, there may be a creative way in which to develop or recreate these items. In each of these situations, I use the "assess, support, and connect" with Amanda and her reported need and struggles for prayer.

Exploring Spiritual Questions

The answer to Question 2 is that the situation may be suited for long-term counseling, beyond interactions in the crisis setting. My main focus would be to affirm and normalize how Amanda feels, remain supportive in her struggles and pain, and plant the seeds for counseling that may be needed later. In particular, I would share, "In situations like these, when we are unable to find answers, it is common to question, 'Where is our God when we need him/her most?' 'Why did God leave us alone?' 'What have I done to deserve this?' and 'Why am I being punished?'"

All are questions aimed at trying to understand horrible things that happen. Sometimes things happen and there is no understanding, but I would want to know how this may be affecting Amanda at the moment and how she can gain some control over an uncontrollable situation. In my experiences with this kind of searching for meaning to explain the "why," once a person can redefine what the "why" means for him or her and gain some control over the situation, the focus starts to shift from the "why" to actions of "how I can get through this." Often in these cases, the relationship with the survivor's higher being is repaired or shifts.

Ethical Issues

DMH workers always should be cognizant of many potential ethical issues. Working with Amanda, I would want to make certain I do not go outside the limits of my scope of practice as a DMH worker that were set forth by the ARC leaders. If assigned in a compassion support unit, DMH workers should provide support, not diagnosis and treatment. In actuality, diagnosis never should be made in an immediate disaster because the time frame is limited and the level of severity cannot be assessed appropriately.

In disaster situations, survivors affected by a catastrophic situation often experience normal reactions to abnormal events. The reactions may resemble various symptoms of mental health issues but do not indicate the presence of actual mental health disorders. DMH workers need to understand that these reactions are common and normal in disaster situations. They also need to keep good boundaries and make certain that survivors know the limits of the crisis worker–survivor relationship. Interactions with crisis survivors often are minimal (ACA, 2013). Therefore, setting up clear boundaries and expectations of the DMH worker's role will help avoid potential accusations of abandonment.

As a DMH worker, I must not promise anything I cannot deliver, and I must make certain that I am practicing within my competencies as assigned by the ARC. If I am assigned a support role in this situation, I should not represent myself as a licensed professional counselor. I also must adhere to the practices and protocol set forth by the lead agency. If I am supervising counseling students, I must make certain that they are practicing only at their current competency level (Webber & Mascari, 2009).

As a DMH worker, I must recognize my own limits and know when I need to address my personal issues that, if left unaddressed, could affect the survivors I am working with. Crisis workers in all settings often experience job dissatisfaction, burnout, and vicarious and secondary traumatization. I must be able to address and respond to my personal reactions and experiences and seek help so as not to do harm to others. Keeping personal issues at the forefront and following best practices should decrease ethical complaints and concerns and provide support against any accusations.

In sum, as a compassionate DMH worker assigned to Amanda, I would hope to alleviate her emotional suffering, improve her situation with my interaction in the present, provide support, connect her to resources, and provide her a safe environment to the best of my ability. "For in a multitude of counselors, there is safety" (Proverbs 11:14, New King James Version).

References

American Counseling Association. (2013). *Fact sheet #10: 1:1 crisis counseling.* Retrieved from http://www.counseling.org/docs/trauma-disaster/fact-sheet-10---1on1-crisis-counseling.pdf?sfvrsn=2

Association for Spiritual, Ethical, and Religious Values in Counseling. (2009). *Competencies for addressing spiritual and religious issues in counseling.* Retrieved from http://www.aservic.org/resources/spiritual-competencies/

McGlothlin, J. (2013). Emergency preparedness. In L. R. Jackson-Cherry & B. Erford (Eds.), *Crisis prevention and intervention* (2nd ed.). Columbus, OH: Pearson/Merrill Prentice Hall.

Webber, J. M., & Mascari, B. J. (2009). Critical issues in implementing the new CACREP standards for disaster, trauma, and crisis counseling. In G. R. Walz, J. C. Bleuer, & R. K. Yep (Eds.), *Compelling counseling interventions VISTAS 2009* (pp. 125–138). Alexandria, VA: American Counseling Association.

 ## Reflections

Tracey E. Robert and Virginia A. Kelly

The increase of natural disasters, terrorist attacks, and trauma seen in recent years has required counselors to seek up-to-date training in trauma and psychological first aid. There is a growing need for counselors to be available nationally and globally and for them to understand how to work with victims.

This case and response underscore the point that the skills needed for disaster mental health counseling can be enhanced by traditional counseling skills, but they are *different* skills. Disaster mental health counseling requires a practical approach to providing a human response to traumatic events—as mentioned in the case, the "ministry of presence." In such counseling, the spirit, from the Latin *spiritus*, or *breath*, can help ground and stabilize the client. Disaster mental health counseling with a spiritual focus can be beneficial in the following ways:

- The method of caring by the mere presence of the counselor or responder underscores the importance of "being," not necessarily "doing."
- Discussion of basic needs and survival after a disaster allows for integration of the client's religious or spiritual coping mechanisms.
- Discussing the spiritual distress that occurs at the time of disaster response is an important element of healing.

• • •

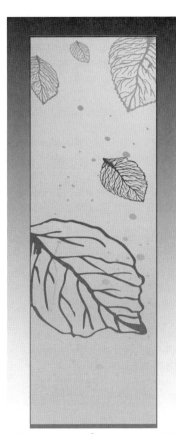

Section III

Spirituality
and Specific
Disorders

Chapter 14 Eating Disorders

Case
Dana Michie

Katie, a 56-year-old White woman who had attended a hospital in-patient eating disorder program, was referred to me for individual outpatient treatment. She had been struggling with anorexia nervosa since she was 13 years old. Katie reported that she was unhappy about the weight she had gained while in the hospital, although she knew that maintaining and gaining weight would be part of her treatment plan, along with addressing her anxiety and depression. Katie was afraid that, left to her own devices, she might not continue to progress.

Background

Katie had lived in a northeastern state her entire life. She had been married for more than 30 years and had three grown children. She met her husband, John, while a senior in high school, and they married shortly after she graduated. She attended college to become a teacher but left once she became pregnant; she did not complete her college education.

Katie described her marriage as "good." She reported that both she and John had been focused on the children and that they maintained fairly conventional roles. John was a teacher and coach and was the family's wage earner, while Katie remained a stay-at-home mom. She said she loved this role while the children were growing up, but after the children had grown, she was lonely because John was still very busy with teaching and coaching and often came home late after games. Katie was deeply religious and active in her church. She attended weekly Bible study and other church activities. Both Katie and John attended church regularly.

As a child, Katie had been slightly overweight and was often teased at school and called fat. She was molested by a family member, causing much inner conflict and making her feel bad about her body and herself. She never spoke of this molestation to anyone for fear of losing the love of the family member who molested her. Katie's eating disorder developed at about age 13. As she began to grow tall and lean, the teasing at school stopped and, for the first time in her life, she felt a sense of empowerment. She vowed that she would never be fat again.

In high school, Katie was raped by five members of the football team when she was on her way to the parking lot returning home from a dance. She said she went home and cried for a long time. She never spoke about this incident to anyone until years later, feeling that no one would believe her because she was unpopular and the boys who raped her were very popular.

Incident

Katie was hospitalized for an extremely low body weight in addition to depression and anxiety. As part of her step-down treatment plan, she was recommended to me for counseling. In addition to having an eating disorder, Katie was diagnosed with anxiety and depression. She reported that she was very lonely at home and spent most of her days alone. Because of her anxiety, she would rarely go out on her own and she had to force herself to go out to perform routine activities, such as keeping doctor appointments. Grocery shopping produced high anxiety, and Katie avoided many social activities because they centered around food. Katie was conflicted about having too much time alone because it allowed her to restrict food. Although she wanted to lose weight, she didn't want to go back to the hospital.

Discussion

My primary goals in working with Katie were to help her maintain her weight gain, reduce her anxiety, keep her mood stable, and address the sexual trauma that was the precipitating factor for her hatred of her body and the eating disorder. Because Katie shared that she liked to write short stories, I chose to work with her using poetry therapy. I hoped that if Katie could cultivate a new identity as a poet, she would eventually release her identity as an anorexic.

Katie selected Psalm 51 from the Bible as a poem she would like to work with. I asked her to read the psalm out loud and then to select a word, image, or line that spoke to her. She identified verses 6 and 7, which state, "Behold, thou desirest truth in the inward being; therefore teach me wisdom in my secret heart. Purge me with hyssop, and I shall be clean; wash me, and I shall be whiter than snow."

Katie said that these lines gave her strength to put aside the eating disorder to become "clean and white" again and that the eating disorder was none of that but rather a dark, lonely existence. "If I am cleansed of this darkness, there will be a new way for me to be in the world that will bring me happiness and joy," Katie said. The eating disorder had become the coping mechanism Katie used to deal with her sexual trauma. Being "cleansed" by God's love and forgiveness helped her feel released from the trauma and hence the eating disorder.

Then she selected verses 10 through 12, which state, "Create in me a clean heart, O God, and put a new and right spirit within me. Cast me not away from thy presence, and take not thy holy Spirit from me. Restore to me the joy of thy salvation and uphold me with a willing spirit." These lines also encouraged Katie to put aside the eating disorder. She said, "With God's help I can make all things new and right again within me, and through him I can find deliverance and salvation from the eating disorder."

This process of reading and discussing poetry inspired Katie in many ways. It helped her develop her voice, and she began to write poetry. It helped her work on her social anxiety by allowing her to speak out in public venues about her journey with an eating disorder. Also, as I had hoped, it helped her see herself other than as an anorexic. Katie wrote and self-published a book of poetry about her eating disorder journey. She now calls herself a poet. This work has given Katie a sense of self and a voice in which to speak of her struggle toward recovery.

Questions

1. Katie struggled with eating on a daily basis and maintaining a healthy body weight. How might a counselor further explore this problem?
2. An important piece of Katie's recovery lies in her developing self-esteem. How might a counselor help her explore this issue more deeply?
3. Religion played an important role in Katie's life. How might a counselor further explore the integration of religion into her counseling?

Response

Jocelyn Novella

Katie's case is a complex one in that she not only has long-term anorexia nervosa but also has had multiple incidences of sexual trauma. Before I address the specific questions asked, I would emphasize the importance of a holistic approach to Katie's treatment. A framework for this holistic treatment plan includes the following:

- eating/physical health;
- behavioral health—immediate psychological states and triggers that lead to physical symptoms;
- family-of-origin history, role in keeping family secrets, role in current nuclear family;
- spiritual beliefs about place in the world, right to exist, specific religious beliefs;
- Eriksonian developmental issues around identity, especially those related to attachment and trauma (Erikson, 1968);
- trauma and current posttraumatic stress disorder (PTSD);
- self-esteem and major points in life that have affected it; and
- family psychiatric history, to rule out predisposition (e.g., anxiety disorders with agoraphobia, depression, bipolar disorders; Garner & Garfinkel, 1997).

From an evidence-based perspective, remarkably little research provides guidelines for the most effective counseling techniques for anorexia nervosa, especially in adults with a lifetime history (Wilson, Grilo, & Vitousek, 2007). Most research that shows efficacy is focused on family therapy with adolescents (Wilson et al., 2007). This lack of research makes choosing a treatment strategy for Katie more difficult. However, extensive research has been done, especially in the past few years, on effective trauma treatment and the benefit of prolonged exposure therapy for improving outcomes after trauma (Taylor et al., 2003). This method will be an integral part of her care.

In reviewing this case with the referring counselor, I would emphasize two key points: (a) that anorexia nervosa is the deadliest of psychiatric disorders because of the combination of physical health decline and suicide and (b) that because Katie has been engaging in restrictive behavior for 43 years, it can become quite intractable, requiring constant monitoring and evaluation in collaboration with a medical doctor who has expertise in working with patients who have eating disorders (Johnson, 1991). Because of these factors, the counselor should constantly assess whether Katie needs to return to an increased level of care, either partial hospitalization or inpatient.

Eating and Weight Issues

The first question addressed eating and weight issues, a key part of the treatment plan. Although these issues need to be resolved for Katie to recover, they are merely an external symptom of all the complex feelings stirring underneath. While the counselor is trying to build trust for the client to allow herself to be vulnerable, these daily eating behaviors need to remain fairly healthful.

The first step is to take a full behavioral history of Katie's eating disorder, recording details about fluctuations in body image at various ages (e.g., issues with being overweight when young) and specifics on her eating and weight throughout her life. Any purging behaviors, such as overexercising, using diet pills or laxatives, or vomiting, should also be tracked in this history. The goal is similar to that in taking a full substance abuse history from a client who has a drug addiction: to establish triggers for worsening behaviors and discover other positive coping strategies that work for the client (Vandereycken & Pieters, 1978).

I would suggest using a food diary to track the connection between moods and triggers for restrictive eating behaviors. Cognitive–behavioral therapy (CBT) may be used to interrupt the process of having a negative feeling, followed by a negative self-image thought, and then restricting food intake or overexercising to release that feeling. CBT also can address Katie's growing agoraphobia, especially around any activity that is food related (Pike, Walsh, Vitousek, Wilson, & Bauer, 2003). The counselor should look for any positive coping strategies the client already uses to maintain healthy eating and should brainstorm new behaviors the client could try. This is a collaborative process—the client is constantly giving feedback to the counselor about what is working, while the counselor is helping the client remain committed to trying new strategies.

Addressing the Self-Esteem Issue

The second question addresses another focal point in the treatment plan framework: self-esteem. I would commend the referring counselor for finding an avenue to "Katie's own voice" through her interest in Biblical psalms and writing her own poetry. This process is crucial in both trauma and eating disorder treatment because clients often feel they do not have the "right" to a voice or to assert themselves. Arthur Crisp and other researchers have described anorexia nervosa as a desire not to grow up or, in the extreme, to make oneself take up little to no space (Crisp, 1997). This definition is symbolic of a lack of voice in the world and, from an existential point of view, ties into a sense of spirituality (meaning and purpose in life). Does Katie feel there is a reason she exists? Does she feel she "deserves" life?

Identity development is a key element of self-esteem. Katie has limited her goals in life to take on a conventional female role in her current family. The counselor could explore with her whether this was a purposeful choice or whether she felt some sense of obligation to focus on others' needs versus her own. An exploration of Katie's occupational and life goals could enhance her identity development.

Richard Bolles's workbook *What Color Is Your Parachute?* (2013) might be a useful resource.

Establishing a solid foundation of identity has been difficult for Katie because of her traumatic sexual experiences. Children who are molested often feel they are "dirty" and blame themselves for the adult having sexual interest in them. Also, when a family member or other person who is supposed to love and support them betrays that trust, it can remove the sense that any adult can be trusted. The family-of-origin dynamic can be changed completely, even if one of the parents is not the offender. The loneliness and deception involved in keeping the secret with the perpetrator often causes survivors to identify themselves as "liars," "colluders," and no longer "good children" (Berrett, Hardman, O'Grady, & Richards, 2007).

To treat this trauma, prolonged exposure therapy and cognitive processing therapy have had great success with PTSD that resulted from military service or sexual abuse/assault experiences (Taylor et al., 2003). I would recommend that the referring counselor become trained in one of these techniques or refer Katie for additional work with a trained practitioner. These self-esteem and family-of-origin issues are part of the reason why family therapy has been shown to be so effective with adolescent anorexics (Wilson et al., 2007). Because Katie is an adult and family therapy with parents is not an option, this work may have to be done in individual sessions, with the counselor teaching Katie some "re-parenting" techniques. Re-parenting also occurs in the relationship with the treating counselor.

The counseling relationship is a key to establishing trust of others and a sense of worthiness in the client (Isserlin & Couturier, 2012). As everyone from Rogers (1961) to Yalom (2005) has emphasized, the relationship can be the most healing aspect of counseling, which is especially true with both eating disorders and trauma treatment. When a client constantly focuses on what is "wrong" with herself, as Katie does, a counselor can be a strong voice for what is right. This process does not entail empty compliments; the client will sense that this is disingenuous and lose trust. It is about showing the client that she deserves to be respected, her thoughts and opinions are important, and she has the right to assert herself and "take up space" in this world.

Integration of Religion and Spirituality

I would again compliment the referring counselor on finding a way to work with Katie's religious beliefs to reestablish her self-esteem. Exploring Bible psalms gives great insight into Katie's sense of what is important in her life, what her God means to her, and how God's "help" can allow her to let go of her eating disorder. Often, an eating disorder replaces God as a source of comfort for the client, so a "mature faith and spirituality can serve as a resource and healing influence for women with eating disorders" (Berrett et al., 2007, p. 374).

When exploring Katie's religious views through her poetry and these psalms, the referring counselor should keep in mind that these are windows into how Katie sees herself in the world. If she is reinforcing her view of herself as "dirty" or "undeserving," these feelings can be discussed in session. For example, Katie asks God to "create in me a clean heart...and put a new and right spirit within me." Understood in this statement is that her current "spirit" is not "right" or "clean." Although she can look to God to "cleanse" her, sometimes these "dirty" feelings can cause clients to feel that God is disappointed in them. Marsden, Karagianni, and Morgan (2007, p. 9) stated that when clients "were unable to live up to the supposed standards of their God figure, their sense of guilt, shame, and failure was exacerbated."

Bryant-Davis et al. (2012) stressed how important it is for the counselor to explore some of these thoughts with the client. A good place to start would be to have Katie examine her religious, and even existential thoughts, on how God creates or allows spirits to become "unclean." The counselor might ask Katie these questions: Does she see her molestation as a child or rape in high school as being choices she made? Does she see them as happening to her? Does she believe her God "blames" her or sees her as unclean because of what happened?

Marsden et al. (2007) also emphasized the importance of locus of control, which is external in many clients with an eating disorder and in many trauma survivors. The counseling relationship encourages the client to find an internal locus of control. The treating counselor could emphasize to Katie that some faiths believe that, just as God creates persons with free will, He or She gives them the right to make choices and decide to control that which they are capable of controlling. The Serenity Prayer used by Alcoholics Anonymous could help Katie adjust her locus of control:

> God grant me the serenity
> to accept the things I cannot change,
> courage to change the things I can,
> and wisdom to know the difference.

Relaxation, meditation, and yoga have been used as "spiritual" treatment for chronic adult anorexics (Long, Fitzgerald, & Hollin, 2012). These techniques, part of an Eastern philosophy of mental, physical, and spiritual wellness, connect mind and body. Katie could be encouraged to explore these spiritual interventions and Eastern spirituality as a supplement to her current religious beliefs.

A Useful Strategy

Providing the best care in a case like Katie's has many aspects, and the counselor can be most effective by following a structured treatment framework. Attending to spiritual issues is a useful strategy for enhancing a client's self-concept and recovery.

References

Berrett, M. E., Hardman, R. K., O'Grady, K. A., & Richards, P. S. (2007). The role of spirituality in the treatment of trauma and eating disorders: Recommendations for clinical practice. *Eating Disorders, 15,* 373–389.

Bolles, R. (2013). *What color is your parachute? A practical manual for job-hunters and career-changers* (2013 ed.). Berkeley, CA: Ten Speed Press.

Bryant-Davis, T., Ellis, M. U., Burke-Maynard, E., Moon, N., Counts, P. A., & Anderson, G. (2012). Religiosity, spirituality, and trauma recovery in the lives of children and adolescents. *Professional Psychology: Research and Practice, 43,* 306–314.

Crisp, A. (1997). Anorexia nervosa as flight from growth: Assessment and treatment based on the model. In D. M. Garner & P. E. Garfinkel (Eds.), *Handbook of treatment for eating disorders* (2nd ed., pp. 248–277). New York, NY: Guilford Press.

Erikson, E. H. (1968). *Identity: Youth and crisis.* New York, NY: Norton.

Garner, D. M., & Garfinkel, P. E. (Eds.). (1997). *Handbook of treatment for eating disorders* (2nd ed., pp. 34–49). New York, NY: Guilford Press.

Isserlin, L., & Couturier, J. (2012). Therapeutic alliance and family-based treatment for adolescents with anorexia nervosa. *Psychotherapy, 49,* 46–51.

Johnson, C. L. (Ed.). (1991). *Psychodynamic treatment of anorexia nervosa and bulimia* (pp. 57–58). New York, NY: Guilford Press.

Long, C. G., Fitzgerald, K., & Hollin, C. R. (2012). Treatment of chronic anorexia nervosa: A 4-year follow-up of adult patients treated in an acute inpatient setting. *Clinical Psychology and Psychotherapy, 19,* 1–13.

Marsden, P., Karagianni, E., & Morgan, J. F. (2007). Spirituality and clinical care in eating disorders: A qualitative study. *International Journal of Eating Disorders, 40,* 7–12.

Pike, K. M., Walsh, B. T., Vitousek, K., Wilson, G. T., & Bauer, J. (2003). Cognitive behavior therapy in the posthospitalization treatment of anorexia nervosa. *American Journal of Psychiatry, 160,* 2046–2049.

Rogers, C. (1961). *On becoming a person: A therapist's view of psychotherapy.* London, England: Constable.

Taylor, S., Thordarson, D. S., Maxfield, L., Fedoroff, I. C., Lovell, K., & Ogrodniczuk, J. (2003). Comparative efficacy, speed, and adverse effects of three PTSD treatments: Exposure therapy, EMDR, and relaxation training. *Journal of Consulting and Clinical Psychology, 71,* 330–338.

Vandereycken, W., & Pieters, G. (1978). Short-term weight restoration in anorexia nervosa through operant conditioning. *Scandinavian Journal of Behaviour Therapy, 7,* 221–236.

Wilson, G. T., Grilo, C. M., & Vitousek, K. M. (2007). Psychological treatment of eating disorders. *American Psychologist, 62,* 199–216.

Yalom, I. D. (2005). *The gift of therapy.* New York, NY: HarperCollins.

Reflections

Tracey E. Robert and Virginia A. Kelly

Eating disorders are life threatening. Adolescents and young adults are most at risk, but eating disorders are on the rise in adult men and, as seen in this case, adult women. These increases have expanded the need for mental health professionals to be aware and responsive. Helping clients find meaning and purpose in their life and assisting them to see how their own voice matters are important goals of therapy for clients with eating disorders. Lack of self-acceptance and history of previous trauma causing loss of trust and safety are key challenges to the counseling process. Using a spiritual focus in counseling can improve the process in the following ways:

- This focus supports a climate of safety in which clients can share their innermost secrets and provides a protective factor to discuss their distorted self-images.
- Holistic care for clients provides a wellness model that addresses the mind, body, and spirit and is highly effective for recovery.
- Integration of the client's own religious or spiritual perspectives provides resources for healing and expands the spiritual intervention options the counselor might suggest, such as mindfulness, spiritual bibliography, and prayer.

• • •

Chapter 15

Sexual Addiction

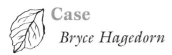

Case

Bryce Hagedorn

Thom, age 37, initially sought counseling in an attempt to help his wife, Claire, break an addiction to food (restrictive type). At the end of the second session, Claire stated that she did not have a problem with food and that it was her husband who required therapy because of his controlling nature. Soon thereafter, Claire filed for divorce, leaving Thom emotionally devastated and highly anxious about the future. He felt his life was crumbling away at the thought of divorce from the woman who had provided a salve to a set of emotional wounds. These wounds had not been revealed thus far, but they were disclosed once a trusting relationship had been established.

Background

Thom was born in upstate New York and raised as an only child. His father owned an electrical business, which kept him very busy, and his mother was a homemaker. The family was very involved with the church at the mother's direction—she was a deaconess, often attending religious services multiple times each week. As such, Thom reported having a very strong faith base and requested that counseling sessions maintain a Christian focus.

Six months into counseling, Thom began to reveal a history of sexual behaviors that started with early exposure to pornography at age 11. In sharing his sexual history, he noted that his first sexual experience at age 12 was unsolicited and shameful: A neighborhood boy 4 years older fondled Thom while they both viewed pornography. This behavior occurred on three occasions over the following 2 years but ceased when the older boy left for college.

To complicate matters, Thom's mother caught her son several times looking at pornographic magazines and masturbating; each time, she delivered a severe spanking. These spankings involved Thom pulling down his pants and leaning against the wall; while his mother spanked him, she would recite various biblical texts to him. He also would be required to seek God's forgiveness the next time the family was at church.

The final spanking that Thom remembered occurred when he was 16. This episode was particularly traumatic in that it occurred in the family's garage, with the garage door open, exposing the incident to the neighbors. Thom's shame resulted in his roughly pushing his mother away from him. During the altercation, Thom's mother tripped over a bicycle, fell, and broke her arm.

Thom's father, who, up to this point, had been oblivious to Thom's use of pornography and the resulting spankings, was called to the hospital and delivered a verbal assault on his son in the middle of the reception area. Emotionally absent up until that time, Thom's father heard only his wife's report of the events and concluded that his son had assaulted her. He made the proclamation that Thom could no longer live in the home; thus, he was sent to live with his aunt in New York City.

Thom's aunt, a religious woman, took him with her to church two or three times per week. Thom once caught sight of his aunt coming out of the shower and felt "hooked" to seek additional opportunities to see her undressed. Hence, he spent great amounts of time and energy in various scenarios that would provide these opportunities.

Feeling ashamed of his behavior, Thom began to hit himself, using various methods to punish his body, such as belts and hairbrushes on his legs and buttocks, yet the voyeurism continued unabated. Fantasizing about seeing other women undressed resulted in his turning his voyeuristic activities to others in the apartment building where he lived with his aunt. Each time Thom caught sight of a naked woman, he would masturbate, punish himself physically, and then prostrate himself on the altar of his aunt's church, begging to be delivered of his behavior.

Two years later, Thom entered college. There his sexual behaviors exploded, with him using pornography more and more, engaging with multiple sexual partners and prostitutes, and frequenting adult bookstores and strip clubs. His voyeurism and self-punishment also continued but were redirected toward the pornography that he viewed (those that contained voyeurism) and the acts that he paid others to perform (spankings by prostitutes).

Then, during Thom's senior year, he met Claire, and all of these sexual behaviors came to a grinding halt: Claire provided him with a "safe haven," a strong religious foundation, a sense of self-control, and a salve to the emptiness he felt. During 15 years of marriage with

Claire, Thom went on to become a successful businessman, an active leader in his church, and an involved father of three children whom he coached to athletic stardom. During those years, Thom's previous sexual behaviors reportedly never manifested.

Incident

After Claire filed for divorce, Thom's semblance of order and self-control crumbled. He shared that he had been experiencing extreme obsessive thoughts about walking around the neighborhood where he lived with the hope of catching sight of someone undressing. Not allowing himself to act on these thoughts, Thom turned his energy toward an increase in religious practices, such as increased memorization of Bible verses and attendance at religious services. He also increased other practices that resulted in physical discomfort, including restricting his food intake; not allowing himself to sleep more than 5 hours; running to the point of causing painful shin splints; and even eating uncomfortably spicy foods, which caused him gastric distress. Having already accepted a diagnosis of sexual addiction, Thom struggled greatly with being in the present moment, honoring his body as a gift, and understanding how God could care about him, let alone love him.

Discussion

Thom and I worked together for 18 months, unraveling the connections that had been formed among sex, pain, shame, and religiosity. In that time, I used the sequential family addictions model (Juhnke & Hagedorn, 2006). Treatment progressed from motivational interviewing, solution-focused therapy, cognitive–behavioral therapy, and family systems theories to object relations theory.

At the 16-month mark, enough trust had been established for me to use object relations theory and thus create a holding environment where Thom could feel valued and safe. In this therapeutic space, Thom was encouraged to "be" and "act" without fear of my abandoning him. At the same time, the re-parenting that occurred allowed me to gently confront Thom about his behaviors, challenge him on his views of God, and keep him in the present moment. Mindfully unpacking some of his most shameful moments resulted in his being able to freely express emotions that had thus far been repressed. During this time, Thom's two mantras that aided his commitment to focus on the present were "I'm struggling well" and "Okay God . . . SHIT . . . okay."

Questions

1. Given the interaction of sex, pain, shame, and religiosity, how would you proceed with addressing Thom's ongoing self-injurious behaviors?

2. Using Thom's preferred Christian lens, how would you address his notions of a loving God who cares about and loves him unconditionally?

3. How would you explain and address Thom's apparent 15-year hiatus from sexual addiction, during which he was very successful (building a business from the ground up, becoming a successful leader in his church, coaching his three children to athletic stardom)? How would you help him understand why he felt like it was all crumbling away at the thought of divorce?

References

Juhnke, G. A., & Hagedorn, W. B. (2006). *Counseling addicted families: A sequential assessment & treatment model.* New York, NY: Brunner-Routledge.

 ## Response

Craig S. Cashwell and Hallie Sylvestro

The case of Thom, though complex, depicts a common vignette for those who struggle with sex addiction, which affects about 6% of the population (Carnes, 1992). Thom came to counseling in a highly vulnerable state. Initially thinking he was presenting because of his wife's problems, Thom found his world unwinding. Now, in the early stages of midlife, he faced dissolution of his marriage, accusations from his wife about his controlling nature, and what appeared to be the reemergence of impulses to engage in voyeurism, impulses that had been dormant for 15 years.

Thom's case cannot be fully understood from a single conceptual framework. Accordingly, the use of the sequential family addictions model (Juhnke & Hagedorn, 2006), an integrated sequential model, is logical. In addition, Thom's struggles can be examined through the respective lenses of the following:

- paired-associate learning,
- trauma theory,
- negative religious coping, and
- sex addiction.

We first discuss Thom through each of these lenses. Then we respond to the specific questions provided at the conclusion of the case presentation.

Paired-Associate Learning

Thom's early sexual experiences were complicated. At a young age, 11, he was exposed to pornography. Fully understanding how and where would be helpful. Thom had his first sexual experience with another person, watching pornography with a 16-year-old boy who also fondled him, when he was only 12. This experience would occur three times between ages 12 and 14, ending only when the older boy left for college. Thom described these experiences as "shameful." In this regard, we can see that he paired his early sexual experiences with shame. Unknown are what messages Thom might have already received from family, friends, and his religious community about same-sex relations, but given the prevalence of homophobia in society, he probably had received some negative messages that further increased the shame.

Between ages 12 and 14, Thom naturally experienced sexual arousal from pornography and being fondled. Therefore, it was the sensorimotor experiences (arousal, excitement) that became paired with shame. The secret nature of these behaviors likely began to lay the groundwork for later addictive sexual behaviors.

The paired association between sex and shame was magnified when Thom's mother delivered a "severe spanking" while reciting Bible verses when she found him looking at pornographic magazines. It would be important to explore this more fully with Thom, including whether his mother's status as a church leader might have led him to conflate her with God. If so, Thom's understanding of God and religion entered the equation that associated sex and shame. The paired-associate equation for Thom starts to look like this:

Sexual behavior = Sexual shame = Religious judgment = Religious shame

Thom experienced additional shame for developmentally normal sexual behaviors and his mother's harsh religious judgment, which may easily have become conflated with God's judgment. The incident at age 16 only reinforced these connections. Thom was publicly shamed and humiliated by his mother's harsh punishment and then overwhelmed by the punishment that occurred where neighbors could see it. Although his response in trying to escape the shaming experience seems warranted, it resulted in injury to his mother, a severe reaction from his father (who did not take time to hear Thom's side of the story), and, ultimately, rejection/abandonment from his parents. Researchers have found that images of God often have parallels based on parenting style, particularly for men (Chou & Uata, 2012). It follows that Thom may have felt abandoned by God, as well as by his parents.

The paired associations continued to be reinforced when Thom became obsessed with seeing his aunt—also a highly religious woman—in various states of undress. In response to this obsession, Thom may have introjected his mother's belief that sexual thoughts and actions must be punished. Without his mother to punish him, Thom began to punish himself. At this point, he had begun a spiral into a pattern of increased sexual preoccupation, sexual acts, shame, and punishment. He begged for God to deliver him but remained trapped in an addictive cycle in which shame became fuel for ongoing sexual preoccupation and actions.

Trauma Theory

Thom's early sexual history was fraught with trauma. Sexual arousal was paired with shame, as well as extreme punishment and judgment. A full exploration of the effects of trauma on developing sexuality is beyond the scope of this response, but research shows that early trauma is present in most persons who seek treatment for sex addiction (Carnes, 1992). Thom's self-abuse can be understood as a function of trauma recapitulation, a tendency among trauma survivors to reenact the trauma experience (van der Kolk, 2007).

Negative Religious Coping

Thom's case also might be understood through a lens of negative religious coping (Pargament, Smith, Koenig, & Perez, 1998). Little information is provided about Thom's religious beliefs. To provide effective counseling, it would be important to assess his beliefs more fully. Given what we know about Thom's early history of religiosity and abuse, he probably had a "less secure relationship with God, a tenuous and ominous view of the world, and a religious struggle in the search for significance" (Pargament et al., 1998, p. 712), characteristics of people who engage in negative religious coping. We also would want to conduct a comprehensive exploration with Thom on whether he felt he was being punished by God for past actions and whether he saw God as someone who loved him.

Sex Addiction

The case explains how for much of his life Thom has struggled with addictive sexual behavior, referred to by researchers as *compulsive sexuality* (Allen & Hollander, 2006) or *hypersexual disorder* (Kor, Fogel, Reid, & Potenza, 2013). As debate continues about whether out-of-control sexual behavior is best viewed through an addiction lens, most experts agree that problematic sexual behavior is indicated by sexual behaviors that contradict personal values, include a cycle of preoccupation and resultant shame, continue despite efforts to change behaviors and avoid negative consequences, and include withdrawal symptoms when efforts are made to stop the behavioral cycle. In this response, we describe Thom's problematic sexual behavior with the term *sex addiction*.

In a number of ways, Thom's early life created the perfect storm for a sex addiction. Carnes (1992) found that 77% of sex addicts come from rigid families and 68% come from families that are both rigid and disengaged, which seems to typify Thom's family. Carnes further found that 97% of sex addicts experienced emotional abuse; 72%, physical abuse; and 81%, sexual abuse. Given what we are told about the punishment Thom's mother used and his early sexual experience with the older boy, he appears to have experienced all three. Thom's early trauma history and poor family functioning set the stage for the "explosion" of addictive sexual behavior in his college years, a period of opportunity and high stress that often fuels the addictive cycle.

Self-Injury in Sexual Addiction

In answer to Question 1, it is not surprising that Thom engaged in self-injury. Carnes (1992) found that 11% of sex addicts engage in some form of self-injury, and as many as 80% of those who self-injure experienced childhood trauma (Wester & Trepal, 2005). Ascertaining the function of the self-injurious behavior would be a good first step in addressing it. Thom probably self-injured to deal with overwhelming emotions of shame. At the outset of counseling, treating the sex addiction would be important because acting out sexually at this point might leave Thom in a shame spiral that would place him at high risk for self-injury. A counseling goal would be to help Thom develop coping strategies to deal with his overwhelming emotions. Over time, helping Thom untangle his sexuality from his early trauma history and religious beliefs would be important in beginning to develop a healthy sexuality.

Because Thom's case is complex and multifaceted, focusing on his early counseling sessions would be important. Although this process would be coconstructed with Thom, likely interventions would include the following:

- Develop a sobriety plan that would help Thom identify sexual behaviors that would constitute a lapse in sobriety, "slippery-slope" behaviors (behaviors that do not constitute a lapse in sexual sobriety but that are early warning signs of a possible relapse), and healthy behaviors (a holistic wellness plan). Thom would be directed to engage in his wellness plan on an ongoing basis and particularly when struggling with slippery-slope or relapse behaviors.
- Participate in a 12-step group, such as Sexaholics Anonymous or Sex Addicts Anonymous. Also, Thom should be encouraged not only to attend but also to get a sponsor and begin working a 12-step program of recovery.
- Develop an inventory of secrets and consequences (Carnes, 2008) to be shared with his counselor and a sponsor, if he has one.
- Develop a "fire drill" plan to implement in times of strong cravings and impulses to sexually act out (Carnes, 2008).

- Contract for a period of sexual abstinence (including masturbation) for 90 days to allow the natural neuroplasticity of the brain to counteract addictive behavior. Addictive sexual behavior induces plasticity in the brain in a manner similar to drug use (Olsen, 2011).
- Develop a healthy sexuality plan with his counselor after 90 days of complete abstinence. Unlike chemical addictions, where the only goal is complete abstinence, the long-term goal of sex addiction treatment is the development of a healthy sexuality.

Trauma work likely will be necessary. However, this work should not be started at the outset of counseling because it might serve as a trigger for additional acting out.

Assessment of Religious Beliefs

Regarding Question 2, this strategy would initially involve an assessment of how Thom views God. Asking Thom to describe God, how God views him, and whether God has forgiven him for things he has done in the past that he regrets all would help paint a picture of how Thom views God. After this assessment, we might discuss with Thom what Christian text tells him about how God loves him and then encourage him to locate scriptures that highlight this. Thom might draw from scriptures such as the following:

> Psalm 103:12—"As far as the east is from the west, so far has he removed our transgressions from us."
> Luke 15:11–32—The parable of the prodigal son
> Matthew 9:36—"When he [Jesus] saw the crowds, he had compassion on them, because they were harassed and helpless, like sheep without a shepherd."

Asking Thom to look through God's eyes might be possible *only* after determining from ongoing discussion that he views God as personal and loving. In addressing how God might have felt toward him during his experiences between ages 11 and 16—being molested by a neighbor, punished by his mother, and abandoned by his parents—it would be critical that this dialogue focus on mercy, compassion, and forgiveness rather than punishment and sin. Experiencing God's love and compassion for him as a child rather than just thinking or talking about it may allow Thom to begin the important work of self-forgiveness.

Attachment and Sex Addiction

In answer to Question 3, men with a sex addiction often have been shown to have insecure attachment, with both higher anxiety and avoidance than nonaddicted control groups (Zapf, Greiner, & Carroll,

2008). Thom's marriage may have provided a safe haven and secure base unlike anything he had ever experienced. With the strength that this safe haven provided, he could be sexually healthy and successful in his work and church lives. However, he never addressed the underlying mechanisms (trauma; abuse; paired associations among sex, punishment, and abandonment) of the addiction that were part of his insecure attachment style. We do not know the details of his wife's declaration that he was controlling, but it would be understandable if he developed anxious attachment strategies out of his fear of abandonment and if he reacted in ways that his wife experienced as controlling.

So, although Thom was not sexually acting out, he was far from well. His wife asking for a divorce probably brought up his previous experiences of abandonment by his parents, triggering overwhelming emotions and impulses to resume acting out sexually. In the short term, Thom needs help developing coping strategies (such as identifying triggers, working on healthy emotional regulation, following a daily wellness plan, having a daily spiritual plan, and otherwise creating a lifestyle balance) and a supportive community (church, support groups) to help him deal with overwhelming emotions, stay sexually sober, and begin the longer-term healing process. For longer-term recovery, Thom could explore his spiritual beliefs and practices more fully, healing the trauma of abuse experienced in the name of religion and creating a personally meaningful and positive spiritual life.

References

Allen, A., & Hollander, E. (2006). Sexual compulsions. In E. Hollander & D. J. Stein (Eds.), *Clinical manual of impulse-control disorders* (pp. 87–114). Arlington, VA: American Psychiatric Publishing.

Carnes, P. (1992). *Don't call it love: Recovery from sexual addiction*. New York, NY: Bantam Books.

Carnes, P. (2008). *Facing the shadow* (2nd ed.). Carefree, AZ: Gentle Path.

Chou, H. T. G., & Uata, D. (2012). The impact of parental discipline on the image of God. *Mental Health, Religion & Culture, 15*, 677–688.

Juhnke, G. A., & Hagedorn, W. B. (2006). *Counseling addicted families: A sequential assessment & treatment model*. New York, NY: Brunner-Routledge.

Kor, A., Fogel, Y. A., Reid, R. C., & Potenza, M. N. (2013). Should hypersexual disorder be classified as an addiction? *Sexual Addiction & Compulsivity, 20*, 27–47.

Olsen, C. M. (2011). Natural rewards, neuroplasticity, and non-drug addictions. *Neuropharmacology, 61*, 1109–1122.

Pargament, K. I., Smith, B. W., Koenig, H. G., & Perez, L. (1998). Patterns of positive and negative religious coping with major life stressors. *Journal for the Scientific Study of Religion, 37,* 710–724.

van der Kolk, B. (2007). The developmental impact of childhood trauma. In L. J. Kirmayer, R. Lemelson, & M. Barad (Eds.), *Understanding trauma: Integrating biological, clinical, and cultural perspectives* (pp. 224–241). New York, NY: Cambridge University Press.

Wester, K. L., & Trepal, H. C. (2005). Working with clients who self-injure: Providing alternatives. *Journal of College Counseling, 8,* 180–189.

Zapf, J. L., Greiner, J., & Carroll, J. (2008). Attachment styles and male sex addiction. *Sexual Addiction and Compulsivity: The Journal of Treatment and Prevention, 15,* 158–175.

 Reflections

Tracey E. Robert and Virginia A. Kelly

The significant loss of the anchor Thom had found as a young adult has led him to engage in behaviors he thought were a part of his distant past. Thom's compulsive sexuality, dormant for many years, has been reignited, as his current behaviors signify a relapse of his addictive tendencies. The pairing of this deviant sexual behavior with shame and religion creates a complex scenario that involves multiple layers, including a resurfacing of significant trauma and profound confusion regarding the roles of religion and God. Using a spiritually based counseling approach can improve the process in the following ways:

- It can help Thom cognitively disentangle his addictive behaviors from his conception of God and religion and may give him access to a healing spiritual presence within his life.
- It can provide Thom access to a compassionate, loving sense of spirituality that can help him deal with and heal from the trauma of his abusive childhood.
- It can provide a means of conceptualizing Thom's sexual behavior as an addiction (a disease). This conceptualization may allow him to use a spiritually based 12-step recovery model that includes the development of a healing relationship with a "higher power."

• • •

Section IV

Substance Abuse

Chapter 16

Alcoholics Anonymous and Addiction

Case

Ford Brooks

Conway, a 58-year-old White male, was a veteran of addiction treatment services. His first attempt at sobriety had started 20 years earlier, and he had put together no more than 6 months of continuous sobriety since that time. His treatment protocols included detoxification and inpatient, outpatient, and partial modalities. He had a long history of depression that stemmed back to his youth.

In his prime, Conway had been a lawyer at the top of his field. Now he stood to lose his license to practice law as a result of complaints to the state bar association for incompetence and intoxication. Having been referred by the bar association's professional impairment program, he called for an appointment, sounding intoxicated on the phone.

Background

Conway was raised Catholic and continued to practice Catholicism along with his attendance at Alcoholics Anonymous (AA) meetings. His practice of law was nonexistent because of the constraints outlined by the bar association. They were requiring that he attend outpatient alcohol and drug treatment, attend five AA meetings weekly, maintain daily contact with his sponsor, and comply with random drug/alcohol screenings. His license had been suspended but could be petitioned for reinstatement at a later date.

Conway's medical condition was significant and pronounced. As a result of his drinking, he suffered from peripheral neuropathy, which affected his gait and balance along with his ability to speak coherently. In short, he sounded and looked like he was intoxicated even when he was not. He also was taking two prescription drugs, an antidepressant and Antabuse, which, should he drink alcohol, would make him violently ill.

Although Conway and his wife, Mary, lived in the same house, they had been estranged for many years and slept in separate bedrooms. She was of little support in his recovery, having given up on him years prior after many broken promises and extramarital affairs. She attended Al-Anon with regularity and created a life for herself that only minimally involved Conway. His main support came from his sponsor, a few contacts in AA, and his daughter, who also was a lawyer and worked out of his office. The bar association considered him a chronic relapser, resulting in the structured plan with a guarded prognosis for continuous sobriety.

Through all of Conway's time in treatment and brief stints at recovery, he maintained an active practice of his Catholic faith. Upon entering outpatient treatment, he shared that his connection to God and faith in getting sober were waning. He was losing hope that the God he had worshipped since childhood was going to be able to save him. He believed, by his own report, that he was unsalvageable, which contributed to his depression. From his viewpoint, what he had left was the possibility of practicing law with his daughter, and that was all.

Another issue Conway struggled with was his sexual promiscuity, which by his report continued to affect his value system and his desire to live an honest and sober life. He said that on many occasions he would drink after having had a liaison with another woman, feeling guilty and ashamed but temporarily fulfilled. Issues with women also affected his faith, and he felt that somehow God was punishing him for his dalliances.

Incident

Upon his referral from the bar association's professional impairment program, Conway presented for his appointment on time and appeared oriented and sober. For the next 90 minutes, he described a litany of treatment protocols he had been involved with and this most recent relapse after 2 months of sobriety. He described his attendance at AA as sporadic prior to his relapse. Conway also stated that, although he had a sponsor, he did not use him for help in his recovery as much as he needed to. Rather, he sought the comfort and support of a newly sober woman in AA. However, their relationship failed, and she relapsed at the same time as Conway.

For the first time in his attempts at recovery, Conway was feeling more hopeless than ever. He denied any current suicidal ideation but shared that the internal conflict between his belief in God and walking a path of honesty and good works was continually compromised by his thirst for female companionship and sexual gratification, which was followed by drinking. He acknowledged a "hole in the soul" that throughout his life he'd tried to fill. He expressed his self-loathing: "How will I ever stay sober?" he asked. He believed that God had turned his back on him and that he was truly alone in this world.

Conway experienced physical progression of his alcoholism along with this internal dissonance. He had liver damage as well as balance and coordination issues. Both his eyesight and his memory were poor, and he looked much older than his stated age of 58. With tears in his eyes, he expressed that he did not believe he had another chance at recovery and that this might be his last shot. He was terrified he wouldn't be able to stay sober.

Discussion

After sitting with Conway for 90 minutes, I thought that this probably was the first time he had been able to honestly express his terror and shame regarding the relapses and the relationships with other women. His defenses, both physical and emotional, had protected him for all those years and then, after yet another failed relationship and relapse, he saw very little hope for putting his life together. He had few supporters of his efforts even though he had been in 12-step meetings for almost 20 years. He had burned bridges with many of those in his life who depended on him for support and technical expertise (family and clients). Now he was, for all intents and purposes, a broken man. He was in a very dark time trying to keep it all together.

Questions

1. What efforts might you make as a counselor to explore Conway's internal angst regarding his faith and his relationships with other women?
2. How would you help Conway discern the differences between spirituality and religion given his Catholic faith?
3. In terms of surrender, how might you help Conway identify his "mini" surrenders so as to help him turn his "will and life over to the care of God" (to quote AA's Step 3)?
4. It seems from Conway's presentation that he was close to a spiritual, if not physical, death if he didn't turn his life around soon. What would you be compelled to say with regard to this?
5. How will this time be different in Conway's treatment, and how can spirituality be a significant aspect of his growth and learning?

Response
Oliver J. Morgan

My initial gut response to reading about Conway was to surrender to prayer. This is not unusual in my way of working—seeking a prayerful or contemplative attitude toward the work of psychotherapy seems an appropriate first step in doing what I call "spiritually sensitive counseling" (Morgan, 2007a; Morgan & Jordan, 1999)—but this time, with this set of case details, I felt *driven* to prayer.

A "dark power" hangs over this case. It's not the mounting symptoms of physical deterioration related to alcohol abuse (peripheral neuropathy, liver damage, deficits in balance and coordination, impaired eyesight and memory) that seem sinister. Nor are the escalating emotional and moral degradations (sexual promiscuity, family estrangement, internal dissonance, depression, and loss of hope) so distressing. These are not uncommon elements in the lives of those who chronically relapse into addiction or who seek professional help for long compulsive careers. Conway's presentation is all too familiar, and yet there is an element of "darkness" here that is arresting. Prayer seems to be the only appropriate response. Faced with Conway's dark despair, his "hole in the soul," counselor and client may need to search out a source for hope.

Searching for Hope

Lying underneath many of the questions in this case study is Conway's hopelessness. The power of his compulsions, with both alcohol and sex with other women, mortally terrifies him (Question 1). He knows that the need for comfort and thirst for union lie beyond his strength. The solace he previously found in religious practice is waning and at risk (Question 2). He has "turned his life over" so many times already—how can he believe this time might be different (Questions 3 & 5)? His spiritual crisis is real (Question 4).

However, here he is, willing to take a "last shot." He acknowledges so much already: the long history of depression, the alcohol addiction, the sexual promiscuity, the guilt and shame. He continues to take action steps—attendance at 12-step meetings, use of a sponsor, cooperation with the professional impairment program, submission to an Antabuse regimen, attendance at counseling. These mini-surrenders are not the actions of someone who is "unsalvageable."

I would begin to address all of these issues by explaining that, in our initial sessions, we are scouting out reasons for hope. Conway acknowledged chemical dependency and sexual compulsivity as reasons for seeking counseling. I would build on this honesty and explain that we know a great deal more about these conditions and how they are interconnected than we did when he began the treatment treadmill 20 years ago.

A Way to Proceed

There may be an inner toxic logic to the existence of multiple addictions (compulsions) and their roots in Conway's early experience (Miller, 2002). Failure to understand and account for them can lead to chronic relapse and an existential downward spiral. "Sexual addiction often coexists with chemical dependency and is frequently an unrecognized cause of relapse" (Schneider, 1991, p. 7). Conway is not alone, and knowing there are possibilities can be empowering.

First, how can the counselor meet Conway where he is, authentically and empathically? Knowing what we now know about addiction, multiple addictions, and chronic relapse, I would listen carefully to (a) his history with alcohol, including any family history with dysfunction and/or chemical abuse; (b) his relationship with depression and sexual compulsivity; (c) the potential for linkages to a comorbid sexual addiction; and (d) the possible connections with trauma (Morgan, 2009; Schneider & Irons, 2001). Our initial sessions assessing the dimensions of his addictions and their potential roots in trauma and family dysfunction, as well as how we frame our work together, would become the platform for counseling (Morgan, 2007b).

Second, we need to know about Conway's early family life, relationships, and potential traumas and how they might be connected to ongoing life patterns. This information is gathered through empathic psychosocial history taking, acknowledgement of challenges and strengths as well as deficits and losses, and collateral information from family members and others. Another source is instrumentation, such as the Family Health History and Health Appraisal questionnaires from the Adverse Childhood Experiences Study of the Centers for Disease Control and Prevention (1997); the Sexual Addiction Screening Test (Carnes, 2013); and PATHOS, another sex addiction screening instrument (Carnes et al., 2012). Empathy, acknowledgement, warmth, curiosity—the basic Rogerian virtues—are in themselves spiritual interventions (Morgen, Morgan, Cashwell, & Miller, 2010; Stanard, 2007). They establish trust and a working relationship that facilitate genuine encounter.

Third, it would help to know the patterns of ritualization and reinforcement that often bind these multiple addictions together (Schneider, Sealy, Montgomery, & Irons, 2005). For example, Conway may be afflicted with a pattern of reciprocal relapse to alcohol abuse after a relapse to compulsive sexual behavior, or vice versa. In addition, relapse to sexual compulsion or alcoholic drinking may follow a period of overeating or workaholism or some other compulsion. These compulsions can be triggered by external stressors that need to be addressed or internal emotional needs, such as a search for fulfillment or perfection (Hagedorn & Moorhead, 2010).

Understanding the patterns and triggers that drive Conway's behaviors may benefit the process of recovery. A history of the interactions and a "functional analysis" of patterns of use (Smith & Meyers, 2004; Smith, Meyers, & Austin, 2008) would help clarify what's happening and demystify the causes of relapse. They might also help break down isolation and build solidarity with other compulsive users.

Suffering Understood

Early trauma, or at least family patterns of dysfunction or emotional disengagement, may form a likely scenario in Conway's past. Helping Conway seek empowerment through such knowledge could be a catalyst for hope. Such knowledge may also bring exoneration. Sometimes realizing that one did the best that was possible for survival can bring a measure of peace and the strength to move forward. Conway needs to find that way forward. He is entangled in a very dark trap.

On the one hand, Conway's fear of being "unsalvageable," his sense that God has "turned his back" and might not save him after so many failed attempts at treatment, might be seen as a kind of reverse pride, the opposite of the humility needed for recovery. Does he see himself as too bad for God to redeem, as though his sins are greater than anyone else's (Pruyser, 1976)? Is his God only "the one who punishes" and never "the one who forgives"? Do his shame and despair make him seem like unredeemable damaged goods? Is this the hidden obstacle to his recovery? Perhaps.

On the other hand, I suspect something different and more destructive is at work. An unholy trinity of trauma, addiction, and shame reside at the core of Conway's heart. The dark power of this unholy trinity can function like a god, imperiously commanding attention and demanding tribute (Grant, 1996; Morgan, 2009). It can rivet one's attention on the negative.

This dark deity shatters faith and dignity. It isolates those enslaved to it from any sense of human communion or the availability of grace. It destroys hope and places tragedy, not love, at the center of one's personal narrative (Jordan, 1986). It demands Conway's soul.

We know that unaddressed trauma and shame are often the driving forces in multiple relapse to addiction (Norman, Tate, Anderson, & Brown, 2007). These three sisters also can conspire to make recovery impossible. If some version of this reality is discovered in Conway's experience, then how do we work toward recovery and healing? How do we ensure that this time will be different in Conway's treatment? Here, we are assisted by an active, multifaceted spiritual approach (Garrett, 1996; Morgen et al., 2010).

Spiritual Catalysts

First, Conway must work to reconnect with himself and his deepest desires. Learning mindful techniques and pursuing Catholic devotional prayers and practices that have meaning for him—including partaking in the sacraments, journaling, seeking personal reflection, reading spiritual texts, and attending Matt Talbot Catholic retreats and/or AA retreats—can help Conway rediscover himself as a deeper spiritual being.

This step can also help Conway accept the truth of himself, the truth of "essential limitation" (Kurtz & Ketcham, 1993). This acceptance can allow for imperfection, for mistakes, for being human—a human who is flawed and loved. This is Conway's spiritual birthright (Morgan & Jordan, 1999). Acknowledging this truth empowers and sets one free. It also opens the possibility for true mutuality and community (Morgen et al., 2010).

Second, spiritually sensitive counseling can help Conway build a sense of connection and communion with others. This sense would go a long way toward breaking the grip of isolation and shame that can trigger addiction. Helping Conway redouble his efforts with his AA sponsor and participate more actively in meetings would be a big step forward. Using church groups and other venues of support would help. Bible studies, aerobic exercise groups, online communities, and volunteer work can all help Conway occupy his time and build a supportive community.

Third, connecting with nature has helped many of those struggling with addictions recover playfulness and innocence in their lives. Refocusing their attention away from themselves and toward creation and nature all around them can be an expanding experience. Recovering a sense of self within the world and its ecology, within God's plan— whether through the mountains, forests, oceans, or a leaf—helps one find meaning and comfort. Connection with creation is also part of our spiritual heritage. It can help put addiction in its place.

Fourth, learning the process of self-examination and confession is a vital spiritual skill in recovery. The "fearless moral inventory" of AA's fourth and fifth steps can aid in this self-review and process of self-acceptance with the help of Conway's sponsor or a compassionate priest. This inventory leads naturally to taking action through the making of amends and remaining vigilant toward one's choices in the present and future. Sharing and working through the inventory can also provide the aware counselor with opportunities for dealing with negative thinking, destructive cognitive schema, and shaming from the internal critic.

In my mind, these areas of work constitute both a compassionate and a muscular spiritual response to Conway's recovery needs. They require commitment, motivation, and action. Grounded in a counselor's wisdom and care, they can provide a way forward against the dark powers that now hold Conway in thrall.

References

Carnes, P. (2013). Sexual Addiction Screening Test (SAST). In *Recovery zone*. Retrieved from http://www.recoveryzone.com/tests/sex-addiction/SAST/index.php

Carnes, P. J., Green, B. A., Merlo, L. J., Polles, A., Carnes, S., & Gold, M. S. (2012). PATHOS: A brief screening application for assessing sexual addiction. *International Institute of Trauma and Addiction Professional, 1,* 29–34. doi:10.1097/ADM.0b013e3182251a28

Centers for Disease Control and Prevention. (1997). Family Health History and Health Appraisal questionnaires. In *Adverse Childhood Experiences (ACE) study.* Retrieved from http://www.cdc.gov/ace/

Garrett, C. J. (1996). Recovery from anorexia nervosa: A Durkheimian interpretation. *Social Science & Medicine, 43,* 1489–1506.

Grant, R. (1996). *The way of the wound: A spirituality of trauma and transformation.* Oakland, CA: Author.

Hagedorn, W. B., & Moorhead, H. J. H. (2010). The God-shaped hole: Addictive disorders and the search for perfection. *Counseling and Values, 55,* 63–78.

Jordan, M. R. (1986). *Taking on the gods: The task of the pastoral counselor.* Nashville, TN: Abingdon.

Kurtz, E., & Ketcham, K. (1993). *The spirituality of imperfection: Storytelling and the search for meaning.* New York, NY: Bantam.

Miller, D. (2002). Addictions and trauma recovery: An integrated approach. *Psychiatric Quarterly, 73,* 157–170.

Morgan, O. J. (Ed.) (2007a). *Counseling and spirituality: Views from the profession.* Boston, MA: Lahaska.

Morgan, O. J. (Ed.) (2007b). "They come to us vulnerable": Elements of the sacred in spiritually sensitive counseling. In *Counseling and spirituality: Views from the profession* (pp. 25–44). Boston, MA: Lahaska.

Morgan, O. J. (2009). Thoughts on the interaction of trauma, addiction and spirituality. *Journal of Addictions & Offender Counseling, 30,* 5–15.

Morgan, O. J., & Jordan, M. (1999). *Addiction and spirituality: A multidisciplinary approach.* St. Louis, MO: Chalice.

Morgen, K., Morgan, O. J., Cashwell, C., & Miller, G. (2010). *Strategies for the competent integration of spirituality into addictions counseling training and supervision.* Retrieved from http://counselingoutfitters.com/vistas/vistas10/Article_84.pdf

Norman, S. B., Tate, S. R., Anderson, K. G., & Brown, S. A. (2007). Do trauma history and PTSD symptoms influence addiction relapse context? *Drug and Alcohol Dependence, 90,* 89–96.

Pruyser, P. (1976). *The minister as diagnostician: Personal problems in pastoral perspective.* Louisville, KY: Westminster John Knox.

Schneider, J. P. (1991, November 1). How to recognize the signs of sexual addiction: Asking the right questions may uncover serious problems. *Postgraduate Medicine—Sexual Addiction, 90.* Retrieved from http://www.sexualrecovery.com/wp-content/uploads/2011/03/recognizesigns.pdf

Schneider, J. P., & Irons, R. R. (2001). Assessment and treatment of addictive sexual disorders: Relevance for chemical dependency relapse. *Substance Use and Misuse, 36,* 1795–1820.

Schneider, J. P., Sealy, J., Montgomery, J, & Irons, R. R. (2005). Ritualization and reinforcement: Keys to understanding mixed addiction involving sex and drugs. *Sexual Attraction & Compulsivity, 12,* 121–148.

Smith, J. E., & Meyers, R. J. (2004). *Motivating substance abusers to enter treatment: Working with family members.* New York, NY: Guilford Press.

Smith, J. E., Meyers, R. J., & Austin, J. L. (2008). Working with family members to engage treatment-refusing drinkers: The CRAFT program. In O. J. Morgan & C. H. Litzke (Eds.), *Family interventions in substance abuse: Current best practices* (pp. 169–194). New York, NY: Haworth Press.

Stanard, R. P. (2007). Remembering the lessons of the angel. In O. J. Morgan (Ed.), *Counseling and spirituality: Views from the profession* (pp. 127–138). Boston, MA: Lahaska.

Reflections

Tracey E. Robert and Virginia A. Kelly

This case and response demonstrate the dance between light and dark, hope and shame, spiritual distress and healing that is central to AA and addiction. Spirituality has been at the foundation of the AA philosophy and integrated into the 12-step recovery process since its inception.

The response deepens the conceptualization of the case and focuses on the core issue of shame and the use of hope as an intervention. The responder states that he and the client need to search for hope. Hope research provides evidence that this spiritual virtue has helped fight loneliness and the isolation St. John of the Cross referred to as the "dark night of the soul."

The responder also links early trauma and abuse as potential sources for the client's addictions and failing faith. In exploring these root causes, the client and counselor can identify triggers and patterns that might be cause for relapse. Multiple addictions can be complex, and sorting through this web requires much effort and a strong working alliance. Morgan's response provides a structured, clear outline for taking action that easily can be written as a treatment plan. A spiritual focus for counseling AA clients can be beneficial in the following ways:

- The use of the client's faith and the spiritual path offered through AA can provide a structure to enhance the therapeutic alliance.
- Intentionally integrating hope, the spiritual virtue, throughout the sessions can provide light and a way out of a process of repeat failures.
- The need for community can be met with the support of the counseling relationship, continued participation in AA, and the validation that the client is seeking.

• • •

Chapter 17 Families and Addiction

Case

Jennifer M. Cook

Judy Taylor, a 42-year-old White heterosexual agnostic female, is married to Gary Taylor, a 41-year-old African American heterosexual Catholic male. They have been married for 18 years and have four children, Chuck, 19; Tina, 16; and 11-year-old twins, Jordan and Connor. When Judy made the appointment, she reported Tina had been skipping school, staying out all night without permission, smoking, and drinking. Tina's school counselor had suggested the family seek counseling when Judy told her, "We don't know what to do anymore." Judy told me she and Gary could not agree on how to stop Tina's defiant behavior and were "at the end of their rope."

Background

For many years, Judy and Gary had prided themselves on being a close-knit family. They ate dinner together almost every night, had family night each week, and genuinely enjoyed each other's company. Their house was the place where all of their children's friends would come to hang out, and they hosted barbeques and family gatherings on weekends. Judy and Gary met when they were in college, and their friends often joked that they were still in love like college kids, laughing, entertaining friends, and stealing kisses when they thought no one was looking.

However, their family dynamics had changed about 7 months earlier. Judy remembered the change being almost simultaneous with Chuck leaving for his first year of college in another state. The day after Judy and Gary returned home from taking their son to college, Gary began to withdraw from the family, spending large periods of time alone in the garage. Now, almost every night, Gary came home from work, barely spoke to anyone, changed into different clothing and retired to the garage, where he worked on one of his "projects." Often, he stayed in the garage late into the night, and he rarely joined the family for dinner.

Over time, Tina started spending every evening with her friends, and Judy and the twins started eating dinner in front of the TV. Friends had stopped coming over to hang out, and there had not been any family and friend gatherings since before Chuck left for school. Gary and Judy spent very little time together. Their communication had dwindled, and frequent arguments ensued, especially about the children. Gary was furious when she gave Chuck permission to spend Christmas skiing with a friend and his family without talking to him about it first.

In January, Judy became enraged with Gary when he unilaterally decided that Tina's problems were related to being in public school and that she needed a more "Godly environment." Gary removed Tina from school, enrolled her in a private Catholic school, and shared this information with Judy via text: "Stop at the store and pick up some school uniforms for Tina on your way home. She's going to Catholic school now."

Judy noticed a change in Tina about 2 months into the school year. Her grades, which had always been As and Bs, dropped to Cs and Ds. Judy began to get calls from the school indicating that Tina was skipping class and eventually that she was missing entire school days. When Judy would confront Tina, she would say, "It's no big deal, everything's under control," and lock herself in her room. When Gary would confront Tina, they would get into shouting matches and she would leave the house. Any time Judy or Gary had an argument with Tina, the couple would end up fighting with each other and Gary would retreat to the garage.

Incident

The family presented for counseling after a tumultuous weekend during which Tina had not come home for 2 days. When Judy and Gary could not reach Tina, Gary searched Tina's room with the hope of discovering clues to her whereabouts. As Gary looked through Tina's things, he found two empty liquor bottles in her closet underneath a pile of clothing. As he dug further, he found an empty cigarette pack, a lighter, and a homemade bong fashioned from a soda bottle.

Gary yelled for Judy to come into Tina's bedroom to see what he had found. Astonished, Judy began to cry. Gary screamed at Judy, "This is all your fault! You kept Tina away from God with your agnosticism! If you would've let me raise her the way I wanted to, in the church, this would've never happened!" Judy yelled back, "Chuck never did any of this, and he never spent one day in Sunday School!"

As the couple yelled at each other, Tina walked into the doorway, staring at her parents in disbelief. She screamed at them to get out of her room, which they did, and she slammed the door behind them. Gary retreated to the garage. When Judy found him, he was sitting on the floor, drinking a beer and crying. Judy moved toward him and said, "We really need some help."

Discussion

When the Taylor family presented for counseling, blame was the theme of our initial sessions together. Each person thought it was important to determine the cause of Tina's behavior, and Judy and Gary each thought the other was at fault, while Tina sat silent. Initially, Gary and Judy chose not to include the twins, Jordan and Connor, in their family counseling sessions because they felt Tina was the "problem" and that the boys had nothing to do with Tina's problems.

I asked Tina when she began drinking and smoking cigarettes and marijuana. At first, she did not want to share many details. Eventually she opened up and revealed that she started drinking after she saw her dad drinking in the garage. She shared, tearfully, "I just wanted Chuck to come back for things to be normal again. And when I saw Dad drinking every night, I thought, maybe that would make me feel better. And it did, because when I was drinking, I forgot about Chuck, and I didn't miss him."

Gary discussed how painful it was for him when his oldest son left for college and how out of control he felt when Judy let Chuck spend Christmas with his friends. He shared that he felt isolated and alone and that the only way to feel okay was to be alone and to drink. Gary stated that at first he had only "one or two beers" and that before long he was getting drunk every night. When I asked Gary whether he ever used drinking to cope before, he put his head in his hands and whispered, sheepishly, "Yes, when I was 17, right after my father died." He shared that he stopped "with God's help" and through a support group at his church.

I conceptualized the Taylor family case through the lens of a family in transition and McCubbin and McCubbin's (1989) Typology Model of Family Adjustment and Adaptation. To normalize the family's experience, I shared with them that they had been in a state of adjustment and stress since Chuck had gone away to college. Each family member had experienced different and similar pileups of stressors and had chosen a different way to cope with the situation. I emphasized that their individual strategies for dealing with the situation were not wrong or bad. When an individual person's stress and coping mechanisms collide with other family members' stress and coping mechanisms, problems occur.

Judy and Gary admitted that they responded very differently to Chuck's departure, but they still wanted to demonize the other's reactions and coping strategies. What they agreed on was that Tina should not be drinking or doing drugs to cope with her pain and that they needed to help her find another way. Gary and Judy began to realize that Tina was not the "problem" and that the entire family was struggling. At this point, they decided it was important to include Jordan and Connor in their family counseling sessions.

I asked the Taylors to identify their family strengths and the ways they are resilient and asked each family member to identify his or her personal strengths and resiliency. I hypothesized that the Taylor family structure is regenerative, resilient, and rhythmic (McCubbin & McCubbin, 1989) and that the family temporarily got off course because they experienced a development they did not anticipate would affect them. I shared this hypothesis with the family. At first, they found it difficult to remember their cohesiveness because of the pain they were currently experiencing. With guidance, they agreed to try to recapture who they were.

The family identified their strengths, such as enjoying being together, laughing, being lighthearted, valuing social justice, and working on service projects together, and having open communication. Judy identified her strengths as being loving, practical, and quick-witted. Gary reported his strengths as being a hard worker, believing that God can get him through any situation, and having creativity. Tina struggled to identify her strengths, but her parents helped her discern that she is smart, kind, and funny. Connor shared that he is funny and smart, like his sister, and Jordan said he is a good friend and an awesome baseball player. Using a strength-based resiliency model, I asked the family to strategize how they could use their strengths to support one another and adapt to a new form of daily living with Chuck away at college. They reinstituted family meals and game nights, and they planned a barbeque with family and friends at the end of each month.

Gary decided he would join a support group at his church to help him reduce his drinking, and Tina said she volunteered to go with him. Tina began individual counseling, and she dedicated herself to being drug and alcohol free. Judy committed to individual counseling, and she agreed to go on a church couples retreat with Gary to try to better understand why his faith was so important to him. Judy's openness to understanding Gary's faith inspired him to apologize to her for blaming their family problems on her agnosticism. The family continued regular therapy sessions for several months.

Questions

1. The counselor conceptualized the family's problem in terms of being a family in transition and the Typology Model of Family Adjustment and Adaptation (McCubbin & McCubbin, 1989). In addition, a strength-based resiliency perspective was used to help the family ascertain their strengths so they could move through their adjustment and into adaptation. What are some other ways to conceptualize this case?
2. Religion/spirituality is important to Gary, and his religious/spiritual beliefs strongly shape his worldview. Religion/spirituality is not an important part of Judy's life, and her worldview is shaped by nonreligious/spiritual beliefs. How could this family's counselor help them see value in both perspectives?
3. Gary chose to attend an alcohol-reduction support group to help him decrease his drinking behaviors. What would it be like to be Gary's counselor if you believed alcohol abstinence was the only way to help Gary with his drinking?

References

McCubbin, M. A., & McCubbin, H. I. (1989). Theoretical orientations to family stress and coping. In C. R. Figley (Ed.), *Treating stress in families* (pp. 3–43). Philadelphia, PA: Brunner/Mazel.

 Response

Robert A. Dobmeier

The counselor's use of the Typology Model of Family Adjustment and Adaptation (McCubbin & McCubbin, 1989) was helpful in that it brought into focus the hypothesis that Chuck going off to college created a crisis for the family. After the initial disequilibrium that was created when the family was left without Chuck's stabilizing influence, the remaining members began to pull together. With the counselor's help, they were able to adjust to the family's loss and adapt to their new circumstances without Chuck living in the home.

Structural Family Therapy

In response to the first question, the case also might be conceptualized from a structural family therapy perspective. Gary's strong reaction to Chuck's going away to college seems to suggest that something was amiss in his relationship with Judy. One of the premises of structural therapy for couples is that "normal and expected milestones in a couple's life can create problems" (Long & Young, 2007, p. 56). The family needs to be able to adjust its organizational structure and rules to respond to developmental events (Gladding, 2007).

Another premise of structural therapy for couples is that their problems develop and are maintained in the context of family relationships. The whole family needs to be involved when dealing with the couple's problems (Long & Young, 2007). Gary and Judy eventually recognized that all members of their family needed to participate in counseling.

One might wonder why Chuck's leaving for college was so disruptive to the family. It appears Gary was distraught about Chuck's transition in that he withdrew from the family and resorted to drinking as he had done as a teen when his father died. A third premise of structural therapy for couples is that unhealthy alliances between family members (a cross-generational alliance with a child) can empower the child at the expense of one member of the couple.

From a structural perspective, the couple represents a subsystem within the family. Ideally, there are healthy boundaries that define familial subsystems, especially for the adult couple of the family unit. In the event that this subsystem is compromised, the possibility of enmeshment—an excessive amount of cohesion among family members (Long & Young, 2007), such as a parent and a child—can occur. This kind of enmeshment should be explored between Chuck and one or both of his parents.

When Gary and Judy first sought counseling for the family, they appear to have been scapegoating Tina in that they identified her as the family member who had a problem. However, when Tina acknowledged that she began to drink and smoke marijuana in response to her father drinking, Gary and Judy began to recognize that they needed to look more deeply at what was taking place in the family.

In the resiliency model of family stress, adjustment, and adaptation (McCubbin & McCubbin, 1991), a family's ability to respond to demands is dynamic and interactional. Once Gary and Judy were focused on Tina and her needs, Gary was willing to address his own drinking and recognized that Judy's agnosticism did not bring on the changes going on in the family. In an effort to create unity in her family, Judy offered to attend a church couples retreat with Gary. Tina committed to give up drinking and drug use and volunteered to join her father in a church support group to reduce drinking. The individual family members recognized that the family needed to work together to regain stability and adapt to life without Chuck at home, and they showed their resiliency by adjusting their own strategy for coping so that the family could thrive.

Spiritual Competence

The second question asked how the counselor might help Gary and Judy see value in their divergent views about religion/spirituality. The Association for Spiritual, Ethical, and Religious Values in Counseling

(ASERVIC) offers 14 spiritual competencies (ASERVIC, 2009) to help counselors address spirituality or religion in counseling.

Competency 7 states, "The professional counselor responds to client communications about spirituality and/or religion with acceptance and sensitivity" (ASERVIC, 2009). In working with Gary and Judy, the counselor should offer acceptance and sensitivity but refrain from taking sides by recognizing and affirming each of them in their respective beliefs. The counselor may thereby become a role model for Judy and Gary as to how they might begin to offer acceptance and sensitivity to each other in their religious/spiritual beliefs.

Competency 10 states, "During the intake and assessment processes, the professional counselor strives to understand a client's spiritual and/or religious perspective by gathering information from the client and/or other sources" (ASERVIC, 2009). Should Gary or Judy raise the role of religion in their relationship during the assessment, the counselor should strive to grasp the meaning that religion holds in their relationship and in their family. The counselor should seek to understand the purpose religion holds for Gary and would do well to invite Judy to talk about her core values that she reports do not include a religious or spiritual emphasis.

In the ASERVIC White Paper, spirituality is defined as a capacity and tendency that is innate and unique to all persons (ASERVIC, 2005). Agnostic belief can reflect a worldview wrought from a genuine search for values (Cashwell & Young, 2011). If it becomes apparent during the assessment that religion plays an essential role in Gary and Judy's relationship, the counselor should invite them to talk about this essential role with each other. Are there common areas in their respective value systems that heretofore have gone unrecognized? One likely common area is Tina—both seem committed to helping her and keeping their family strong.

Competency 11 states, "When making a diagnosis, the professional counselor recognizes that the client's spiritual and/or religious perspectives can (a) enhance well-being; (b) contribute to client problems; and/or (c) exacerbate symptoms" (ASERVIC, 2009). In listening to Gary and Judy express their beliefs, the counselor should pay attention to the impact of Gary's religious beliefs on his well-being, that of his wife, and that of the whole family. Gary might be encouraged to project himself into his wife's shoes to recognize her genuine search for well-being in herself, their marriage, and their family.

Harm Reduction Versus Abstinence

In Question 3, the case introduced the harm reduction model, which states that persons who have abused or been addicted to a substance can learn to control their use (Moss-King, 2013). Gary's attendance at an alcohol-reduction support group suggests that he believes he can drink alcohol responsibly. Other authors in the addictions field espouse the abstinence model, which states that one who has been addicted to a substance must give up any use of the substance to prevent relapse. A counselor who works with Gary and advocates the abstinence model is likely to view any use of alcohol as Gary's denial or minimization of his dependence on alcohol. The counselor may be concerned that Gary's abuse of alcohol will worsen unless he gives it up.

The abstinence model often is associated with a view of addiction as a disease. The person becomes increasingly dependent on the substance psychologically and physically. The disease of alcoholism renders the person helpless to control his drinking or his life (Schaffer & LaPlante, 2005). The counselor is likely to view the problems in Gary's marriage and in the family as resulting from his alcoholism.

In the United States, the Alcoholics Anonymous (AA) 12-step abstinence model is the preferred treatment for persons who have had a problem with alcohol use (Lemanski, 2001). Among the 12 self-help steps that AA advocates, the alcoholic must (a) recognize that he or she is powerless over alcohol, (b) believe that one is in need of a greater power to restore one to sanity, and (c) turn one's will and life over to God as God is understood by the person (AA, 2013). Gary's counselor probably would advise him to forgo the alcohol reduction support group in favor of joining an AA group. The counselor also might recommend that Gary's significant others—Judy, Tina, and Chuck—attend an Al-Anon group to help them recognize enabling behaviors and learn to create appropriate consequences for his abusive drinking.

The counselor is likely to encourage Gary to make amends with his wife and children for the harm he has brought to the family as a result of his problem drinking. The counselor might note that Gary admitted to abuse of alcohol only during two periods of his life, when his father died and when his son moved away to college. The counselor might wonder how Gary could go 24 years between these two events without his problem drinking recurring and whether Gary is being honest about his use of alcohol throughout his adulthood. The counselor may think that consultation with Gary's significant others is required to verify his account of his alcohol use.

Introducing motivational interviewing (Chamberlain, 2013) might invite and challenge Gary to look honestly at the benefits and liabilities of his current alcohol use. Such interviewing is based on the readiness for change model (Prochaska & DiClemente, 1983), in which the willingness to seek help for substance abuse is viewed as essential for treatment to be effective.

References

Alcoholics Anonymous. (2013). Chapter 5: How it works. In *The big book online* (4th ed., pp. 58–71). Retrieved from http://www.aa.org/bigbookonline/en_tableofcnt.cfm

Association for Spiritual, Ethical, and Religious Values in Counseling. (2005). *White paper.* Retrieved from http://pacounseling. org/whitepaper.rtf

Association for Spiritual, Ethical, and Religious Values in Counseling. (2009). *Competencies for addressing spiritual and religious issues in counseling.* Retrieved from http://www.aservic.org/resources/spiritual-competencies/

Cashwell, C. S., & Young, J. S. (2011). *Integrating spirituality and religion into counseling: A guide to competent practice* (2nd ed.). Alexandria, VA: American Counseling Association.

Chamberlain, L. L. (2013). Assessment and diagnosis. In P. Stevens & R. L. Smith (Eds.), *Substance abuse counseling: Theory and practice* (5th ed., pp. 122–154). Upper Saddle River, NJ: Pearson.

Gladding, S. T. (2007). *Family therapy: History, theory, and practice.* Upper Saddle River, NJ: Pearson.

Lemanski, M. (2001). *A history of addiction recovery in the United States.* Tucson, AZ: Sharp Press.

Long, L. L., & Young, M E. (2007). *Counseling and therapy for couples.* Belmont, CA: Thomson Higher Education.

McCubbin, M. A., & McCubbin, H. I. (1989). Theoretical orientations to family stress and coping. In C. R. Figley (Ed.), *Treating stress in families* (pp. 3–43). Philadelphia, PA: Brunner/Mazel.

McCubbin, H., & McCubbin, M. (1991). *Family assessment inventories for research and practice.* Madison, WI: Family Stress, Coping, and Health Project.

Moss-King, D. A. (2013). Individual treatment. In P. Stevens & R. L. Smith (Eds.), *Substance abuse counseling: Theory and practice* (5th ed., pp. 188–202). Upper Saddle River, NJ: Pearson.

Prochaska, J. O., & DiClemente, C. C. (1983). Stages and process of self-change of smoking: Toward an integrative model of change. *Journal of Consulting and Clinical Psychology, 51,* 390–395.

Schaffer, H. J., & LaPlante, D. A. (2005). Treatment of gambling disorders. In G. A. Marlatt & D. M. Donovan (Eds.), *Relapse prevention: Maintenance strategies in the treatment of addictive behaviors* (pp. 276–232). New York, NY: Guilford Press.

 Reflections
Tracey E. Robert and Virginia A. Kelly

Addiction is known as a common and devastating disease. More than half of adults have reported that one or more of their close relatives has a drinking problem. Illicit drug use has increased, especially among young adults. As the problem grows, so does the need for effective counseling. Less recognized is that addiction affects the whole family, not just the family member with the addiction. In this case, the parents' differing belief systems and coping mechanisms, family members' responses to the launching of Chuck, the loss felt by Gary and Judy, and Tina's response with substance use led to chaos and a breakdown of family structures.

This case and response focus on the use of careful spiritual assessment as a springboard to identifying underlying issues of family tension and coping mechanisms. The use of a family therapy response to substance abuse has long been recommended. An understanding of how family members are influenced by their religious and spiritual beliefs and how this affects their overall well-being can only increase its effectiveness. We think that a spiritual focus can improve family counseling in the following ways:

- A spiritual assessment identifies elements for supporting participants' belief systems.
- Discussion of joint and individual spiritual values and beliefs can produce a climate of safety and connectedness to address chaotic and disruptive coping mechanisms.
- Increased self-awareness can enhance the opportunities and options for change.

• • •

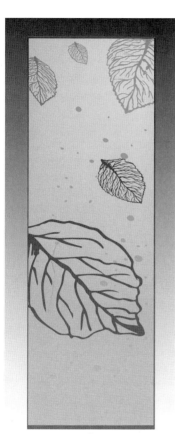

Section V

Career

Chapter 18 ## Career Issues Over the Life Span

Case
Tracey E. Robert

Cheryl, a 45-year-old single White woman, came to counseling because she was experiencing anxiety attacks at work and at home. She and I had worked together for more than 20 years at various career transition points in her life. Cheryl was concerned about the future of her current position and the career path she had chosen in print publishing, a shrinking industry. She said, "Just when I thought I had finally figured out what I wanted to do, my life is falling apart."

Background

Cheryl came from an upper-middle-class Presbyterian family. They attended religious services every Sunday and frequently participated in community suppers. Cheryl's family greatly valued education. Her father was a successful entrepreneur with multiple degrees, her mother was a talented artist, and her older sister had pursued the arts and business in her academic path. Cheryl and her sister had attended private schools throughout their childhood, and the expectation was that they would attend prestigious colleges. Both siblings had been accepted at elite academic institutions but had failed to complete their degrees.

When Cheryl was 20, she left college because her future career path was undecided. She tried working in two industries before deciding that the business world was not really for her. At age 25, Cheryl came to me for counseling and indicated she had a lack of direction and purpose. I referred her to my career change workshop, where she explored her interests, values, and skills.

Cheryl realized that she enjoyed writing and decided to pursue a literature degree with hopes of working in the publishing industry. She excelled in her classes, especially the ones that focused on creative writing, and felt that she had found her niche. To support herself while attending school, Cheryl continued to work part-time in a job she didn't like.

At age 31, Cheryl graduated and returned to counseling to start the job search and try to move into the work world with a focus. She demonstrated some anxiety about the job interview process, describing herself as shy and socially awkward. Diligent and committed to the job search process, Cheryl soon landed multiple job interviews with book and magazine publishing companies. We practiced interviewing skills, and she demonstrated strong communication skills and seemed prepared for the process.

During the following 2 months, we met several times as Cheryl dealt with rejections, delays, and offers. She finally was offered a book publishing position that allowed her to write and work directly with authors. Her initial anxiety about the interviewing had been reduced by practice and by the coping skills she had learned when she left college.

Cheryl described that she found solace and comfort in music and going on meditative walks. Her music interest provided a social outlet, and she was able to start attending concerts again because she was gainfully employed. Cheryl's anxiety seemed to have faded away.

For the next 10 years, Cheryl enjoyed uninterrupted employment. Then, at 41, her company was sold and she returned to counseling to transition to another position. With counseling support, she obtained another job in publishing and worked in her new company for several years.

Incident

Cheryl came to me for counseling again at age 45 because her feelings of anxiety started to resurface. Her current employer had discussed cost reductions and layoffs, and she anticipated losing her job—a process she had been through before. Cheryl's manager reassured her that her job was not at risk, but she knew the signs of change and was experiencing panic attacks. Cheryl's symptoms had started to recur when she heard about the companywide cost-cutting efforts. Her past experience suggested that her position could be at risk because it was not revenue producing. She had been laid off before and then rehired but eventually lost that position—all the while being praised as a top performer.

The mixed messages from Cheryl's employers and her deep-seated concern that she was at risk led to breathing problems and heart palpitations. Her doctor wanted to prescribe antianxiety medication, but she did not like the way it made her feel, so she refused. She felt she was "losing her center" and didn't know what to do. She thought she had thoroughly explored her career options and had selected a career that was a "perfect fit," but the state of the economy didn't seem to agree. Cheryl's anxiety symptoms increased with time, and she didn't feel she could function at work. She asked for a leave of absence and entered treatment for her anxiety.

Discussion

In working with Cheryl, my primary goal was to help her identify the root of her anxiety symptoms and learn new coping skills. Because she loved music, I integrated the use of music lyrics with journaling and mindfulness meditation to help her cope with the anticipation of change. We explored Cheryl's religious beliefs as a source of spiritual comfort, but she noted that she had stopped attending church while in college and instead found comfort in nature.

Cheryl described a loving, supportive family and childhood. Both parents supported her striving to find something that she was passionate about as they had successfully followed their dreams. However, Cheryl emphasized that achievement and high expectations were part of the culture at home. Her parents were happiest when she "settled down" and finally had a career and not just jobs. They viewed work as a vocation and did not entertain the idea that one could have multiple careers over one's lifetime.

Cheryl's ability to continue to find work in a shrinking industry was commendable. However, she could not see beyond this industry and started to feel panic that she would fail. I used work adjustment theory and attachment theory to conceptualize Cheryl's struggle. I hypothesized that her self-esteem was strongly connected to her work and that she had focused most of her time—and her life—on work. Cheryl had some outside interests, but her social life revolved around work and she had stopped attending concerts and listening to her music.

Because the career process had been challenging—Cheryl reported feeling overwhelmed with needing to find another career—a good focus seemed to be using the work adjustment model and helping her find her transferable skills. The use of cognitive–behavioral strategies, including mindful walking and meditation, helped reduce her panic and anxiety symptoms. As a result of our work together, Cheryl discussed the possibility of a career transition, not necessarily a total career change. She also shared a desire to expand her social connections and expressed interest in attending a group for mindfulness meditation and joining the Sierra Club for hiking and walks in nature. Taking these steps allowed Cheryl to reduce her anxiety and start to think of the future again.

Questions

1. Cheryl had a rocky road for 25 years as she moved from jobs to a selected career field that was shrinking. How might a counselor guide her in the new world of work?
2. Integrating personal and career goals is important for effective counseling. What career interventions would you suggest to help reduce Cheryl's anxiety?
3. How might a counselor further explore the spiritual domain in this case, and what other spiritual interventions might support Cheryl's career exploration?

 ## Response
Larry D. Burlew and W. Matthew Shurts

Cheryl, a midlife worker, perceived that she may need to make an involuntary career transition. This perception created anxiety that resulted in her taking a leave of absence from her job. Using cognitive–behavioral strategies, her counselor helped reduce her anxiety symptoms enough so that she was willing to begin a career exploration process. The counselor also helped her identify how her identity was heavily aligned with her worker role with a narrowly defined occupational self-concept. By using a work adjustment model, the counselor helped her consider transferable skills, thus allowing her to consider a potential career change. The counselor also helped her realize that she could find a better balance among her work, social, and spiritual roles rather than rely solely on work for life satisfaction and meaning.

We recommend that the counselor frame Cheryl's case from Super's (1990) developmental life span, life-space approach. Cheryl most likely viewed herself as being in the maintenance stage of career development, thinking of merely preserving the achieved status she had already attained. This view would explain why, when faced with a potential involuntary career transition, she had an intense reaction that involved anticipatory grief and led to her taking a leave of absence.

While working, Cheryl seemed to create an imbalance in her life roles, allowing the worker role to dominate her identity and setting aside her spiritual and social life roles. This imbalance left her feeling empty with respect to developing friendships, socializing, and involving herself in spiritual activities that would make her feel peaceful. Her occupational self-concept was narrowly defined—as might be expected for a person who followed one career path for an extended period—which made the thought of a midlife career change difficult and stressful.

Career Diamond

Considering Questions 1 and 2 on career guidance and interventions, we suggest beginning the counseling process by using Andersen and

Vandehey's (2006) career diamond as an initial intervention and applying both existential and narrative approaches to the process. As a visual tool, the diamond allows clients to recycle into the exploration stage of Super's (1990) model and revisit the developmental tasks of crystallizing and specifying a career choice within a global economy. Cheryl seemed to be seeking more than just another career choice; she seemed to want to find meaning in her life by integrating other life roles along with the worker role. In addition, she was struggling with the detour her life story had taken, feeling like she was off the path she had envisioned.

The diamond starts with awareness (labeled with the letter *A* at the beginning of the diamond) that change is occurring and that a decision is needed (Andersen & Vandehey, 2006). The awareness involves an expanding of self-awareness (who I am in relation to the world of work) at the top of the diamond and an expanding of external awareness, or factors to consider in the career decision-making process, situated at the bottom. The expanding awareness leads to a clearer "vision of self in the world of work" (Andersen & Vandehey, 2006, p. 32).

This vision is similar to Frankl's (2006) view of finding meaning regardless of the situation one finds oneself in (e.g., an involuntary career transition). It also aligns with the narrative career counseling tenet that persons are constantly constructing their ongoing personal life story and trying to make meaning from that life story (Campbell & Ungar, 2004; Gibbons & Shurts, 2010). The vision is at the center of the expanding part of the diamond, which is what the client is moving toward through exploration and self-awareness. Once clients reach the vision, they move toward the other end of the diamond and make an informed decision.

In beginning the counseling process, the counselor can help Cheryl understand that she is recreating her vision and reauthoring her life story and that these processes will help her develop a renewed sense of meaning in her life. Cheryl can start this journey by plotting herself on the diamond in terms of her current level of self-awareness. She can address factors, such as transferrable skills and importance of various life roles, in creating a new vision of herself in the world of work. Then, she can plot herself on the lower half of the diamond with respect to various external factors related to the world of work in a new global economy. This visual tool allows the client to expand her awareness and move closer to her vision; so at the beginning of each session, movement on the diamond can be assessed and changed as growth occurs.

Career Lifeline

Another visual tool that might aid Cheryl in eliciting patterns and themes from her past is a lifeline exercise (Gibbons & Shurts, 2010). This simple activity involves having the client recollect important events from her life, noting them on a horizontal lifeline starting at birth and culminating in the current date. Cheryl would be asked to include some of the events that stood out in her memory, not necessarily involving her career/job.

The goal is to give Cheryl enough freedom to select events that have personal meaning. After completing the list of events, she would be asked to title each event and provide a one- or two-sentence description of the event's impact on her current experience. The counselor's role during this process is one of offering encouragement and noting themes that appear to arise across the events (e.g., the role that spirituality played in her life; times when she lacked social engagement). With knowledge of these patterns across the life span, Cheryl will be in a more informed space to address her career flux.

Cheryl will choose where she wants to begin the journey of awareness. To address Question 1, she can "expand knowledge of external factors that will impact [her] decision" (Andersen & Vandehey, 2006, p. 33). We would begin this exploration with career stories, a narrative technique suggested by Inkson (2007). He defined a career story as a "personal moving perspective on our working life" (Inkson, 2007, p. 231) and stated that the narrated story creates patterns from the past and allows a client to find a *plausible* story for the future. Inkson (2007) added that "we must constantly reconfigure the story to take account of new events" (p. 234).

New World of Work

With respect to external factors and the new world of work, Cheryl can begin her story with her journey in the publishing industry and how that industry changed over the years. She can address how the industry emerged into the 21st century, along with its many job titles created by the burgeoning global economy and technology. She can consider what frightens her about the nature of the new world of work that Young and Collins (as cited in Inkson, 2007) claimed "can [now] be expected to be increasingly discontinuous (p. 232)." In some ways, her *fear* of change resulted in living a restricted existence, narrowing her identity to the worker role (Frankl, 2006).

From this initial, more personal aspect of her story, Cheryl can broaden her awareness of the new world of work and gain a fresh picture of the exciting challenges and opportunities in a global economy, both within the publishing industry and in other related professions. The counselor can guide Cheryl in her awareness of the external factors via bibliotherapy and Internet research. For example, Young and Collin's (2000) book *The Future of Careers* can provide a fresh view of how to manage oneself in the new world of work. Internet articles, such as "Today's Global Job Market—Nature of the International Job Market" (Global Opportunities, 2013) and James Turck's "Ten

Traits of a Valuable Employee" (2013), can demonstrate the desired qualities of the new worker in a global economy.

Internet sources can help Cheryl generate a broader story of the global job market and examine new possibilities for using her transferrable skills that she identified with her counselor. For example, Cheryl likely would benefit from joining and participating in online and in-person communities that focus on career transitions. The information she gleaned would be helpful, and connecting her with others who may be struggling with career transitions might help normalize the situation and decrease her self-doubt.

In terms of integrating a spiritual component into this process, numerous churches offer support groups for persons who are going through career transitions (e.g., http://www.bumc.net/career). Multiple websites and online groups have been created to address similar situations. One notable resource is Tripping on the Ladder (http://www.trippingontheladder.com), an online community created by and for people who are undergoing career transitions or engaging in professional reflection. The offerings vary widely. Cheryl might find the discussion forums and ideas about how to renew and replenish oneself and manage stress quite helpful. More tangible career-focused forums about how to reinvent oneself and success stories from persons who have successfully navigated a career transition also might help.

During Cheryl's external awareness process and expanding story constructing, she should journal on what she is learning about the global economy and how it adds to her emerging vision of herself and her overall career identity. Cheryl is free to reconfigure her career story any way she wants and is responsible for choosing the aspects of the new world of work to add to her story (Frankl, 2006). As she learns more about the external factors on the diamond, she moves herself closer to a new vision that involves many avenues and alternatives for consideration.

Life Roles and Career Beliefs

In considering the top half of the diamond and personal self-awareness, Cheryl seems aware of what her goals are: perhaps changing careers, expanding her social connections, and reengaging in spiritual activities. These goals involve three interacting life roles: social, worker, and spiritual; however, because Cheryl was living a restricted existence, she was more fully engaged in the worker role to the exclusion of the social and spiritual roles.

We suggest that the Career Beliefs Inventory (CBI; Krumboltz, 1991) be administered because it might identify where Cheryl is putting up barriers to making an existential commitment to change the balancing of these three important life roles. Then, we suggest using a developmental technique used by Larry D. Burlew, the Life Role Balance Circle (based on Super's [1990] life-career rainbow). The client draws a circle and assigns a percentage of time she is involved in each life role, up to 100%. Cheryl already expressed a need to spend more time in her social and spiritual life roles, so then she must reassign percentages to the various life roles, including being an adult child, that are less discussed in the case. From this reassigning, she must decide how she will reallocate her time for new behaviors and roles.

To expand Cheryl's self-awareness, each life role must be explored in more detail. By reconfiguring her career story and integrating information learned about the new world of work, the counselor can help Cheryl create a new vision of who she wants to be as a worker. This exploration is not just about skills, personality traits, and values. It provides a comprehensive picture of where she sees herself in the new world of work, how she wants to integrate her life roles (e.g., reduction of percentage of time spent in the worker role), what the work environment would be like, how she would interact with colleagues, and what retraining or updating she needs to act on this awareness.

Additional Career Interventions

The counselor may use several interventions to integrate Cheryl's vision into a life career plan that implements decisions she will make about her reconfigured career story. Any career plan format can be used, but Burack and Mathys's (1980) model is especially helpful because it represents a visual journey in arches that unfold over time. Each arch should address a particular part of her vision to include work and leisure projects, particularly related to this midlife transition into the new world of work, while achieving a better balance of life roles.

Using the interventions to follow, the counselor can help Cheryl identify goals that would be included in her career plan. A creative arts intervention, such as drawing an image of a worker within the ideal work environment and with a better life role balance, can be useful. If additional assessment is needed, a number of career inventories can be administered (e.g., the Self-Directed Search [Holland, 2012] and the What Seems Necessary for My Happiness Scale from the CBI [Krumboltz, 1991]). At this point, Cheryl can integrate her knowledge about the new world of work by inserting herself into the ideal work environment, visually representing what would bring her meaning. If she struggles with the visual representation, career imagining through career fantasy exercises or guided imagery can be used "to engage the intuitive left-brain hemisphere and to eliminate the critical thinking that often discounts possibilities" (Andersen & Vandehey, 2006, p. 194).

Because Cheryl wants to expand her social connections, the counselor could assess her view of herself as "shy and socially awkward" and whether that is still how she sees herself as a midlife woman. She can be referred to a support group for women in midlife career change or for midlife women in transition to hear other women's perspectives. She also could be guided to use social media to begin connecting with other persons to network for possible job opportunities.

Exploring the Spiritual Domain

Considering Question 3, reconnecting Cheryl with her religion as an aspect of her spirituality is an important avenue to explore, keeping in mind that this is now part of the reconfiguring of her career story. Cheryl's religious beliefs could come up through the existential and narrative work noted earlier (e.g., lifeline activity; discussions of meaning). However, a more intentional focus on her current versus her desired religiosity during this time of transition can provide an opportunity to enrich her spiritual life and deepen the meaning-making process.

Internet resources and bibliotherapy can prove helpful in this realm because a plethora of resources are available that address career transitions from a Christian perspective. In "Career Change as God's Calling?"—a brief Internet article authored by career counselor Gina Delapa (2009)—she shared personal lessons learned during her career transition. For a more detailed resource, Cheryl could be directed to Susan Britton Whitcomb's (2008) book, *The Christian's Career Journey: Finding the Job God Designed for You.* Cheryl would be encouraged to use these sources as catalysts for in-session exploration of how reconnection with her religious practice and perhaps a deeper faith could become a strong supporting character in her new career story.

References

Andersen, P., & Vandehey, M. (2006). *Career counseling and development in a global economy.* New York, NY: Lahaska Press.

Burack, E. H., & Mathys, N. J. (1980). *Career management in organizations: A practical human resource planning approach.* Lake Forest, IL: Brace-Park Press.

Campbell, C. G., & Ungar, M. (2004). Constructing a life that works: Part two. An approach to practice. *The Career Development Quarterly, 53,* 28–40.

Delapa, G. (2009). *Career change as God's calling?* Retrieved from http://www.relevantmagazine.com/life/career-money/blog/18064-career-change-as-gods-calling

Frankl, V. (2006). *Man's search for meaning.* Boston, MA: Beacon Press.

Gibbons, M. M., & Shurts, W. M. (2010). Combining career and couples counseling for college students: A narrative approach. *Journal of College Counseling, 13,* 169–181.

Global Opportunities. (2013). *Today's global job market—Nature of the international job market.* Retrieved from http://www.globalopps. org/papers/BreakgIntoGlobalJobMkt.htm

Holland, J. (2012). *SDS Form R professional manual.* Lutz, FL: PAR.

Inkson, K. (2007). *Understanding careers: The metaphors of working lives.* Thousand Oaks, CA: Sage.

Krumboltz, J. D. (1991). *Career beliefs inventory.* Palo Alto, CA: Consulting Psychologist Press.

Super, D. E. (1990). A life-span, life-space approach to career development. In D. Brown & L. Brooks (Eds.), *Career choice and development: Applying contemporary theories to practice* (2nd ed., pp. 197–261). San Francisco, CA: Jossey-Bass.

Turck, J. (2013). Ten traits of a valuable employee. *Real Truth, 11.* Retrieved from http://realtruth.org/articles/100108-004-society.html

Whitcomb, S. B. (2008). *The Christian's career journey: Finding the job God designed for you.* Indianapolis, IN: JIST Works.

Young, R. A., & Collin, A. (Eds.). (2000). *The future of careers.* Cambridge, UK: Cambridge University Press.

 ## Reflections
Tracey E. Robert and Virginia A. Kelly

This case underlines the impact of an imbalance between life roles; in this case, a heavy focus on the work domain resulting in neglect in the spiritual and social domains. Developmental tools, such as the lifeline and a focus on expanding the client's self-awareness, can tap into the beliefs and values that drive the client's decision making and enhance the counseling process.

Integrating spirituality into the career counseling process can include exploring whether the client wants to reconnect with his or her familial and early beliefs. We would caution that the counselor must make sure that this reconnection is what the client wants, not just assume it would help fill the void. Many churches and faith-based groups have provided valuable help to many during their job and career process. In this particular case, the client might want to search for meaning in another belief system and not return to her early roots. Integration of spirituality into career counseling over the life span provides these benefits:

- support and strategies for dealing with transitional events and accompanying loss,
- identification of clients' talents or gifts and a calling or purpose that draws them to a certain field or career, and
- guidance to explore deep issues of meaning and mattering in their life and the world.

• • •

Chapter 19
Job Loss

Case

Edina L. Renfro-Michel

Joseph, a 36-year-old White male, was referred to counseling by his unemployment caseworker, Ronald. Joseph had not been attending his training sessions on time, and he missed several meetings with his caseworker. When Ronald confronted him about these behaviors, Joseph said, "Ever since I was laid off, I have felt lost, without direction or meaning in my life. What is the point?"

Background

Joseph was born in the Midwest to middle-class parents. An only child of working parents, he often was home alone after school, a situation he was determined not to repeat with his children. Joseph's father was an electrician, and his mother was a secretary for a local water company. He shared that his parents were atheist, even though they celebrated Christian holidays like Christmas and Easter. Joseph did not remember discussing religion or spirituality when he was growing up. "We just didn't talk about God or religion," he said. "The subjects were taboo in our house. We talked about Santa and the Easter Bunny, but God was not a part of the equation."

Upon high school graduation, Joseph began working as a sheet metal inspector in an automobile plant. At 25, he was promoted to supervisor. Shortly after his promotion, Joseph married Anna, an elementary school teacher. He stated that he and Anna had a strong marriage.

Joseph and Anna had two children, Duncan, 7, and Isabelle, 3. When they were expecting Duncan, they decided that Anna should stay home to provide stability for their children. Joseph stated, "It is important that the children have a constant parent, one who is with them and can help them with homework or issues with friends. I didn't have that. I was often alone and didn't have anyone to talk to about school problems."

Joseph thrived in his supervisory position, often working overtime, sometimes up to 60 hours a week. He enjoyed meeting the plant management's productivity challenges in creative ways. A natural mediator, Joseph was an effective liaison between management and the workers. He described being a supervisor as "important."

Incident

Joseph had been laid off when the automobile plant closed 2 years earlier. Anna went back to work to help provide for the family until Joseph was able to find employment. He registered with the state unemployment office and began meeting with Ronald on a monthly basis. At first, Joseph was excited to spend some time with his family, but as the unemployment continued, he began questioning his life purpose. Because there was a lack of employment for automobile factory workers in the area, Ronald suggested that Joseph participate in state job training to change his career.

Joseph chose to begin training as a welder because the job prospects were good. The work was not enjoyable, but he completed his training. When asked about his lack of interest in welding, he said, "As long as I can provide for my family as a welder, it is fine that I don't like the work." He obtained three interviews for welding positions but could not find employment.

Joseph's unemployment insurance was discontinued, and he became despondent. Ronald recommended that Joseph complete job search training to learn résumé writing and interview skills for his new career. After a few weeks, Joseph was late for several training sessions and missed his monthly meeting with Ronald.

Joseph decided there was no point in continuing the training, meeting with Ronald, or applying for jobs because obviously there was no employment in his future. "I want to go back to work and provide for my family," he said. "I have lost my calling, and I know I won't ever find a job like the one I had. I just don't have any hope. I don't have any meaning in my life."

Discussion

Joseph stated that his main goal in counseling was to "move past the interview process and become an employee." As his counselor, I focused on the deeper issues of lack of meaning in his life and his feelings of despondency. From a work adjustment theoretical orientation, we discussed how Joseph's work was a strong part of his identity and how his psychological need to do "important" work was a contributing factor to his success in the automotive industry.

Joseph had lost his identities as a supervisor, mediator, and primary income provider for his family. Losing his primary identities caused Joseph to feel that he was lost and that his life was lacking in meaning. During our work together, Joseph discussed a "feeling of needing to be connected to something bigger than myself, a higher consciousness." However, he had difficulties contemplating spiritual development because he believed that religion was synonymous with spirituality.

After Joseph discussed his feelings of meaninglessness, I asked him to create a list of aspects in his life that currently, or in the past, provided him with a sense of fulfillment. The two themes that emerged were "making a difference" (both at work and with his family) and spending time with his family. Both of these themes were surprising to Joseph, because his primary foci in terms of identity had been making money and finding employment.

When asked what would be a dream job, regardless of money or education, Joseph stated, "Something where I can help people solve problems or find connections with others." Upon further processing of this information, Joseph said, "I never thought about these things before; now I am more confused about what I should do. I need to go back to work to help my family, but maybe I also want to go back to school for a different kind of training. And a large part of me just wants to go back to bed."

Questions

1. Given Joseph's difficulties finding work, how could a counselor help him develop strong interviewing skills?
2. Joseph lost his sense of self and meaning in his life. What else might a counselor do to help him redevelop these?
3. How might a counselor help Joseph better understand his interest in spirituality, and how it might be helpful in his job search and his life?

 ## Response

Jane Goodman

The emotional impact of job loss is often underestimated. It involves stages of grief that have been compared with the stages of mourning after a death—persons frequently experience great despair and hopelessness before traveling the journey toward hope. The stages of grief described by Kübler-Ross (1969) were adapted by Goodman and Hoppin (1990) for job loss. They include relief or shock and denial, emotional release, depression and physical distress, panic and guilt, and anger and hostility; in the best-case scenario, they culminate in renewed hope and rebuilding. Joseph seemed to be toggling between depression and guilt over not providing for his family.

Spencer and Adams (2002) described the transition process as one that includes losing focus, falling into a pit, and then climbing out of the pit and finding meaning in the experience. Joseph apparently was struggling in the pit, and his feelings of confusion and perhaps depression demonstrated this condition. Bridges (2004) talked about transition in terms of an ending, a period of confusion, and a new beginning. We can see Joseph in this formulation as a person struggling in a period of confusion. Bridges, in his preface to the second edition of *Transitions* (2004, p. xii), distinguished transitions from simple change in that transitions require an inner reorientation and a change in self-definition; they are psychological, not simply situational.

Schlossberg (Anderson, Goodman, & Schlossberg, 2012) described four aspects of any transition, including job loss: the situation, the self, the support, and the strategies. In Joseph's case they include the following:

- *The situation.* Joseph lost a job he really liked and felt successful in. His wife's return to work helped financially, but that was not the family plan, and he wanted and needed to work soon to contribute to their expenses. He was used to working long hours, and the enforced time at home was troubling to him. His training as a welder had not paid off in terms of employment. He had no other education beyond high school.
- *The self.* Joseph was in a state of confusion regarding who he was, what was important to him, and how he related to his own spirituality. His very identity was in flux, and this was causing him a great deal of angst.
- *The support.* We do not have a lot of information about Joseph's support system. We know his wife went back to work when he was laid off, but we don't know the feelings around this decision. We have not heard anything about other external supports, and Joseph's internal supports also were problematic.
- *The strategies.* Joseph was looking to the counselor to help him develop strategies to manage the decisions around employment and education, but it seems he also was hoping to get some help in figuring out what was important to him and how this tied in with his desire for a spiritual connection.

Two-Pronged Approach

It has been said that one of the most important goals of counseling is instilling hope. Joseph was in desperate need of hope and dreams, and his statements about feeling meaningless and looking for something "bigger than myself, a higher consciousness" provide us with clues to this need. It appears that helping Joseph find, or find again, his spiritual self would be indicated. To paraphrase the name of a popular musical, he may find that he has an amazing dreamcoat.

Working with Joseph calls for a two-pronged approach. He needs, for financial and emotional reasons, to find work, so job-hunting skills must be addressed and addressed promptly. While doing this, however, the counselor would be right in pursuing his deeper need for finding meaning in life as well as work. It seems appropriate for Joseph to look at both short- and long-term goals. The short-term goal would be for him to find any work that would help him support his family; the long-term goal would be for him to make some decisions about pursuing further education and following his dream of work that allows him to solve problems, make connections, and "make a difference."

Question 1 asked about helping Joseph improve his interviewing skills. It is easy to imagine the impression he made as he interviewed. Depressed clients tend to present themselves without affect or as so self-deprecating as to convince an employer that they will not be good employees.

Joseph had not had to look for work since his late teens, when he began to work for the employer who recently laid him off, so there is no reason to believe he had any idea how to present himself in an interview. The counselor should go back to the basics and teach him how to research a position, prepare for the interview, develop a strong paper résumé, develop a strong electronic résumé, and practice actual interviewing. Given Joseph's shaky sense of self, the emphasis should be on finding his strengths as an interviewee and only gently correcting his weaknesses. Presenting himself positively and assertively is more important than being highly skilled. Recording his practice interviews and playing them back would allow him to provide his own feedback. The counselor's job would be to keep him from being too hard on himself.

To help Joseph find new meaning in life—meaning that previously was provided through his work—it would be important to convince him that continuing to see the counselor, even after he has found new work, is worth his while. He could then explore the kind of work he would like to pursue long term, plan for what education or training he might need, and develop an action plan that would lead him toward this goal. In Joseph's case, using Savickas's (2003) questions would be an appropriate way to proceed, helping him get in touch with needs and desires that he perhaps never considered. These questions include the following:

1. What is your earliest recollection?
2. What do you like to do in your free time?

3. Do you have a favorite saying or motto?
4. Whom do you admire? Whom did you admire growing up? How are you like or different from these people?

The counselor also could engage Joseph in values clarification activities, art therapy activities, and other activities that engage a client in discovering or uncovering wishes and dreams—indeed, ways of trying on that dreamcoat.

Job Search and Spirituality

To help Joseph begin to connect with his spirituality, the counselor could ask him to consider times when he experienced what Csikszentmihalyi (1996) called "flow," the experience of being "in the zone." The counselor could ask him such questions as "When have you felt that time didn't exist?" and "When have you felt 'lost in the moment'?" As he remembers these times, Joseph might see a connection with something larger than himself, whether he considers it a deity or simply a oneness with the universe.

Joseph might be aided by finding a religious organization that fits with his beliefs and becoming involved in its activities. These activities would provide him with the opportunity to "make a difference" even before he finds that opportunity in his work life. It also would provide a sense of belonging and support. However, if organized religion does not feel appropriate to him, he can still pursue his spirituality individually and continue his quest to have a meaningful life.

References

Anderson, M. L., Goodman, J., & Schlossberg, N. K. (2012). *Counseling adults in transition: Linking Schlossberg's theory with practice in a diverse world*. New York, NY: Springer.

Bridges, W. (2004). *Transitions: Making sense of life's changes* (2nd ed.). Cambridge, MA: DeCapo Press.

Csikszentmihalyi, M. (1996). *Creativity: Flow and the psychology of discovery and invention*. New York, NY: Harper Perennial.

Goodman, J., & Hoppin, J. M. (1990). *Opening doors: A practical guide to job hunting* (2nd ed.). Rochester, MI: Continuum Center, Oakland University.

Kübler-Ross, E. (1969). *On death and dying*. New York, NY: Macmillan.

Savickas, M. L. (2003, September). *The career theme interview*. Paper presented to the International Association of Educational and Vocational Guidance, Bern, Switzerland.

Spencer, S. A., & Adams, J. D. (2002). *Life changes: A guide to the seven stages of personal growth*. San Luis Obispo, CA: Impact.

Reflections

Tracey E. Robert and Virginia A. Kelly

The connection between work and spirituality has been described as a key component of job satisfaction, life satisfaction, and work adjustment. One component of spiritual well-being, existential well-being, has been defined as finding meaning and purpose in life. In many cultures, this need is met through work. In Joseph's case, the centrality of work in his life contributed to a deep sense of loss when he was laid off, and the counselor and responder addressed the deeper existential issues of loss and direction in life. From a wellness perspective, integration of the spiritual domain was critical.

The mechanics of the job search (interviewing, networking, and résumé writing) are helpful action steps in the counseling process. As seen in this case, the client's inner life influences the outcomes—Joseph's lack of direction and purpose in life led to frustration and failure to be reemployed. Integration of the work and spiritual domains expands the client's options and offers multiple interventions to address the stages of loss and career transition. Opportunities to nurture workers' inner strengths through their spirituality may indeed be beneficial for job and overall life satisfaction. Integration of spirituality into career counseling provides the following benefits:

- More intentionally identifying the client's perception of meaning and purpose in life and feeling a sense of community enhance career decision-making skills.
- Integration of career metaphors, such as road map, journey, resources, season, and growth, provides interventions to tap into the strengths of the client's inner life.
- An enhanced sense of spiritual well-being can increase coping skills and resilience.

• • •

Section VI

Diverse Populations

Chapter 20
Islamic Identity

Case
Taysier El-Gaili

Mona, a 39-year-old Sudanese Muslim, was raised in a diverse cultural environment. She experienced many traumatic events and painful experiences, and she struggled with both her religious faith and how to interact with divergent belief systems. Mona had gone to counseling for ongoing but fragmented conflicts in her faith, culture, and identity, coupled with difficulty in adapting to her own culture, which resulted in multiple visits. She stated, "I failed to identify myself with my home country or my fellow men and women. I just felt I did not belong."

Background

Mona moved from Sudan to Saudi Arabia with her family when she was 6 years old after experiencing war trauma when she was 5. This trauma constantly invaded her dreams until she was almost 18, when she moved to Egypt to obtain a bachelor's degree.

Within the multicultural diverse environment Mona grew up in, she received American education throughout her life. She attended intermediate and high school in Saudi Arabia in a dual-language (Arabic and English) school following the American education system. Her bachelor's degree was from the American University in Cairo, and her master's degree was from a Sudanese University in Khartoum. Mona then enrolled in a post-master's program in the United States.

Mona's father tried to reinforce her Sudanese identity in various ways. However, she struggled with that identity because she had not been a part of the Sudanese community until the age of 30. Mona had lived in a Western compound in the Eastern Province of Saudi Arabia since she was 9. She lived a typical expatriate's lifestyle, but none of the Sudanese families at the compound had kids her age, and none of the students at her school were Sudanese. When Mona went to the American University in Cairo, she tried to identify herself with the Sudanese community but felt she didn't belong. Her many differences included her Arabic accent that was not typical Sudanese, her clothing style, her liberal attitude, and her daring personality.

After living in Sudan for more than 7 years, Mona reported a change in her personality characterized by excessive anger, unnecessary defensiveness, occasional anxiety, and crying episodes. This behavior created challenges with relationships and conflicts around intimacy that were faith based and could have been the result of lack of clarity of what she wanted in a partner. She dated several men, including a conservative Arab Sudanese, a liberal American Muslim, a liberal Sudanese, and a liberal non-Arab non-Muslim, the last being the love of her life for the past 4 years.

Mona's conflicts with the Arab conservative man were related to opposing belief/value systems, but complications in her relationship with the love of her life were about religion and conflicts between her desires and her faith. Her religion prohibited her from marrying a non-Muslim without him converting, and her own values rejected living with him without marriage. She asked, "Why did God bring my beloved in my path if He knows we cannot be together?" Ironically, Mona became more spiritual, thinking of God more and feeling His presence wherever she went.

Mona perceives herself as a free soul who refuses to be repressed by cultural or religious ideologies. She managed to identify her own cultural values, but she seemed to be struggling to find peace with her spiritual and religious identity. Although she felt repressed with Arab Muslim men because of their restrictive cultural ideologies, she felt liberated with the love of her life. However, she was the one who imposed religious and spiritual restrictions in their relationship. The conflict mainly revolved around her religious and moral beliefs about premarital sexual intercourse; eventually, Mona became pregnant. She believed that everything happens for a reason, and she was struggling to find the reason behind her experience with the love of her life. The only one she found was to bring her closer to God!

A year earlier, the man she was truly in love with had proposed marriage, but Mona's family refused the marriage proposal, so she left her country with him. She needed to know whether she could live with him and go against her religious and cultural beliefs. A few months later, they broke up because of constant conflicts about intimacy and her feelings of guilt.

Mona found out that she was pregnant after they broke up and decided to keep the baby because of her faith. When she told the man about the pregnancy, he did not offer to convert to her religion and marry her. Instead, he told her to abort the baby because it was not her decision alone and "he never donated to any sperm bank." Feeling devastated, Mona told her brother and her mother, who came to her place, assaulted her, and tortured her physically and emotionally.

Mona ran away to another African country and told an ex-countryman about her situation, and he then proposed to marry her. When they called her mother to proceed with the marriage, her mother came to stay with her and seemed at first to accept the idea of the marriage. Mona's mother waited until after the baby was delivered then continued her abuse of Mona in all its forms. Mona, her mother, and the baby traveled back to Sudan. Mona's mother arranged for someone to take the baby away and for a Sudanese married man to marry Mona.

Incident

Mona came to counseling this time because she had run away from her home country a third time after being emotionally and physically abused by her mother. She had two major anger episodes in which she broke glasses and mobile phones in her house. Mona felt that she was deceived and betrayed even by her husband, who was passive when she told him about what she was going through and the unbearable torture.

Mona said that if it weren't for her faith, she would have killed herself to put an end to her pain and torture. She explained that she had a liberal Islamic upbringing even though she was living in a radical Islamic country. She identified herself as a spiritual woman with an ample mutual love of the Creator. She said, "I was angry with Him, but I knew deep inside me that somehow He chose what's best for me because I was sure He loved me, but I'm really tired and need some pampering from Him."

Mona expressed the need for space to heal and to gain control over her life. She also needed to find work outside of Sudan and "reconciliation with God."

Discussion

In dealing with Mona, it was crucial to explore the spiritual and religious dimensions in depth. I integrated her Islamic faith and used her belief in a spiritual power to access internal and external resources. Mona expressed the strength she gets when she reads the Quran or prays. She said, "I talk to Him and ask Him to interfere; I ask Him to forgive me and not to punish me by taking my baby away from me." I encouraged this spiritual healing and used Islamic storytelling as a therapeutic tool to foster forgiveness and to instill hope.

Mona's relationship with God was very important in helping her make major decisions. However, she was angry with God for allowing her mother to abuse her and for taking the baby away even though she knew that He knew the other option was to abort the baby, and then He would be angry.

Mona's Arab African culture values the venting and sharing of details of even daily events. Thus, I was able to introduce free association as a tool for gaining insight. Mona was angry with her mother about her mother's reactions. We explored together her mother's strict background and religious upbringing in a conservative Sudanese culture that associated having a baby outside of marriage with shame and stigma. For Mona, there was only God, whom she did not want to upset with an abortion. I discussed with Mona the role of the religious leader in the Sudanese culture, the possibility of talking about the issue with him, and the prospect of asking him to talk to her mother or mediate between them.

It seemed that Mona needed to better know herself as existing in the middle of opposite belief systems. I used the Haeri model as a spiritual and psychological developmental tool for gaining self-knowledge. The model, based on Sufi ideologies, focuses on the positive energy created through the love of God and His prophet.

Because Mona reported that sometimes she felt she got lost trying to find out who she truly was, I used a psychodynamic approach to explore her persona, the mask she was wearing to protect herself. We discussed the idea that wearing a mask may have been a result of being raised in many cultures and undergoing an enduring search for identity and needing to belong. The persona functioned in Mona's life as an ego defense mechanism that preserved her image to allow for smooth socializing and acceptance from the society of which she happened to be part.

The persona hid her anxiety and her greatest fear, being married to a Sudanese man. We would need to explore this more. It was not clear whether it was a matter of being ashamed to let others see her fear or that she was not allowed to even express her fear because it was in total opposition to her persona.

Mona seemed confused about her relationship with her husband in her arranged marriage. She did not know whether she should trust him and his intentions in still wanting to be with her. Mona discussed her persistent dreams and fears that her husband had cast a spell on her to be able to marry her and that what she was going through could not be God's plan for her.

Together, we processed the Islamic-faith-based cultural beliefs regarding black magic and the evil eye as clearly stated in the Quran and the sayings of Prophet Muhammad. We examined the protective measures in Islam as well as the treatment from both the evil eye and black magic, using specific verses from the Quran.

Mona's cultural and spiritual upbringing supported the use of dream analysis. This strategy focused on the feelings associated with her dreams and with symbolic interpretations from the Quran. This dream analysis fits with a psychodynamic model.

We processed the Islamic belief that God provides different strengths in different circumstances. In this belief system, with each situation she would be protected, punished to be purified, and then prepared. Prophet Muhammad taught people this prayer: "God, behold, I ask you for a faith that brings joy to my heart with a firm conviction such that I realize that nothing happens to me unless you have prescribed it for me and I feel pleasure at what you have allotted to me, O the most merciful of those who have mercy."

We then explored how, in Mona's case, God's plan might be the best plan for her and that she was being asked to consider a new experience with her husband, to find pleasure in appreciating what she had, and to count her blessings. This reframing allowed her to view her situation more objectively.

I asked Mona how she could improve the quality of her life, focusing on her gratitude for all her blessings. I asked her whether she had found God's grace and if she felt that her faith was being tested. I supported her through her pain and suffering to empower her to discover her inner strength and potential.

Questions

1. How would the counselor guide Mona in interpreting her antagonistic relationship with her mother?
2. How might a counselor help Mona understand the roots of her conflicting beliefs to be able to intervene and assist her in striving for a balanced Islamic identity?
3. How could a counselor explore the pattern of running away from trauma and abuse in Mona's life?
4. How might a counselor explore Mona's spiritual development and persona and shadow?

 Response
Abigail H. Conley, Sylvia C. Nassar-McMillan, and Anjabeen Ashraf

When continuing counseling with Mona, the counselor should conceptualize this case through the intersections of identity development, cultural development, spiritual development, and healing. Mona is dealing with many issues and transitions that affect her personal well-being, including surviving abuse from her family, being estranged from her child, adjusting to a new arranged marriage, and reconciling with God. We suggest that the counselor explore Mona's identity development through the lens of her diverse cultural experiences, religious beliefs, and interpersonal strengths for an integrated sense of self.

Family Relationships

The first question asks how the counselor might help Mona interpret her antagonistic relationship with her mother. The counselor should begin with an examination of the family structure in Mona's culture of origin. In more collectivist cultures such as Mona's, community, and particularly, family are salient constructs (Nydell, 2012). Family serving as a central tenet for Mona may explain the degree of distress she has faced in making certain life decisions that she knew would conflict with familial wishes. For Mona, even in the face of the trauma inflicted by her mother, cutting relational ties may not be viewed as a viable option.

The counselor should determine what Mona desires. Does she want to see her mother again? Does she want to attempt a dialogue? If she does want to start a dialogue, how would she feel comfortable doing this? Would she prefer to communicate through email, phone, a relative, or a religious leader? A role play or empty-chair technique may be useful here to help Mona articulate what she would say to her mother.

If Mona chooses not to continue a relationship with her mother or to limit interaction with her, it may cause dissonance and anxiety within her because, from a cultural standpoint, that may be unheard of or frowned upon (Dwairy, 2006). In that case, the counselor may help Mona come to terms with her choice and reconcile it with her current needs and cultural framework.

Exploring the concept of religious abuse and how it might connect to the other types of abuse Mona suffered might be useful. Religious abuse is "mistreatment of a person who is in need of help, support, or greater spiritual empowerment with the result of weakening, undermining, or decreasing that person's spiritual empowerment" (Johnson & Vanvonderen, 1991, p. 20). The abuse Mona suffered at the hands of her brother and mother seems intricately related to her behavior falling "out of line" of her family's cultural and religious expectations and appears to have been intended to disempower her. Mona exhibits the manifestation of internal states (e.g., anxiety, depression, and self-hatred) that are physical and psychological repercussions of religious abuse. The counselor could help Mona process how being abused has affected her relationship with her family and her religious and cultural identity.

Social support is another important element to consider here because Mona has lost a large form of support: her family. Mona's struggles, though traumatic and unique, are similar to the universal struggle of identity and spirituality for all human beings as they move toward authenticity. To normalize her experiences, the counselor may want to explore persons with whom Mona has connected who may share similar backgrounds, struggles, and religious identity formation. The counselor may consider connecting Mona with a religious community.

Because the Haeri model based on Sufi beliefs was used with Mona previously, the counselor might consider finding a Sufi community center and connecting her with a representative there. Mona seems to be highly spiritual, and the Sufi tradition focuses on spirituality and a relationship with God (Fadiman & Frager, 1997). Encouraging Mona's connection with others who accept her religious journey may give her a foundation and sense of belonging from which she can begin to piece together the parts of her identity.

Understanding Conflicting Beliefs

The second question asks how a counselor could help Mona understand the roots of her conflicting beliefs to work toward achieving a balanced Islamic identity. In many cases, religious and cultural identities are intricately intertwined. In Mona's case, the following four key considerations relate to her conflicted "Islamic" identity development: (a) all three of Mona's countries of origin and residence (Sudan, Saudi Arabia, and Egypt) are Arab countries, spread across the Middle East/North Africa (MENA); (b) Arab and Muslim values have considerable overlap; (c) there is a wide range of diversity among Arab countries; and (d) Mona has undergone the acculturation process (loosely defined here as becoming reintegrated into a different culture) at least three times over her lifetime. These considerations, explored with Mona, can help her achieve a more balanced identity.

Sudan, Saudi Arabia, and Egypt are members of the League of Arab States (Encyclopedia Brittanica, 2013). Spanning the MENA region, they all are predominantly Muslim, although other religions are represented on smaller scales. Largely because of this Muslim majority in the region, Arab and Muslim cultural values often are intertwined (Nassar-McMillan, 2010).

Several key values are religious faith and the importance of family life, which is patriarchal in structure. However, the ways in which these values manifest in daily family and community life can vary substantially across countries according to the region or even the immediate subregion (Nassar-McMillan, Ajrouch, & Hakim-Larson, 2014). In other words, the intraethnic diversity needs to be understood both generally and specifically. For example, the political regime and corresponding sociocultural milieu may represent a wide spectrum of relative conservatism—or, conversely, liberalism—that may subsume both religious behaviors and individual rights on the basis of issues such as family hierarchy and gender. The counseling process could be used to cocreate meanings and definitions—in essence, Mona's experientially based perceptions of these varied country-specific cultures.

Juxtaposed on this backdrop of potentially dramatic range of diversity in cultures across Sudan, Saudi Arabia, and Egypt, the process of acculturation needs to be considered broadly and then the specific relevance to Mona's case explored. According to Berry and his colleagues (Berry, Phinney, Sam, & Vedder, 2006), the acculturation process characterizing the immigration experience has four possible outcomes depicted on two perpendicular continua: (a) high versus low preferences on one and (b) heritage culture versus larger society culture on the other. High preferences for both heritage and larger society culture results in *integration*; low preferences for both heritage and larger society culture results in *marginalization*; high preferences for heritage versus larger society culture results in *separation*; and high preferences for larger society versus heritage culture results in *assimilation*. This schema was developed to better understand the immigration process, typically as applied to a single immigration experience.

Mona has transitioned into and out of these cultures at various points, which has added considerable complexity to her cultural (including her religious) identity. The counselor and Mona need to explore not only the various country-specific cultures but also Mona's identification, or lack thereof, to help her self-define who she is in terms of her religious, or Islamic/Muslim, identity, as well as her broader cultural identity.

To assess Mona's mental health from a culturally sensitive standpoint, the counselor and Mona need to explore her cultural identity, worldview, acculturation, and religious identity, and they need to perform trauma assessment (Ibrahim & Heuer, 2013). To promote Mona's resilience in dealing with her current crises and decision-making processes, the counselor could help her identify positive resources, including safety, social support, functional status, identity development, faith, acculturation, and socioeconomic level (Nassar-McMillan, 2010).

Running Away From Trauma and Abuse

Question 3 asks how the counselor could explore Mona's pattern of uprooting her life after experiencing trauma. Given Mona's pattern of coping with trauma by changing her environment, the counselor could coconstruct with her a new narrative of the traumatic events she is dealing with, thus processing Mona's pain without her giving up her identity. With the use of narrative therapy, this construction could draw on different stories from Islam that speak to loss, grief, and strength.

In addition, helping Mona identify how her current participation in her Muslim faith speaks to her current experience of loss and grief might be beneficial. This task could be accomplished by incorporating forgiveness work into counseling. Using the process model of forgiveness therapy (Enright & Fitzgibbons, 2000), the counselor could help Mona move through these four phases of forgiveness: (a) uncovering, (b) decision, (c) work, and (d) deepening. In each phase, it is important to allow for collaboration between the counselor and the client. The counselor should be mindful of allowing Mona to control this process so as not to impose the view that she *should* forgive and thereby reinforce women's traditional gender role socialization related to submission and overpathologizing anger (McKay, Hill, Freedman, & Enright, 2007).

In the uncovering phase, Mona could examine whether, and how, the abuse she has suffered has compromised her life. This phase could involve exploring how her major life transitions, including moving, giving birth, and getting married, are connected to surviving trauma. In addition, the counselor could allow space for Mona to confront feelings of anger, shame, cognitive preoccupation, exhaustion, and fear. Mona also could explore how experiencing trauma has changed her view of the world, including her relationship with her family, her culture, and God.

In the decision phase, the counselor could use psychoeducation to clarify what forgiveness is and is not. He or she should emphasize to Mona that forgiveness is not exoneration, reconciliation, or a forgetting of or denial of the wrongdoer's behavior but rather a process by which she can acknowledge her anger, normalize her rage, grieve her losses, and finally forgive (Wade & Worthington, 2005). It is then up to Mona to decide whether she would like to commit to forgiving on the basis of this understanding.

If Mona decides to proceed with forgiveness, the work phase would be next in the forgiving process. The counselor could help her explore the cultural and religious identity of her family to gain a deeper understanding of context for her mother's and brother's behavior. Without condoning their actions, or blaming herself, Mona could begin to reframe her affect toward her family, herself, and God. In this phase, she might explore her ability to show empathy, to bear pain, and to give the moral gift of forgiveness (even though the perpetrators do not deserve it).

The deepening phase involves finding meaning in suffering. The counselor could help Mona explore the ways in which she has grown as a result of her suffering, along with times she has needed and relied upon forgiveness from others. Exploring how her experiences connect her to others and the idea that she is not alone in her suffering would be useful. In this final phase, the counselor and Mona could coconstruct a new narrative that creates meaning out of trauma. For example, she could explore how her pain has brought her closer to God and whether there is a new purpose to her life as a result of her experiences. This exploration connects to the fourth question, spiritual development.

Spiritual Development

Question 4 asks how a counselor would explore Mona's spiritual development and persona and shadow. To assist Mona in working through the trauma she has experienced and reconcile with God, the counselor could continue with a psychodynamic, insight-oriented approach. The guiding assumption of this theoretical conceptualization is that spiritual development will occur when there is resolution of the psychological conflicts impeding her relationship with God (Rizzuto, 2005). The counselor could use a developmental model of psychoreligious functioning to provide a helpful framework to understand the psychological dynamics underlying Mona's religious concerns.

Using a psychoanalytic perspective, Genia (1995) delineated a hierarchy of the following five levels of spiritual development: (a) egocentric faith, (b) dogmatic faith, (c) transitional faith, (d) reconstructed faith, and (e) transcendent faith. In this theory, people move forward through each stage but may regress or become stagnant at various times in their life. Stage 3, transitional faith, is characterized by spiritual uncertainty and doubt—clients often experience questioning and emotional turmoil and lack a sense of belonging. Stage 4, reconstructed faith, showcases a commitment to faith that is self-chosen, meaningful, and spiritually fulfilling. Clients in this stage are tolerant of religious diversity but may seek a religious community to offer guidance during times of spiritual uncertainty (Genia, 1992).

On the basis of the information presented in the case, Mona seems to be moving into Stage 4, reconstructed faith. When she was dating the "love of her life," who did not share her faith, she began questioning her faith. She asked why God would have brought him into her life, and she grappled with finding consistency between her moral values and her actions. Her faith was strengthened through her experience of not marrying the love of her life and of choosing to have her baby. Because of these experiences and the trauma that followed, she has reconstructed what her faith means to her and has moved back toward adhering closely to her religious doctrines.

A core conflict for Mona is finding her own liberal-Muslim spiritual identity amid her family's conservative Sudanese culture. Living out her self-identified great fear, being married to a Sudanese man, exemplifies this conflict. The counselor should continue to explore the archetypes of persona and shadow to help Mona reconcile her desire to embrace God's plan for her with her anger toward her mother and brother for their abuse and her husband for his indifference to it. Mona is working to count her blessings and find strength in being tested by God while struggling to find peace and acceptance with persons in her life betraying and abusing her. The counselor could continue the practice of dream analysis, assigning Mona the homework of keeping a dream journal and allowing her to construct meaning from her dreams as they relate to her healing and identity development.

Focusing on Mona's spiritual development in counseling also would affect her psychological conflicts related to her suicidal ideation and outbursts of anger. Genia and Cooke (1998) found that, as women begin to reach the later decades of their life, a mature faith orientation may help them maintain a positive outlook on life. Criteria for a mature faith include the following: having a transcendent relationship with a higher power, living in a manner consistent with one's spiritual values, possessing an ability to have commitment without absolute certainty, having an appreciation of spiritual diversity, retaining an absence of egocentricity and magical thinking, placing equal value on reason and emotion, having a mature concern for others, being tolerant and strongly encouraging human growth, struggling to understand evil and suffering, having a deep sense of meaning and purpose, and keeping space for both traditional beliefs and private interpretations (Genia, 1991). The counselor could explore with Mona how matching her worldly wants and needs aligns with the will of God, which would allow for a more mature faith orientation in which she is in harmony with herself, the sacred, and the world (Rafea, Rafea, & Rafea, 2005).

Through the intersections of Mona's spiritual, cultural, and identity development, the counselor could conceptualize the counseling process holistically. Empowering Mona to define her interpersonal interactions through choice and forgiveness, thereby building on her strengths, the counselor could help her in exploring and integrating her multiple identities. Within the frameworks of cultural and religious identity development, the counselor could help Mona move toward resolution and unification of self.

References

Arab League. (2013). In *Encyclopedia Britannica*. Retrieved from http://www.britannica.com/EBchecked/topic/31483/Arab-League

Berry, J. W., Phinney, J. S., Sam, D. L., & Vedder, P. (2006). Immigrant youth: Acculturation, identity, and adaptation. *Applied Psychology: An International Review, 55,* 303–332. doi:10.1111/j.1464–0597.2006.00256.x

Dwairy, M. (2006). *Counseling and psychotherapy with Arabs and Muslims: A culturally sensitive approach.* New York, NY: Teachers College Press.

Enright, R. D., & Fitzgibbons, R. P. (2000). *Helping clients forgive: An empirical guide for resolving anger and restoring hope.* Washington, DC: American Psychological Association.

Fadiman, J., & Frager, R. (1997). *Essential Sufism.* San Francisco, CA: HarperSanFrancisco.

Genia, V. (1991). The Spiritual Experience Index: A measure of spiritual maturity. *Journal of Religion and Health, 30,* 337–347.

Genia, V. (1992). Transitional faith: A developmental step toward religious maturity. *Counseling and Values, 37,* 15–24.

Genia, V. (1995). *Counseling and psychotherapy of religious clients: A developmental approach.* Westport, CT: Praeger.

Genia, V., & Cooke, B. A. (1998). Women at midlife: Spiritual maturity and life satisfaction. *Journal of Religion and Health, 37,* 115–123.

Ibrahim, F. A., & Heuer, J. R. (2013). The assessment, diagnosis, and treatment of mental disorders among Muslims. In F. A. Paniagua & A. Yamoda (Eds.), *Handbook of multicultural mental health: Assessment and treatment of diverse populations* (2nd ed., pp. 362–382). San Diego, CA: Elsevier.

Johnson, D., & Vanvonderen, J. (1991). *The subtle power of spiritual abuse.* Minneapolis, MN: Bethany House.

McKay, K., Hill, M., Freedman, S., & Enright, R. (2007). Towards a feminist empowerment model of forgiveness psychotherapy. *Psychotherapy: Theory, Research, Practice, Training, 44,* 12–29. doi:10.1037/0033-3204.44.1.14

Nassar-McMillan, S. C. (2010). *Counseling Arab Americans.* Pacific Grove, CA: Brooks Cole/Cengage.

Nassar-McMillan, S. C., Ajrouch, K. J., & Hakim-Larson, J. (2014). Biopsychosocial perspectives on Arab Americans: An introduction. In S. C. Nassar-McMillan, K. J. Ajrouch, & J. Hakim-Larson (Eds.), *Biopsychosocial perspectives on Arab Americans: Culture, development, and health* (pp. 1–9). New York, NY: Springer.

Nydell, M. K. (2012). *Understanding Arabs: A contemporary guide to Arab society.* Boston, MA: Intercultural Press.

Rafea, A., Rafea, A., & Rafea, A. (2005). *The book of essential Islam: Spiritual training system of Islam.* Dorset, UK: Book Foundation.

Rizzuto, A. M. (2005). Psychoanalytic considerations about spiritually oriented psychotherapy. In L. Sperry & E. P. Shafranske (Eds.), *Spiritually oriented psychotherapy* (pp. 31–50). Washington, DC: American Psychological Association.

Wade, N. G., & Worthington, E. L., Jr. (2005). In search of a common core: A content analysis of interventions to promote forgiveness. *Psychotherapy: Theory, Research, Practice, Training, 42,* 160–177.

 Reflections

Tracey E. Robert and Virginia A. Kelly

For the past 10 years, the Muslim faith has been the fastest growing religion in the United States. This case and response highlight the many interactions among religion, culture, and immigration that

Muslims and persons of other faiths and cultures often experience. Understanding the multicultural issues clients present as they bring their faith into the counseling process has become even more necessary for counselors to achieve effective outcomes. Counselors also need to recognize the impact of multiple diverse immigration experiences—the barriers, challenges, and trauma caused by global displacement and deportation—and provide comfort and support.

A holistic approach allows the counselor to integrate the spiritual belief system as a resource and provide more effective cross-cultural counseling. Understanding that there is a diversity of practice within the Muslim belief system is important. Muslims and Arabs often are lumped together when, in fact, there are different levels of religiosity among believers as well as different cultural contexts. A spiritually focused approach to counseling Islamic clients offers the following benefits:

- It provides a framework for balancing the issues of culture and religion, clarifying the client's personal identity, and reducing tension and anxiety.
- Spiritual interventions, such as journaling and reading of spiritual works, can provide avenues for self-understanding and forgiveness.
- The journey for integration of the self, and not compartmentalizing life experiences, can lead to wholeness and strengthen the client's resilience.

• • •

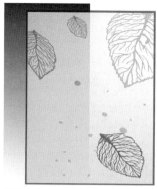

Chapter 21

Lesbian, Gay, Bisexual, Transgender, and Questioning (LGBTQ) Clients

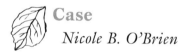

Case
Nicole B. O'Brien

Maria, a 25-year-old White woman, came to counseling for the first time reporting that she was feeling anxiety after a breakup from her first lesbian relationship. She also reported that accepting her sexual orientation within the context of how she was raised was difficult and that this issue was creating problems in her relationship with her mother. She asked, "How can I become who I want to be within my family?"

Background

Maria recently graduated with her master's degree in sports management and chose to live at home with her parents to save money. She was raised in an Italian American family that placed high value on family, traditions, and religion. She had no siblings, but her large extended family, particularly her cousins, were all extremely close, and she considered them siblings. Most of her extended family lived in the same town, and they typically shared all holidays together as well as a monthly family dinner.

Maria described her family as loyal and a bit overinvolved in each other's lives. She appreciated being raised in such a close-knit family but commented on how it had been difficult to become her own person as she grew older because the expectation was that family members stay geographically—and emotionally—close to home.

Maria described her relationship with her parents as caring and supportive. She and her father connected mostly over her participation in sports and their shared enjoyment of watching sports. Her relationship with her mother revolved around cooking, spending time with extended family, and being "best friends." Maria appreciated how close she and her mom were but found it difficult to maintain the role as her friend, particularly as she tried to establish romantic relationships. She described feeling torn between spending time with her mother and pursuing her intimate relationships.

Maria's family went to church every Sunday and celebrated all of the religious holidays. She received her first communion and was confirmed in the Catholic Church, and she attended an all-girls Catholic high school. Maria appreciated that her parents raised her with a sense of connection to a religious tradition, but now she was uncertain about how her Catholic background fit with who she was becoming as an adult woman, especially as she was coming to terms with her sexuality.

Incident

Maria came to me for counseling because she was feeling anxious. She said that these feelings began after she experienced a breakup with an intimate partner 2 months earlier. Maria reported that the relationship, with another woman with whom she had gone to college, was intense. She said that, although this was the first relationship she had with a woman, she had been attracted to women since middle school.

Maria said that she still missed her ex-girlfriend but had just started to put herself in situations to meet other women. However, sometimes she felt guilty about going out to meet women because her parents would not condone it and the Catholic religion considered it sinful.

Although Maria identified herself as a lesbian, she tried to keep her sexual orientation hidden from her parents. Her mother had recently overheard Maria talking to her best friend about a date she had had with a former teammate from college. When her mother approached her and asked her directly if she was a lesbian, Maria denied it and said she was talking about a man with whom she had a date. Her mother told her that she would pray to Saint Jude anyway, just in case Maria had any thoughts of being a lesbian.

Maria talked about how it was becoming hard for her to hide things from her mother and pretend to be something she was not. She said it made her anxious, yet at the same time, she did not want to tell her mother about her sexuality because she thought it would devastate her. Sometimes she wondered if there was any credence to her mom's perspective about homosexuality being something that God did not intend.

Discussion

My primary goals in working with Maria were to help her through the developmental stage of launching and becoming an autonomous adult and navigating the coming-out process. Working from a developmental and systemic model, I tried to understand the issues Maria was facing within the context of the systems in which she was embedded—family, friends, and religious community—and how she could interact with these systems in a way that allowed her to thrive as an individual.

I hypothesized that Maria's feelings of anxiety were completely normative for the developmental life stage of launching, particularly as she was trying to find ways to stay connected with her parents while also being her own person. Further contributing to Maria's stress was her own struggle to accept her sexuality and address it within the context of the significant relationships and values in her life.

I wanted to first validate and acknowledge the difficulty Maria was facing from a strength-based perspective. I also wanted her to witness her own bravery in her decision to explore these issues. She had explained how difficult it was even to pick up the phone for an appointment.

I then asked Maria to talk to me about her sexuality and with whom she had shared this information. She described knowing her sexual orientation from an early age but not acting on it until recently. She talked about gradually informing her friends, all of whom were supportive. Maria felt that this support helped her further explore her sexual orientation. I encouraged her to maintain this support system and "family of choice" during the counseling process.

For many years, Maria participated with her family in a way that aligned with the rules that structured the family. She had been an obedient child, teenager, and young adult. She followed the religious traditions her family established and often sacrificed exploring her own sense of self to be a "good" daughter.

Maria was now at a point where she wanted to establish her own identity but was afraid about how this would affect her relationship with her parents. With the use of circular questioning techniques, we engaged in dialogue that allowed me to understand Maria's perspective of her mother's worldview about family and relationships. With this process, we were able to bring Maria's mother into the counseling room without her actually being there. This technique also enabled us to role play how Maria might talk with her mother not only about her sexual orientation but also about her desire to move out of the house and establish herself as an adult.

Next, I used a postmodern approach of coconstruction and collaboration. Maria and I worked together to create an understanding of religion that went beyond the bounds of tradition and doctrine but that embodied an approach to life that was defined by compassion, kindness, and understanding. Within this framework, Maria could accept herself and her sexuality and have a sense of spirituality that aligned with how she wanted to interact with the world.

Through our work together, Maria was able to come out to her father first. Her father expressed concern for his daughter and the discrimination she would face but was supportive. Maria was also able to invite her mother into therapy to discuss her sexuality and their evolving relationship as mother and daughter. Although these conversations were difficult at times, Maria was able to honor the idea that her mother needed to mourn. Maria's mother also remained engaged in the therapeutic process and wanted to work on her relationship with her daughter.

Questions

1. Maria seemed like she was struggling with launching from her family of origin, but the cultural norm for her family was to "stay close to home." How might a counselor further address launching within this type of family?
2. One of Maria's primary concerns was being honest about her sexual orientation within her family. How might a counselor provide more help with this, especially if she feels that her family would not accept her because of their religious and cultural belief systems?
3. How might a counselor understand the issues Maria brought into therapy within a spiritual framework, and how could spirituality help Maria navigate some of the obstacles she was facing?
4. Maria's presenting issue was anxiety. How might a counselor use spiritual interventions to address this concern?

Response
Anneliese A. Singh

The case of Maria is pretty typical for LGBTQ people. She presents with many concerns—including a recent breakup, anxiety, family stressors, and tensions between her religious upbringing and her lesbian identity—that need to be addressed. I would use a framework of LGBTQ-affirmative counseling based on competencies outlined by the American Counseling Association (ACA, 2010) and the Association of Lesbian, Gay, Bisexual, and Transgender Issues in Counseling (ALGBTIC, 2013).

Because Maria's presenting issues clearly are related to her multiple identities of sexual orientation, gender, race/ethnicity, and religious/spiritual background, I would use an intersectionality theoretical perspective (Warner, 2008) to help me assess how her multiple identities intersect with one another. I also would use a relational–cultural theory (RCT; Baker-Miller, 1977) perspective to work with Maria to identify and explore the supports and barriers to her resilience related to her multiple identities. This perspective also would provide a framework to identify the importance of family relationships and intimate partnerships.

Using the ACA Counseling Competencies

One of the core competencies for a counselor to provide LGBTQ-affirmative counseling is having awareness, knowledge, and skills related to understanding and addressing how societal heterosexism influences clients' well-being and their relationships. Heterosexism includes societal assumptions that LGBTQ clients are not "normal," and heterosexism often is institutionally enforced (e.g., restrictions on marriage and adoption rights). Counselors need to understand that persons may internalize heterosexism as negative beliefs about their sexual orientation, and they need to intentionally assess for these negative belief systems and provide alternative affirmative viewpoints.

The counselor in the case that has been presented is using a collaborative approach with the client to explore the tensions she currently feels. I would add that a counselor working with Maria could explicitly share in the initial meeting an affirmative view of LGBTQ people and validate that many lesbian clients have struggled to reconcile their religious/spiritual beliefs and upbringings with their sexuality.

To conduct a thorough assessment of internalized heterosexism, I would ask Maria how she has internalized negative beliefs about her sexuality because of the tension she is feeling with her religious upbringing. After this assessment, I would provide Maria with examples of persons who have not only reconciled their Catholic faith with their sexuality but also have thriving identities of being both lesbian and Catholic. However, I would not share these examples as the only outcome for Maria. Heterosexism is so pervasive that she may not have ever considered that she could be lesbian and Catholic, lesbian and a person of faith, or lesbian and holding religious/spiritual beliefs different from those of her family.

Sharing the aforementioned information with LGBTQ clients can help counselors develop the foundation for an affirmative counseling environment in which the focus is on the client's experience. The counselor should note that heterosexism causes very real mental health stressors. Another aspect of building a safe counseling environment for Maria would be to use neutral terms, such as *partner*, when assessing relationship status. The counseling environment should include books on LGBTQ issues on the bookshelf and a Safe Zone sticker on the office door.

Clients who have experienced societal oppression related to their sexual orientation, as Maria has, often constantly assess the degree of safety they may have in settings. This assessment of safety is especially true of mental health settings because of myths about conversion therapy (which the ACA has strongly stated to be unethical). Counselors who use the LGBT competencies also should be mindful of the advocacy (Lewis, Arnold, House, & Toporek, 2003), multiculturalism (Sue, Arredondo, & McDavis, 1992), and spirituality (ASERVIC, 2009) competencies.

Sexual Orientation, Culture, and Family

To address the first question of Maria's struggle to launch from her family of origin, the cultural norm for her was to stay close to home, but I would carefully assess and explore her racial/ethnic identity. For example, I would be curious about how Maria defines herself in terms of her race/ethnicity and what influence being Italian American has on her beliefs about family and relationships. Throughout this exploration, I would integrate how Maria's identity as an Italian American intersects with her religious/spiritual identity, gender, and sexual orientation.

Maria seems to have long-standing views of how families are constructed and enacted in Italian American culture. I would collaboratively explore how these views have influenced her definition of family in the past and how she may want to define family for her present and future self. In assessing her gender identity, I would ask what the gender expectations and socialization processes are within Italian American families and how these processes have affected Maria.

Mapping on to these two explorations, I would examine the process of her sexual identity development. Included in this exploration would be an assessment of the extent to which she is connected with other LGBTQ Italian American people (online and offline), the access she has to LGBTQ support groups related to coming out to family, and the coping strategies she has used in her sexual identity development as she has sought to understand its intersection with her religious/spiritual identity.

In addition to counseling, having access to LGBTQ social support and resources would help validate the experiences Maria is having within her family. These resources also would support Maria in defining who she is in relationship to her culture and identity as a lesbian. Throughout our discussions of her family, I would explore the tensions between her as an individual and as a person who is from a collectivist cultural background; the goal would be to identify cultural patterns and dynamics she would like to maintain or shift.

Religious/Spiritual Identity and "Coming Out"

The second question posed was how a counselor might provide Maria with more help being honest with her family about her sexual orientation, especially if she feels that her family would not accept her because of their religious and cultural belief systems. Counseling strategies might include dual assessment of her religious/spiritual identity development and of her sexual orientation identity development.

For example, having discussions with Maria about her past and current religious/spiritual views would provide me with an understanding of her current identity in this domain. If she is strongly adherent to her Catholic upbringing, she may benefit from examples of other Catholic LGBTQ persons who have integrated their religious/spiritual and sexual orientation identities. I would explore how her religious/spiritual beliefs and practices might be used to help her cope with the current tensions she feels in coming out to her family. Interventions might include prayer and bibliotherapy on Catholic LGBTQ persons.

If Maria has begun to question her religious/spiritual identity, she may need time and space to explore issues of grief related to these questions. The counselor in the case study provided Maria with important support and options for deciding who might be the safest person to come out to first and provided a family counseling session. Before these interventions, I would remind Maria that she could share more about her multiple identities with her family when she is coming out if it would be comfortable for her (e.g., "I am a lesbian and a Catholic"). Because families also have coming-out processes, the counselor may continue to explore what stage Maria's family may be in after Maria comes out.

Using a Spiritual Framework

The third question asked how a counselor might understand the issues Maria brought into therapy within a spiritual framework and how spirituality could help Maria navigate some of the obstacles she was facing. I would use RCT (Baker-Miller, 1977) and the ACA-endorsed spirituality and LGBT competencies to develop an LGBTQ-affirmative framework.

My work would be guided by the RCT tenet that emphasizes relationships, rather than sole individuation, as a foundation of mental health. I would use this tenet to explore how Maria might, as the counselor did in this case, develop families of choice for herself and help her mitigate the impact of potentially losing connection with her family when she comes out. The counselor used a strengths-based approach with Maria in exploring her sexual orientation and spirituality. This is a critical approach—recent research has suggested that more LGBTQ persons may identify as spiritual rather than as religious (Halkitis et al., 2009).

Spiritual Interventions for Anxiety

The fourth question asked about Maria's presenting issue of anxiety and how a counselor might use spiritual interventions to address it. I would collaboratively explore with Maria any resilience and coping skills she has developed over her life related to her religious/spiritual upbringing and identity. For example, Maria may find praying, attending church, and performing other rituals of Catholic practice helpful in reducing her stress and increasing her resilience and ability to cope. However, Maria may not feel especially connected with her Catholic upbringing and may want to explore different faith traditions and connect with other LGBTQ persons of faith. In this exploration, I would be guided by the following ASERVIC (2009) competency: "The professional counselor is able to (a) modify therapeutic techniques to include a client's spiritual and/or religious perspectives, and (b) utilize spiritual and/or religious practices as techniques when appropriate and acceptable to a client's viewpoint."

Providing Support and Safety

Because Maria has faced many stressors, I would support her in any questioning of her faith. This questioning can be a normal response, and counseling can provide Maria with a safe place to question—and deepen—her spiritual beliefs.

References

American Counseling Association. (2010). *Competencies for counseling with transgender clients*. Retrieved from www.algbtic.org

Association of Lesbian, Gay, Bisexual, and Transgender Issues in Counseling. (2013). *Association for Lesbian, Gay, Bisexual, and Transgender Issues in Counseling (ALGBTIC) competencies for counseling lesbian, gay, bisexual, queer, questioning, intersex, and ally individuals*. Retrieved from www.algbtic.org/resources/competencies

Association of Spiritual, Ethical, and Religious Values in Counseling. (2009). *Competencies for addressing spiritual and religious issues in counseling*. Retrieved from http://www.aservic.org/resources/spiritual-competencies/

Baker-Miller, J. B. (1977). *Toward a new psychology of women*. Boston, MA: Beacon Press.

Halkitis, P. M., Mattis, J. S., Sahadath, J. K., Massie, D. L, Pitrelli, K. B., & Cowie, S. E. (2009). The meanings and manifestations of religion and spirituality among lesbian, gay, bisexual, and transgender adults. *Journal of Adult Development, 16*, 250–262.

Lewis, J. A., Arnold, M. S., House, R., & Toporek, R. L. (2003). *ACA advocacy competencies*. Retrieved from http://www.counseling.org/Resources/Competencies/Advocacy_Competencies.pdf

Sue, D. W., Arredondo, P., & McDavis, R. J. (1992). Multicultural counseling competencies and standards: A call to the profession. *Journal of Counseling & Development, 70,* 477–486.

Warner, L. R. (2008). A best practices guide to intersectional approaches in psychological research. *Sex Roles, 59,* 454–463.

Reflections
Tracey E. Robert and Virginia A. Kelly

Social justice issues that LGBTQ clients often face include conflicts with their religious or spiritual traditions. Effective spiritual assessment can clarify for the client and counselor how strong the client's spiritual beliefs are and whether he or she actually adheres to traditional practices. Being a part of specific ethnic groups may not be indicative of religious beliefs identified with those groups. In-depth discussions and definitions of values, beliefs, and practices can help LGBTQ clients establish their identities and development. Finding safe havens for their own spiritual practices can be a struggle. Counselors can help identify resources that help. Counseling LGBTQ clients with a spiritual focus can improve the process in the following ways:

- Spiritual genograms and a spiritual lifeline activity can help clients identify important events in their life that have contributed to their spirituality and to their identity.
- The discussion of spiritual values and beliefs can allow for exploration of abuse, anger, and discrimination that clients often have experienced. This discussion can produce a climate of safety and connectedness for better addressing isolation and loneliness.
- It enhances the ability for self-acceptance and acts as a protective factor for clients.

• • •

Chapter 22 # Integrating Religion into Counseling

Case
Jane C. Chauvin

Petra, a 42-year-old woman, came to counseling seeking help for depression, feelings of rejection, and feelings of isolation. This was 5 years after a horrendous natural disaster had destroyed her home, her security, and her way of life. She stated, "During Hurricane Katrina, God abandoned me," and she asked, "How could He have let something like this happen?"

Background

Petra grew up in a large southern city that suffered horribly from the effects of Hurricane Katrina. She had always loved the city of her birth and rejoiced and participated in all of the many parades, festivals, and celebrations that such a multicultural setting provided.

Petra grew up in a Christian home, and her whole family attended their parish church. She also was educated in an elementary school attached to the same church parish. She attended a local church-affiliated high school and then a state university. Petra obtained a degree in business and later an MBA. She was employed by a major utility company in the same city.

Petra met and married her husband, Robert, in graduate school. They continued to reside in the city where both were raised. They had two children, Caitlin, 18, and Bobby, 15. Petra described her marriage as "fulfilling" and happy. Both she and Robert worked outside the home, and their children attended church-related schools. She and her husband were very involved with the children's activities.

As a child and throughout high school, Petra attended church weekly and on holidays with her family. During college, she began to question some of her earlier religious beliefs. As her circle of friends widened, Petra became familiar with a variety of religious belief systems. She began to attend different worship services and to take courses in comparative religions.

With marriage to Robert in the faith in which both were baptized, Petra reverted to the religion of her youth, and she reported that it felt "comfortable." Then, Hurricane Katrina struck.

Incident

In late August of 2005, Petra and her family were living in a middle-to upper-middle-class neighborhood. Their home was the fulfillment of a dream that they were able to realize after student loans for both of them were finally paid off. This new home was a source of pride and accomplishment for the whole family.

When hurricane warnings were announced that August, neither adult was overly concerned because they had lived in a hurricane-prone area all their lives. But when a mandatory evacuation of the city was ordered, Petra and her family packed up and headed out of state. They took a few changes of clothing with them and little else. Everyone thought that they would return home in a few days, maybe without electricity, but life would be pretty much "back to normal."

The hurricane struck, and there were reports of levees breaking and flooding in most of the city, in some places as high as 12 to 15 feet. One of the most severe breaks in the levees had occurred in the area where Petra and her family lived. No house in their immediate area had been spared. News of the devastation was on local and national news 24 hours a day.

Even with all of this coverage, complete with pictures, nothing prepared Petra and her family for what they would find when they were finally allowed to return to the city almost a month later. Their home had been submerged in water for about 3 weeks. One outside wall had been ripped off, and almost nothing inside was salvageable. Mud and debris filled every room, and the smell was horrible. Their beloved neighborhood was a "ghost town" that bore little or no resemblance to the place they had left on that August day, 4 weeks earlier. Devastation was everywhere. Petra felt overwhelmed and hopeless, but she and her family began the sad work of clearing out what remained of their home and eventually rebuilding.

When Petra came to see me, 5 years had passed since the hurricane struck. She described feelings of depression, anger, and isolation. She was back in the new home that had taken her family such a long time to complete. She could not understand why she was not feeling better.

Petra had expected these negative feelings to decrease as things got better in her life. Instead, she described herself as feeling more anxious and sadder than she had felt initially during the long months, and even years, of rebuilding. "I hardly know who I am now," she lamented to me. "Even my faith in God has been shaken."

Discussion

Petra obviously was experiencing posttraumatic stress disorder (PTSD)—feelings of delayed reaction to a major tragedy in her life, one she had not really dealt with entirely when it occurred. The primary goals of therapy were to help her understand what these feelings were and why they were coming to the surface several years later and to help her finally deal with them.

I thought that Petra had been so absorbed with dealing with what had to be done immediately after the tragedy she had pushed down the emotions that had occurred when she first beheld the devastation. These feelings had risen to the surface, along with possible new ones, as Petra's life returned to a more normal pace and she had time and space to really experience the true nature of her losses.

The hypothesis here was that Petra had no choice but to deal with the immediate in her life, and this had taken almost 4 years. During this period, she did not allow herself to truly feel the grief and loss that had been thrust upon her. She simply threw herself into doing what had to be done.

Petra felt that she had no choice and that the uncomfortable feelings she was experiencing might stand in the way of her restoring some semblance of the life she had led before. Not only had she lost her home and many possessions, but her job was at risk and the city itself was slow to recover. Loss was all around her. She likened it to what people might experience in the aftermath of a war. Nothing was the same. Petra's belief in God and her religious faith had always been a source of solace and strength for her, and now she was even questioning this.

Petra needed to first go back through some of the feelings she had suppressed and to allow herself to go through the various stages of grief that she was feeling. Various models of grief therapy were discussed and explained. The anger, hopelessness, and anxiety she was currently feeling were attributed to the sudden and dramatic turn that her life had taken. PTSD was also explained and applied to her situation to allow her to understand why she was experiencing such discomfort years after the actual event.

Petra's religious beliefs had always been an important part of her support system, and she needed to reclaim some semblance of this if she was to deal with her anger and anxiety in a constructive manner. As an adult, she had to sort through her beliefs and her feelings around religion and spirituality and recognize what she truly wanted to embrace at this stage of her life.

Questions

1. Petra suffered tremendous loss in Hurricane Katrina and never fully grieved that loss. How might a counselor help her recognize and embrace the various stages of grief?
2. Petra expressed many feelings during the process of rebuilding, not only about her house but also about her life after a natural disaster. These feelings were now coming back to haunt her. How might a counselor help her understand and work through PTSD?
3. Petra's religious faith and her belief in God had always been a comfort to her, and now she felt that she had lost this important aspect of her life. How might a counselor help her explore the anger she felt toward God?

 ## Response
Cecile Brennan

Petra responded in a way that is not uncommon for survivors of an ongoing crisis (van der Kolk, 2006). Although Hurricane Katrina was time limited in duration, its effects continued for many years as the extent of the physical, social, and emotional disruption and damage manifested. Petra experienced the intensity of a life-threatening natural disaster; she is now immersed in an emotional and spiritual crisis triggered by the disaster. If Petra's present crisis is viewed as something negative that should be eliminated, she will never come to benefit and grow from her experiences. Petra's challenges are to integrate her experiences into her life and then into her understanding of the world. The first of these challenges is essentially emotional and psychological; the second is primarily spiritual. In both cases, understanding that there is no going back to "how it was" is crucial. Nothing will ever be the same.

Telling Her Story

Listening is at the heart of counseling survivors of a natural disaster (Cooper, 2010; Halpern, 2006). In the midst of the disaster, and often for some time afterward, people operate in survival mode. Attention is given only to determining the next steps needed to survive and to reestablish some sense of equilibrium. During this period, experiences and emotions often are not processed and not psychologically incorporated. Neurologically, intense emotional experiences may not be encoded in language and so reside somewhat outside a person's ability to talk about them (Schacter, 1997).

The first step in working with Petra is providing a safe and supportive space in which she can recount her experiences. A counselor should resist the impulse to try to make everything all right for her. "Everything is fine now," "That is all in the past," and similar comments are not helpful for someone who is still incorporating the experience.

The counselor needs to rely on the core counseling skills of unconditional positive regard, empathetic listening, and rephrasing (Cooper, 2010). This approach encourages Petra to tell the story of her experience. In the telling, she can, perhaps for the first time, put the experience out there—literally outside of herself. In externalizing the event, Petra gains a measure of control over it and begins to separate herself from it. This process does not mean that Petra should deny her feelings. She experiences the feelings, but they do not control her or define who she is.

Once the story has been recounted enough times to lessen its emotional valence, a counselor can interject information about how experiencing and surviving a crisis can affect a person physiologically and emotionally. At this point, discussing PTSD can be helpful. Although labeling clients can be stigmatizing, giving a name to a condition also can have a liberating explanatory power.

Explaining PTSD to Petra can help her understand that her reactions are not uncommon. For example, describing the symptoms of PTSD can inform her about how a life-threatening crisis can affect her very physiology by heightening the response to perceived threats so that every thunderstorm becomes a harbinger of a hurricane (van der Kolk, 2006). A description of PTSD flashbacks can help her recognize that her replaying aspects of the disaster over and over can be seen as an unconscious attempt to gain mastery over them rather than as a sign that she is going crazy (van der Kolk, 2006). With this kind of understanding, Petra can move from being victimized by her circumstances to proactively predicting and planning, and only then responding to, events.

Recognizing Grief

Education about the grief process is just as important as education about PTSD. Grief education can assist in removing both the guilt of grieving and the stigma about not being over the grief and trauma of the experience. The stages of death and dying articulated by Kübler-Ross (1997)—denial, anger, bargaining, depression, and acceptance—are often used to guide people through this process of grief.

If these stages are familiar to Petra, discussing them with her would be useful. However, a common understanding of these stages often explains the grieving process as something that happens to people in an orderly progression. If a person has experienced a period of depression, the next step in the grief process should be, according to a simplistic understanding, acceptance. If, instead, the grieving person experiences anger once more, the grieving process is thought to be aberrant or even pathological. Because of this tendency to pressure people to follow the stages in lockstep fashion, and because empirical studies have shown that not all people go through all of the stages (Maciejewski, Zhang, Block, & Prigerson, 2007; Neimeyer, 2001), looking at other models of the grief process would be useful.

Worden's model of grieving (2008) can help clients understand that grieving is a nonlinear, non-time-limited process. This understanding may help Petra realize that recovering from a traumatic event does not mean that people get better and better until they are returned to their predisaster selves. The grief process may be two steps forward and one step backward. The postdisaster survivor is not the same person as he or she was before the disaster. Life once again becomes more predictable, but the postdisaster normal is not the same as the predisaster normal.

Worden's model (2008) describes the following four challenges or tasks that the grieving person faces: (a) to accept the reality of the loss, (b) to work through the pain and grief of the loss, (c) to adjust to an environment in which the deceased is absent, and (d) to emotionally relocate the deceased and move on with life. In telling the story of her experience, and in sharing her feelings with the counselor, Petra has engaged the first two tasks. As Worden stated, this is an ongoing process that most likely will not have a clearly defined final point.

Continuing to work toward the resolution of these tasks is important for Petra. The counselor needs to attend to whether the grieving process is proceeding toward resolution rather than continuing unabated or even intensifying. If Petra is not moving in the direction of coming to terms with her grief, and if she is experiencing a disruption in her usual sleeping and eating patterns, a psychiatric evaluation is appropriate to determine whether medication is indicated. The goal of medication is to reduce the symptoms sufficiently to allow Petra enough mental space to reflect on her experiences and feelings. If medication is prescribed, Petra needs to understand that receiving medication does not remove the need to continue to talk about the trauma she endured.

Because Petra did not lose a loved one, the third and fourth tasks are expanded to include other losses, such as those of a home, a community, and a sense of safety. Petra needs to be encouraged to mourn these losses in much the same way she would mourn the loss of a loved one. Specifically identifying her losses, labeling them, and recognizing the impact of their absence would enable her to begin to move forward. At this point in the healing process, the counselor might encourage Petra to connect with others who have experienced loss. Being part of a community of people struggling with the same issues often provides strong healing power (Halpern, 2006).

A Spiritual Crisis

Petra also lost her innocence and naiveté, her belief that God somehow protects good people. This loss led to an existential crisis, a spiritual crisis that challenged how she views and understands God. Addressing this spiritual crisis requires a counselor who is comfortable working with spiritual questions.

Although it is recommended that all counselors possess spiritual competencies (ASERVIC, 2009), the reality is that many counselors would feel unsure about how to assist Petra as she works through her relationship with God. In addition, she might be more comfortable speaking with a clergyperson about her spiritual concerns. If this is the case, referring Petra to a clergyperson is recommended. Counselors might develop a referral list of clergy they are familiar with who have some psychological sensitivity and understanding. Referring Petra to a clergyperson who chastises her for her questions and for her anger at God would be catastrophic.

If the counselor and Petra continue to work together on these issues, the counselor needs to be prepared to accompany her on a journey that has no clear destination. Some people who have experienced a crisis of belief end up more confirmed in their faith tradition; others move more in the direction of agnosticism, if not atheism. The counselor should give Petra the lead on this journey and act as a sounding board and a companion. The goal is to help Petra move out of anger and reactivity and into a new understanding of her existence, one that takes into account that inexplicable, seemingly bad things can happen to people for no apparent reason. The goal is not to direct Petra's path toward a reconciliation or a renunciation of her religion.

Bibliotherapy Resources

In following Petra's lead, the counselor could recommend books or other resources that deal with the issues she is grappling with. One classic text is Kushner's *When Bad Things Happen to Good People* (1981). In this recounting of his own struggle to reconcile himself to his young son's chronic illness and death, Rabbi Kushner deals with the kinds of questions that are plaguing Petra. Another useful text is Viktor Frankl's *Man's Search for Meaning* (2006). In this extended reflection on being a survivor of the Holocaust, Frankl describes how meaning and community can be found in even the most dehumanizing environment. Aimed at a Christian audience, *Angry With God* (2001) by psychologist Michele Novotni and Randy Peterson directly addresses the anger and abandonment felt when catastrophe occurs.

Directly addressing her spiritual crisis empowers Petra to search for answers to her questions. Once engaged in this process, she is no longer stuck in reactivity or passivity. She has begun to actively pursue answers to her questions.

Regaining a Sense of Self

Petra states that she hardly knows who she is in the aftermath of surviving the disaster. She feels abandoned by God and bereft of the community she loved. Regaining her sense of self has been delayed by the immediate need to rebuild and physically recover from the hurricane. Through telling her story, learning about the psychological and neurological sequelae of surviving a natural disaster, consciously engaging in the grief process, and actively seeking a resolution to her spiritual crisis, Petra will begin to discover herself anew.

References

Association for Spiritual Ethical & Religious Values in Counseling (ASERVIC). (2009). *Competencies for addressing spiritual and religious issues in counseling.* Retrieved from http://www.aservic.org/resources/spiritual-competencies/

Cooper, J. (2010). Essential crisis intervention skills. In L. R. Jackson-Cherry & B. T. Erford (Eds.), *Crisis assessment, intervention, and prevention* (pp. 55–71). New York, NY: Pearson.

Frankl, V. E. (2006). *Man's search for meaning.* Boston, MA: Beacon Press.

Halpern, J. (2006). *Disaster mental health: Theory & practice.* New York, NY: Cengage.

Kübler-Ross, E. (1997). *On death & dying.* New York, NY: Scribner.

Kushner, H. S. (1981). *When bad things happen to good people.* New York, NY: Schocken Books.

Maciejewski, P. K., Zhang, B., Block, S. D., & Prigerson, H. G. (2007). An empirical examination of the stage theory of grief. *JAMA: Journal of the American Medical Association, 297,* 716–723.

Neimeyer, R. A. (2001). *Meaning reconstruction and the experience of loss.* Washington, DC: American Psychological Association.

Novotni, M., & Peterson, R. (2001). *Angry with God.* Colorado Springs, CO: Pinon Press.

Schacter, D. (1997). *Searching for memory: The brain, the mind and the past.* New York, NY: Basic Books.

van der Kolk, B. (2006). *Traumatic stress: The effects of overwhelming experience on mind, body and society.* New York, NY: Guilford.

Worden, J. W. (2008). *Grief counseling and grief therapy: A handbook for the mental health professional.* New York, NY: Springer.

Reflections
Tracey E. Robert and Virginia A. Kelly

It seems that natural disasters are becoming commonplace. Dealing with the loss of her home, community, and sense of safety shook Petra's beliefs to the core and created spiritual distress and depression. As seen in this case and response, psychoeducation can be a useful tool for reducing PTSD and depression. The deeper spiritual distress, where Petra's formerly strong religious beliefs are challenged, offers the counselor the opportunity to address the spirituality and religion in her life. As mentioned, consultation or referral to clergy might be a helpful adjunct to counseling. However, the counselor's ability to work with the humanistic and existential issues at the core of the spiritual distress can be crucial to a positive outcome. Acting as a guide on this journey, the counselor can integrate spiritual interventions, such as meditation, journaling, contemplative prayer, and bibliotherapy, to accompany the counseling sessions.

In Chapter 13, Amanda also dealt with a natural disaster, but the case and response counselors' roles and approaches were different. In Amanda's case, the counselors were working in a crisis center and were disaster mental health workers with counseling skills; in this case, the counselor was in a counseling setting that allowed for a more direct spiritual approach. However, both infused the spiritual domain into the counseling process to aid the client where they were. Integrating religion and spirituality can improve the counseling process in the following ways:

- Using clients' belief system as a path to reconnecting with their inner self in a safe environment can stabilize and lift their depression.
- Introducing spiritual interventions and using the counseling session to process the experience can increase clients' self-awareness and self-care options.
- Psychoeducation with a spiritual focus can alleviate stress and anxiety around loss of core beliefs and coping responses to crisis and unexpected transitions.

● ● ●

Chapter 23 # Military Families

Case
Cheri Smith

Kelly, a 43-year-old White woman married to an Air Force pilot, came to counseling because she was struggling with several issues. She had been to counseling previously to cope with developmental issues with her children. This time, she sought counseling because she was overwhelmed with a medical issue, her responsibilities in caring for her children, and her husband's third deployment to Afghanistan. Watching the news about and receiving updates from her husband's command exacerbated Kelly's sense of being overwhelmed and powerless.

Background

Originally from California, Kelly did not have a specific hometown. She traveled a lot and moved frequently when she was growing up because her father served in the Air Force. As a result, she was very familiar with the military lifestyle.

After Kelly finished college, she joined the Air Force, where she met Jim, a pilot and squadron commander. They married, and Kelly gave up her career in the Air Force to focus on supporting her husband.

Acknowledgment: Sharon Kingsley assisted in the preparation of this case study and provided a unique perspective. She has been a military dependent almost her entire life. Her father was a career officer in the military, and her son is an officer in the military. Her husband is a major general in the Air Force and is currently serving in Afghanistan.

She served as the lead of the squadron spouses group, where her role included assisting other spouses through deployments. Kelly was involved in advocacy groups for military dependents and in helping other spouses cope with the challenges of military life.

Kelly and Jim had three children: James, 12, Kristina, 11, and Mark, 6. The two older children were in middle school, and the youngest, in first grade. Both parents had a very active role in the local church, having been readers since they had been stationed at the local base. The family went to church on a regular basis, and the older children were involved in the Christian education programs and served as acolytes. Kelly assumed primary responsibility for her children's religious development because her husband was deployed frequently.

Incident

Kelly found a lump in her breast, and after testing, she was waiting for the results. Unsure of the diagnosis, she chose not to tell Jim while he was experiencing the stress of deployment and responsibility for a mission.

Kelly was dealing with managing her children and their school issues. Her oldest child, James, was refusing to go to school at times, so she continually fought with him about school attendance and not turning in schoolwork. James's negative behaviors began after he started at a new school when the family moved to their current base. He was having trouble making friends.

Kristina had trouble when things were less than perfect. She sometimes became overwhelmed because she was trying to make sure that everyone was all right; thus, she did not always get the attention she needed. The youngest child, Mark, was adjusting because this was his first year in a regular school environment. He was misbehaving more because his father was gone, and he was more sensitive to everything and cried easily.

Kelly sought counseling to cope with feeling isolated, experiencing anger, and being overwhelmed having to manage these major issues alone while her husband was deployed. Although she served as a resource person for other squadron families, she found it hard to lean on other spouses for support. Kelly also felt isolated because she couldn't share the information with her husband. She was unsure where to turn to deal with her health and her children.

Discussion

I am a counselor associated with Military OneSource (http://www.militaryonesource.mil), a program that refers military families for counseling. In working with Kelly, my primary goal was to help her identify support systems through a variety of family systems strategies, focusing on her recent diagnosis and her situation with her oldest son.

As Kelly's counselor, I helped Kelly look at positive resources. This process began by researching some of the support systems she had available to her through the military.

First, I tried to identify the supports Kelly needed to have in place as she went through her lumpectomy. She could have the surgery at the hospital on base. The squadron spouses group could supply meals and babysitting and help with car pools for the children. I also discussed with Kelly the steps that she needed to take if she had to share a negative diagnosis with her husband. For example, we discussed what military channels she might need to go through to follow protocol, such as notifying the first sergeant before sharing bad news with her spouse.

Second, we explored how to secure resources for James's school issues. These resources included a school liaison officer (SLO) and an Exceptional Family Member Program (EFMP). The SLO is the central point of contact for military families on school-related matters. For instance, the SLO helps with the transfer of school credits when military families relocate to a new civilian school district. The EFMP is set up to help military families with special needs address the unique challenges they may encounter as they settle into a new installation. I asked Kelly for permission to communicate directly with the SLO. We worked together with the SLO and the EFMP to set up support systems for James.

Because Kelly mentioned she was an active member of her church and her religion was important to her, I explored what inner resources she felt most comfortable using. They included centering prayer, breath work, journaling, meditation, and other self-awareness activities.

Questions

1. Kelly seemed to have become overwhelmed with all of her responsibilities—coping with her own health issues, taking on both of the parental roles, and serving as the leader of the squadron spouses group while her husband was deployed. How might the counselor explore Kelly's coping mechanisms?
2. Military resources were available to Kelly. Because she felt overwhelmed, having so many resources and deciding which ones to use might be more than she could handle. What strategy might best help her identify resources?
3. Religion was important to Kelly. How might a counselor work with her to further explore religious and/or spiritual resources that she can use to develop coping skills?

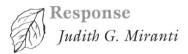

Response
Judith G. Miranti

The characteristics of military families as a subculture can be generalized to other systems that constantly undergo change. However, military families also have unique characteristics and pose unique challenges that call for a deeper level of resiliency and adaptation. They are expected not only to respond to immediate separation but also to embrace this separation for a perceived greater good. The military family in this case is already imbued with a sense of dedication and purpose and has been a member of this subculture and lifestyle for several generations.

General Impressions

In the military mindset, the individual systems that form this culture are subjugated to the overarching strategic purposes of the greater system, as evidenced by the mantra of each branch of military service (e.g., the Marines' "Semper Fidelis" [Always Faithful]). Inherent in this lifestyle is the expected ability to rise to the immediacy of any situation by being prepared to be called into active duty and to undergo deployment. This expectation implies a readiness on the part of each member of the system.

The family in question, particularly Kelly, the spouse left behind, is experiencing additional challenges that warrant systems support. Kelly's resistance to accepting this support is compounded by her deeper sense of possible failure to respond to the demands of the military mindset. Her own perceived limitation—that she cannot measure up to the expectations—is causing her to seek counseling because she fears letting down her immediate family as well as her family of origin.

Several indicators in Kelly's case would warrant screening for depression. Factors to consider include abandonment issues, possible anger over giving up her career, a lack of spousal support in rearing the children, a perceived lack of a support network, and her recent medical findings. Conducting a religious/spiritual assessment to determine Kelly's degree of religious commitment and spiritual values would be helpful for the counselor as he or she applies appropriate interventions. Possible screening for early onset of menopause would be advisable. After analyzing the results and before beginning counseling, the counselor needs to gather additional information. Using the military resources stated in the case, I would want to receive a full report of the two older children's academic and anecdotal records. I also would recommend assessing for childhood depression.

Using Results and Selecting Approaches

Once the assessments have been completed, the counselor could then approach this case from a systems perspective using several appropriate theoretical orientations and interventions. Adlerian approaches—faulty beliefs, early recollections, and lifestyle assessment—could be used to deal with generational issues, including family-of-origin patterns, because Kelly also is a product of a military family. Other possible approaches include solution-focused interventions for short-term results (those in which Kelly believes she has some control), cognitive–behavioral therapy with Kelly and the children, and family systems theory (Corey, 2013).

Military protocol is another factor to be considered. Kelly has to first go to her husband's superior before discussing possible troubling issues with him so as not to put him in harm's way. His position as an Air Force pilot in charge of a squadron is a heavy responsibility, one that Kelly is fully aware of, and knowing this can only serve to compound her feelings of being overwhelmed. Just when Kelly is in need of spousal support, she cannot access it.

The counselor also would want to determine the degree of support Kelly has from her family. What is her relationship with her mother? What are her father's expectations of her? What is the birth order in her family of origin?

Because Kelly is feeling overwhelmed and out of control, identifying issues within her control would be a first step. Then, those over which she has limited or no control would be discussed, along with coping strategies and systems support as suggested by the counselor.

My purpose in suggesting that the counselor first work with Kelly to find short-term solutions would be to help her regain some control over her life. The counselor could address the following issues within Kelly's control:

- the children's adjustment issues and developmental challenges, and
- her parental role and responsibilities.

Then, the counselor could focus on issues over which Kelly has limited or no control:

- her medical condition and the uncertainty of the diagnosis,
- grief and loss issues resulting from her medical condition, and
- abandonment issues resulting from her spouse's deployment and possible strained relations with him.

Family counseling sessions should be conducted once Kelly begins to make some minor adjustments and feels more in control. During these sessions, the children could begin to see how families work together and how roles, responsibilities, and family rules all have a purpose.

Family of Origin

Regarding Question 1, a discussion of ways in which Kelly's family of origin, particularly her mother, coped with issues of deployment, parental responsibilities, and support systems would be helpful because these vertical stressors appear in generational patterns. How does Kelly perceive her parents' expectations, and how does she feel she is measuring up with her mother?

As the therapeutic relationship develops and trust is established with Kelly's counselor, a discussion of short-term resolutions could be explored to reduce her stress. Kelly's resolutions might include the following:

- relieving herself of her leadership responsibilities;
- arranging times for regular exercise, yoga, and meditation as suggested by her counselor while the children are in school;
- finding opportunities to socialize and share parenting responsibilities with other mothers as a participant in the squadron spouses group; and
- talking about her hobbies and activities that are fulfilling.

Developmental Considerations

Regarding Kelly's parental roles, focusing on the developmental issues of her children and normalizing as much as possible what they are experiencing in their new location would be recommended. Middle children often feel as though they have to hold things together. Kristina, the middle child, is trying to find her place in the family; relieving her of the responsibility to make sure that everyone is happy is a first step. Kelly could ask Kristina to make a list of ways in which she could help her and ways in which they could have fun times together. An 11-year-old child is beginning to compare herself to her peers and perceive how she is measuring up. She also is feeling a lack of attention. Finding mother–daughter time together could help.

Mark is on target developmentally. Adjusting to new situations and undertaking initiatives are difficult for a 6-year-old. Exploring with Kelly some ways in which the school could help Mark in adjusting, identifying satisfying rewards for him, and having friends his age to play with would be useful. Children at this age want to please adults, and Kelly's recognizing Mark's achievements is an important piece. Mark also needs to feel a connection with his dad, so scheduling military video conferencing, Skype, or FaceTime is suggested.

Military Resources

Regarding Question 2, as the counselor suggested, exploring and securing resources, including an SLO and an EFMP, would help address James's school issues. Holding parental sessions with teachers and contracting with James at home could ensure continuity between home and school and quell any manipulations James might try. Everyone would be on the same page regarding expectations.

Also, James seems lost without his father, and Kelly is attempting to fill that void, thus increasing her stress levels. Looking at base support and finding ways to engage James with other male figures would be suggested, such as Little League, after-school activities, and tutoring. The counselor might discuss ways to give James face time with his dad while he is deployed. This is the time when James needs a male role model; involving his dad in the process is critical to his mental well-being. Compiling a listing of resources that could support Kelly in her parenting role and identifying with whom she could form a social network would facilitate her accessing them when needed.

Spiritual Resources and Interventions

In answer to Question 3, there are both predictable and unpredictable events in life, and how one copes and perceives the situation can determine the outcome. When faced with a crisis, such as a medical diagnosis that could be life threatening, people often turn or return to their spiritual or religious values and practices (Cashwell & Young, 2011). Exploring Kelly's belief system could highlight internal resources she might have related to spirituality.

Because religion is important to Kelly and her husband, the counselor could begin to explore ways to incorporate interventions appropriate to her religious beliefs and values. Useful tools include the Spiritual Assessment Inventory, which measures spiritual development, and the Spiritual Assessment Scale, a measure of spiritual strengths and weaknesses (Cashwell & Young, 2011). Asking Kelly several informal questions would be useful to the counselor in applying appropriate religious and spiritual interventions. These questions might include the following:

- What gives meaning and purpose to her life?
- To whom does she turn when faced with a crisis?
- Where does she find comfort and solace?
- What does she do that is different from her ordinary way of coping with situations?
- How does she find her sacred space?
- Where does prayer fit in her life?
- How does she bargain with God for positive outcomes? (Burke, Chauvin, & Miranti, 2005).

Other techniques that could be suggested include spiritual bibliotherapy, Bible or scripture readings, meditation, journaling, yoga, and exercise. One spiritual value related to trust is surrender. When someone has no control over a situation or its outcome, this spiritual strategy, according to Frame (2003), seems to have a positive association with psychological and spiritual well-being for persons in crisis.

Role playing as a strategy to address Kelly's anxiety as she awaits a diagnosis would allow her to begin to face the reality of her medical situation and help her relay the information to her husband and children. Talking about the support services and child care she will need should an operation be necessary would help her put plans into place.

The counselor also might tap into the religious and spiritual beliefs of Kelly's children by using creative activities, such as drawings, paintings, dance, and music, that may help them express feelings and relieve stress and depression. Helping the children create their own stories could reveal areas of anxiety and fear. The use of guided imagery activities could be especially helpful with the older children, James and Kristina.

Another way to incorporate the religious and spiritual dimensions would be to see if Kelly is willing to involve her pastor. The counselor needs to find out how Kelly and the children are involved in church activities. Involvement in their church would help the family stay connected with this support system and find ways to be useful and productive.

Conclusions

This case is challenging and complex, with several therapeutic layers. From an individual as well as from a systems perspective, the strategies and interventions recommended may help alleviate some of Kelly's immediate concerns. However, the counselor should use a variety of assessments and outside resources and supports for ongoing family engagement. Doing so would allow the family members to see their problems and concerns in a more global way, thus normalizing as much as possible what they are experiencing. Keeping the family connected, including frequent interactions with her husband, face time with the children, and commitment to the counseling process, would help Kelly and her children better cope with the deployment.

References

Burke, M. T., Chauvin, J. C., & Miranti, J. G. (2005). *Religious and spiritual issues in counseling: Applications across diverse populations.* New York, NY: Brunner-Routledge.

Cashwell, C. S., & Young, J. S. (2011). *Integrating spirituality and religion into counseling* (2nd ed.). Alexandria, VA: American Counseling Association.

Corey, G. (2013). *Theory and practice of counseling and psychotherapy* (9th ed.). Pacific Grove, CA: Brooks/Cole.

Frame, M. W. (2003). *Integrating religion and spirituality into counseling.* Pacific Grove, CA: Brooks/Cole.

Reflections

Tracey E. Robert and Virginia A. Kelly

Military personnel and their families present unique challenges to the counseling process because they face frequent deployments, casualties, and related mental and emotional stress issues as well as the special demands of the military mindset. As stated in the case and response, the use of technology to offer support and comfort within the family structure was an important tool for the counselor to recommend outside of the counseling sessions. Integration of technology and Internet applications in counseling can be exceptionally helpful in working with this population. Military families have access to an array of online counseling services through the Military OneSource website provided by the Department of Defense.

In the military, the spiritual well-being of personnel and their families is the focus of chaplains and pastoral care. However, numerous spiritual interventions are available online and through web applications for counselors to address spirituality for these clients. Sites that offer meditation, sacred prayer reflection, yoga, and tai chi exercises abound. The use of technology and the Internet and integration of spiritual resources can enhance the counseling process for military clients in the following ways:

- Spiritual interventions provided through technology—DVDs, podcasts, videos—can supplement the counseling relationship and improve the client's coping skills.
- The use of technology allows for shared spiritual activities, such as prayer and scriptural readings, that can strengthen the client's familial bonds.
- Spirituality can create community and fight the isolation and separation anxiety that often create barriers for military families.

• • •

Chapter 24 Offenders

Case
Keith Morgen

Jack Miller, a 52-year-old man, had just been paroled after serving a 10-year prison sentence on drug charges. This was his third incarceration since he turned 18. All of his offenses were drug related and nonviolent. Jack was unmarried and alienated from his family and re-entered society with no friends and limited education (he earned his GED in prison) and job skills.

Jack came to counseling as a mandate of his parole agreement. He discussed how he had dismissed all "religious" activities throughout his life, including church attendance and self-help groups. Jack stated that he "wants some purpose in life" but also "doesn't believe in any kind of spiritual thing" because "my life has sucked, so why would any God do that to someone?"

Background

Jack's parents abused him as a child both verbally and physically, but the offenses were never reported to the state he lived in. He reported that his long history of abuse left him feeling "like I was worth crap."

Jack dropped out of school in the 11th grade. His parents disowned him around that time, leaving him homeless. He took up drug dealing (prescription pain pills and heroin) and burglary (cars and homes). He reported that he rarely used substances and "only sold them for the cash."

Jack struggled with crime throughout his adult life and spent his adult years in and out of prison. He occupied his time in prison by selling contraband and keeping to himself. The prison clergy and counselors approached Jack repeatedly to offer him religious and spiritually based support. He dismissed their efforts, stating he was not religious and did not believe in counseling.

Incident

Jack stated that he was seeing me for counseling only because it was a mandate of his parole. Once the mandate expired, he would stop coming to counseling. Jack also could not promise that he would not return to crime, stating that his criminal behavior was the only way he derived meaning in his life. At the end of the first session, he said, "I've been told I'm scum, no good, a loser, since I was a kid by my parents, teachers, cops, corrections, neighbors, and on and on and on. At some point, you just come to believe it."

Discussion

I tend to work with offenders from an existential perspective because many come to me with a predefined negative self-impression forged through years of reinforcement. Numerous core components of existentialism overlap with basic spiritual elements—forgiveness, surrender, freedom, and responsibility. Consequently, conceptualizing the case from a spiritual framework as a search for new meaning in life—which, from a phenomenological perspective, respects Jack's wish for self-definition—can be effective.

However, Jack denounced spirituality and religious matters. Consequently, any solid spiritual-based counseling needed to start with an exploration of why he dismissed spiritual work. Trepidation or resistance toward a spiritual discussion might diminish if Jack understood "spirituality" as a construct for deriving meaning out of life. His issue with spirituality was summed up in an early session in which he stated, "Everyone is always telling me what I am, who I am, and where I need to be. I didn't need a priest or counselor in prison telling me more stuff about me."

The "incident" in this case was not a specific event but rather a prerequisite for working with Jack to reconsider a new life definition not predefined by anyone or anything. This work would require an exploration of Jack's imperfections (spiritual concept of essential limitation), his ability and willingness to confront emotions of shame and guilt (spiritual concepts of surrender and confession), and his openness to learn from previous actions and turn his shame or guilt into a facilitator of change (spiritual concept of humility).

From an existential orientation, I would slowly work with Jack to help him shed his unhealthy self-perception by accepting the discomfort of existential guilt (simply self-acceptance of his own value as a human being) coupled with the realization that his life is not okay and many of the reasons why are his responsibility. In brief, Jack lacked what Paul Tillich termed "the courage to be oneself," which is defined as follows:

> The theological assertion that every human soul has an infinite value is a consequence of the ontological self-affirmation as an indivisible, un-exchangeable self. It can be called "the courage to be oneself." But the self is self only because it has a world, a structured universe, to which it belongs and from which it is separated at the same time. Self and world are correlated, and so are individualization and participation. (Tillich, 1952, pp. 87–88)

Questions

1. How does a spiritually oriented approach enhance counseling for offenders?
2. Jack was attending counseling as a mandate. How would a counselor use spirituality based counseling concepts to facilitate an increased motivation for counseling?
3. Jack's life experience had taught him that he was "worth crap." Because Jack was dismissive of spirituality and was not a religious man, how could a counselor use spirituality to create a more positive self-perception?
4. Spiritual discussions, no matter how framed, are not for everyone. How would a counselor working with Jack know if this line of inquiry was not working or appropriate considering his needs and motivation for counseling?

References

Tillich, P. (1952). *The courage to be*. New Haven, CT: Yale University Press.

Response
Gerald A. Juhnke

There is little doubt that a 10-year prison sentence will change one's life. Being confined to a six-by-eight cell, dealing with constant threats to one's own personal safety as well as the safety of family and significant others who are outside prison, and witnessing brutality among prisoners and injustices between guards and inmates will numb one's humanity, annihilate one's sense of control, and diminish one's sense of life purpose.

Jack survived three incarcerations in his 52 years, the most recent one lasting 10 years. Many states would label him a habitual criminal and eliminate simple parole opportunities. These incarcerations undoubtedly changed his life as well as his perceptions of self and others. Jack reported that he does not believe in "religious" activities and dismissed prison clergy's invitations to participate in what he considered religious groups. However, like many other inmates and ex-offenders I have counseled over the past 27 years, he might find spiritually oriented counseling approaches beneficial and rewarding.

Similar to many ex-offender clients, Jack had a history of perceived disappointments, heartaches, and betrayals. They started in his childhood when his parents were verbally and physically abusive. Spiritually oriented counseling approaches for ex-offender clients can be especially helpful in addressing such long-term histories of disappointments, heartaches, and betrayals and in enhancing counseling efficacy by helping ex-offenders understand the intermingled links among shame, guilt, anger, and forgiveness (Armour, Windsor, Aguilar, & Taub, 2008; Davis et al., 2013; Waldram, 1993).

A Spiritual Lens

Cashwell and Young (2011) stated, "This spiritual way, simply stated, involves developing a lens for seeing the sacred in one's circumstances" (p. 2). Over the years, I have experienced two predominant groups of ex-offender clients. The first group has developed this spiritual lens, embracing spirituality as a means to find new personal meaning, peace, and fulfillment first within and later outside the prison system. Some within this group carry enormous Bibles and constantly quote memorized scripture. Others memorize the Koran and pray aloud during specific prayer times. Still others are quiet about their beliefs—they meditate and focus on their personal spirituality and are mindful. These folks often don't embrace organized religion or typical spiritual beliefs. However, they have developed their spiritual lenses.

No matter how persons in this first group present, loudly self-proclaiming spiritual beliefs to others or introspectively focusing on their private worlds, they have developed Cashwell and Young's stated lens for seeing the sacred in their circumstances. They have come to depend on their spirituality to survive within a world that has stripped them of basic comforts and protective rights that most within society have.

The second predominant group I have experienced are those ex-offender clients who have truncated or extinguished their spiritual beliefs. They have extreme anger toward all so-called spiritual things—especially any higher power that would cause them to endure the living hell of a prison experience.

Allowing Clients to Decide

The fundamental construct in counseling ex-offender clients is to allow them to determine whether spiritually oriented approaches to counseling are suitable for them. Stated differently, one can invite clients to integrate spirituality into their lives and develop their lenses for seeing the sacred in their circumstances. However, counselors must be exceptionally careful not to coerce or force spirituality or spiritual beliefs on their clients. Even the slightest perception that counselors are pushing a spiritual agenda is sufficient for many ex-offender clients to become distant, belligerent, or even enraged. Most believe they have endured far too many injustices and have been robbed of too much time to be badgered by counselors who don't understand their idiosyncratic experiences or losses.

Should any client adamantly deny spirituality or refuse to engage in spiritually oriented counseling, it is imperative that the counselor discontinue spiritually oriented interventions and instead focus on interventions that match the client's beliefs. It has been my experience that once change occurs and greater rapport is established with such clients, the use of spiritually oriented counseling can be revisited and possibly begun.

Facilitating Spiritually Oriented Counseling

So, how does one invite ex-offender clients to participate in spiritually oriented counseling? A statement such as the one below may be helpful:

> Many of my clients who have experienced prison tell me they gained a new understanding of their meaning for existence. Some report they have found a "higher power." Others report they use meditation, prayer, or yoga to gain an inner peace. Still others quote scriptures, use mindfulness, or embrace the Serenity Prayer (Niebuhr & Brown, 1987) asking their higher power to grant them wisdom. Others tell me that they have found spirituality and their personal spiritual experience even differently. Tell me how you have come to find spiritual meaning for your life and what practices you use to create your inner peace and comfort.

This statement offers an open invitation for ex-offender clients to report their spirituality and practices that work for them. It provides a list of possible options that clients might have used and secondarily provides options that they may want to consider. Whatever the ex-offender's spiritual practices—as long as they are legal, ethically acceptable to professional counseling, and safe—they should be embraced and magnified. Thus, if a client responded that she has used the Serenity Prayer (Niebuhr & Brown, 1987) to gain inner peace, counselors should embrace this behavior and take advantage of her use of prayer as a resource.

Counselors might further ask how the client used the Serenity Prayer, how the Serenity Prayer was useful, how she determines when she will use the Serenity Prayer, and what other spiritually oriented counseling interventions she has found helpful (Juhnke, Watts, Guerra,

& Hsieh, 2009). Asking such questions may expand the application of her spiritual resource and promote use of the resource in new areas of the client's life.

Forgiveness

Forgiveness is another especially important topic for ex-offender clients. McCullough, Pargament, and Thoresen (2000, p. 9) defined forgiveness as "a prosocial change toward a perceived transgressor." Enright, Freedman, and Rique (1998) defined forgiveness as follows:

> A willingness to abandon one's right to resentment, negative judgment, and indifferent behavior toward one who unjustly injured us, while fostering the underserved qualities of compassion, generosity, and even love toward him or her. This new stance includes affect, cognition, and behavior. (p. 47)

Some counselors may mistakenly perceive forgiveness as focusing only on the ex-offender's crime victims. Instead, counselors must help ex-offenders identify those who have wronged them and investigate how forgiving those persons can actually help the ex-offender.

For example, Jack reported that his parents were verbally and physically abusive. Until he successfully forgives his parents and others he believes intentionally wronged or harmed him, he very likely will be unable to truly understand or experience forgiveness and unable to truly forgive others. In addition to forgiving others, Jack must learn to forgive himself. If he forgives others but is unwilling to forgive himself, he still holds himself accountable for his previous behaviors, thoughts, and actions. Ultimately, he can never forgive himself. Therefore, he always will be conflicted about pardoning those who wronged him and his healing will be incomplete.

Mandated Clients

Court-mandated clients tend to view the counseling experience as something "done to them" by "the system." This view entraps counselors in the role of being an agent of the court and truncates probability for successful treatment outcomes. Instead, spiritually oriented counselors must refuse this ineffective treatment model and jointly establish a model that empowers both counselors and their clients. Here, counselors explore and understand their attitudes, beliefs, and values regarding spirituality and religion and help their clients do the same. Counselors know themselves and understand how their chosen counseling profession matches their spiritual attitudes, beliefs, and values. They also know how to use their counseling skills and profession to better the world community in which they live and work.

Concomitantly, spiritually oriented counselors see and experience clients as valued cocontributors to the counseling process. Counselors and clients jointly develop and determine client treatment goals and objectives in relation to the clients' spiritual beliefs and knowledge. The intent of counseling then becomes helping clients attain their full potential without succumbing to court-mandated treatment plans or reporting requirements. Thus, the counseling process includes holistic and spiritual exploration of faith, hope, love, and other values.

References

Armour, M. P., Windsor, L . C., Aguilar, J., & Taub, C. (2008). A pilot study of a faith-based restorative justice intervention for Christian and non-Christian offenders. *Journal of Psychology and Christianity, 27,* 159–167.

Cashwell, C. S., & Young, J. S. (2011). *Integrating spirituality and religion into counseling: A guide to competent practice* (2nd ed.). Alexandria, VA: American Counseling Association.

Davis, D. E., Van Tongeren, D. R., Hook, J. N., Davis, E. B., Worthington, E. L., Jr., & Foxman, S. (2013, July 22). Relational spirituality and forgiveness: Appraisals that may hinder forgiveness. *Psychology of Religion and Spirituality.* doi:10.1037/a0033638

Enright, R. D., Freedman, S., & Rique, J. (1998). The psychology of interpersonal forgiveness. In R. D. Enright & J. North (Eds.), *Exploring forgiveness* (pp. 42–62). Madison: University of Wisconsin Press.

Juhnke, G. A., Watts, R. E., Guerra, N. S., & Hsieh, P. (2009) Using prayer as an intervention with clients who are substance abusing and addicted and who self-identify personal faith in God and prayer as recovery resources. *Journal of Addictions & Offender Counseling, 30,* 16–23.

McCullough, M. E., Pargament, K. I., & Thoresen, C. E. (2000). The psychology of forgiveness: History, conceptual issues, and overview. In M. E. McCullough, K. I. Pargament, & C. E. Thoresen (Eds.), *Forgiveness: Theory, research, and practice* (pp. 1–14). New York, NY: Guilford Press.

Niebuhr, R., & Brown, R. M. (1987). *The essential Reinhold Niebuhr: Selected essays and addresses.* New Haven, CT: Yale University Press.

Waldram, J. B. (1993). Aboriginal spirituality: Symbolic healing in Canadian prisons. *Culture, Medicine and Psychiatry, 17,* 345–362.

 ## Reflections

Tracey E. Robert and Virginia A. Kelly

Bryce Hagedorn described a need for offenders in counseling to embrace change, stating, "The only thing one needs to change is everything." He added that counselors who work with offenders also need to be open to the change process but that just as offenders often resist change, so do many counselors.

Some counselors do not see how they can integrate spirituality into traditional theories of counseling. The conceptualization in this case is helpful in this regard. The case also points out that much of the work in prisons is faith based and may not be a good fit for all offenders. Being culturally sensitive to offenders' belief systems is necessary for effective counseling. Also, the discussion of spiritual values, beliefs, and virtues (e.g., forgiveness and hope) has to be supported by the client. Caution in the use of language and concepts is recommended. Counseling offenders with a spiritual focus can improve the process in the following ways:

- Embracing the client's beliefs and resources facilitates the movement to change, allowing for freedom of choice for those who do not feel that they have any.
- Spiritual interventions can be effective with resistant offenders when connecting to the core issues of self and finding meaning.
- The process of developing a personal spirituality can provide offenders with protection and comfort and thus contribute to their willingness to change.

● ● ●

Section VII

Spiritual Interventions

Chapter 25

Mindfulness Meditation

Case
Paige Greason

Michael was a 22-year-old fifth-year college student when he came to counseling after a breakup with Maggie, his girlfriend of 2 years. The breakup triggered a downward spiral into depressive symptoms that were out of character for Michael. He was finding it difficult to engage with his friends and was struggling to make it to classes each day. Although the breakup was his idea, Michael couldn't get over the fact that he had "let Maggie down."

Background

Michael was the third child in a family of four. His mother was a professor at a local university, and his father was an attorney at the town's major law firm. Michael's older sister was finishing her PhD, and his other sister had just started chiropractic school. His younger brother had just finished high school and was looking forward to starting his college career at a large state university. The family, of European American descent, placed a high value on education. The expectation was that the children would get an advanced degree, focus on building a solid career, and ride that out until retirement.

Michael enjoyed a relatively successfully high school career. He was voted the treasurer of both his junior and senior classes and was a copy editor for the yearbook. Michael did well academically and was voted into the National Honor Society. He had a small group of core friends and was generally viewed as a shy but nice guy. Michael sang in the choir with his younger brother at the Presbyterian church his family had attended since before he was born. He started a volunteer organization to provide art therapy to the homeless in his community.

Since coming to college, however, Michael struggled to find his way, in terms of his career path and his relationships. His initial intention was to major in business, but after 2 years of a less-than-stellar performance in those classes, he decided to switch to computer science because he suspected he could find a good job with that background. However, Michael never felt inspired or fully engaged in the work, and his grades reflected this lack of enthusiasm.

During this time, Michael developed a very small group of acquaintances, but he didn't feel particularly close to anyone—until he met Maggie. They became romantically involved within a month of meeting each other at an on-campus party. Maggie had a troubled adolescence and a significant history of depressive symptoms. Michael began to spend much of his time trying to help her feel better about herself. His family was very concerned about the relationship and let him know that they didn't think he was making a wise decision. His family's concern fueled his desire to stay with Maggie because he believed he was the only one who understood her.

One year into the relationship, Michael began to recognize that he was feeling more drained than inspired by his time with Maggie. He never voiced this thought to anyone, because he felt he would be judged for having stayed in the relationship so long. Michael noticed that when he returned home to his childhood church, he would often cry silently in the church pews. As a result, he became concerned for his mental health.

When Michael voiced these concerns to Maggie, she became suicidal and later was admitted to the local hospital for suicidal ideation and self-harm. Michael felt tremendously responsible and remained with Maggie for another year. However, after a summer apart when Maggie seemed to have found a good friend at a summer camp, Michael got up the nerve to suggest a breakup. Maggie did not take the news well and again was admitted to the hospital. Despite this, Michael held to his belief that returning to the relationship was not the right choice for him, much to the delight and celebration of his friends and family.

Incident

The whole experience was a tremendous blow to Michael's sense of self. He always thought of himself as a helper—someone others could count on—and here he felt he was a failure for not being able to cure Maggie's depression and was a "loser" for leaving her when she was down.

Michael's relationship issues, coupled with his inability to find a major that connected with his soul, left him feeling not just sad but despondent. He began to think that something was terribly wrong with him and that he was basically unlovable. He felt helpless to change his situation and could only picture many years of living a lonely, empty life. To make matters worse, he felt bad about feeling bad.

Having come from a "good family" and "having nothing really to complain about compared to people like Maggie" only made things worse. Michael's friends and family thought he should be happy now because he was free of this relationship. Their perception only added to his pain. He began to pull away from his friends and spent much of his time sleeping or ruminating about his plight. Michael came to counseling at the urging of his roommate, who was concerned that he had lost weight and was unwilling to leave the apartment.

Discussion

I worked with Michael from a mindfulness-informed perspective. My first objective was to help him develop self-compassion around the decisions he had made and the struggles he was experiencing. I conceptualized much of Michael's current struggle as a self-critical meta-emotion around the very real initial hurt and pain of the relationship loss and the search for a meaningful career path. Michael had experienced the inevitable pain that comes with living life, but he was turning this pain into suffering by focusing on the mismatch between where he was and where he thought he should be both emotionally and academically.

I taught Michael some mindfulness techniques to help him begin to connect with the wisdom of his senses and observe his experience nonjudgmentally. Through these exercises, Michael began to get some distance between his thoughts about his experience and his actual experience. He realized that his thoughts were just thoughts—not facts—and he began to notice that he could have moments of presence when he felt alive and connected to those around him, much to his surprise.

Michael developed an ability to "watch" his thoughts and shift his attention when he noticed that he was headed down into an old, ineffective mental groove. Most important, he began to ride the wave of feelings and emotions that are a natural part of life's rhythm. Rather than try to push difficult feelings away—whether they were the result of external events or an internal thought process—Michael began to simply observe the changing current of his life.

Michael was armed with a deeper awareness that his struggles were a natural part of his creative process of becoming, rather than an inherent flaw. He allowed himself to connect again with those things that brought him peace, including singing and volunteering. He began to watch old belief patterns when they arose and took steps to move into his life from a place of being grounded in his deeper knowing.

Questions

1. A key issue for Michael was balancing his own needs with the needs and expectations of people around him, specifically his family and girlfriend. How might a counselor help Michael explore this dynamic?
2. Michael was at a pivotal transition in his life. What are some of the important developmental issues that could be addressed in counseling?
3. Being in the church environment seemed to open Michael to his emotional life. How might his spirituality and sense of connection to the church be explored in counseling?

 ## Response
Bobbie A. Birdsall

Michael appears to be dealing with several issues: life span development, career development, and spiritual development. A wellness model gives cohesiveness to all these issues. Spirituality is concerned with persons' search for meaning, purpose, and value in life (Wiggins, 2003).

In a holistic model for wellness and prevention over the life span, Witmer and Sweeney (1992) placed spirituality at the center of a wheel. The Wheel of Wellness provides a comprehensive framework for understanding and integrating salient facets of life, including work, love, and friendship. This model allows the counselor to address many important facets of a client's life and provides a strong foundation for the integration of religion and spirituality into the counseling process. Integrating Michael's spirituality into his journey on a spiritual path toward wholeness is a developmental goal.

Balance and Well-Being

The first question asked how a counselor might explore the dynamic of balancing Michael's own needs versus family and relationship dynamics. Having Michael go through the components of the Wheel of Wellness to identify areas where he has a high sense of self-regulation as well as domains where he needs to increase self-regulation would be a good starting place to explore personal growth. Research supports the role of mindfulness in fostering well-being and self-regulated behavior (Brown & Ryan, 2003). The counselor's use of mindfulness interventions is relevant in this situation because mindfulness also has been linked with well-being in students (Lynch, Gander, Kohls, Kudielka, & Walach, 2011).

The counselor's attempt to use a mindfulness-informed perspective comes from a strong evidence-based practice. Mindfulness describes a mental state of consciousness characterized by awareness in the present moment without judgment (Barnes & Lynn 2010). This awareness includes one's sensations, thoughts, emotions, images, and awareness of the environment. Practicing mindfulness can help break depressive cycles of thinking, provide alternative ways of understanding one's thoughts and feelings, and allow choices of responding (Mason & Hargreaves, 2001).

Mindfulness-based therapy (MBT) often is used to alleviate depression and to help a client accept what is currently happening in his life. Several studies have shown that MBT is effective with anxiety and depression (Brown & Ryan, 2003; Hofmann, Sawyer, Witt, & Oh, 2010; Mason & Hargreaves, 2001). Because Michael exhibited symptoms of depression, I would administer the Beck Depression Inventory (BDI). The results of the BDI along with the counselor's informal assessment of depression would help define the alleviation of depressive symptoms as a treatment goal.

Virtually all spiritual traditions have created meditative practices. Huxley (as cited in Miller, 1999, p. 68) described mindfulness as follows:

> The full value of meditative practices is best understood as tapping into the universal potential for the human mind to transcend its preoccupation with negative experiences and to become more comfortable with the experiences of compassion, acceptance, and forgiveness. The most significant clinical application of mindfulness is the capacity to adopt an "observing self."

The metacognitive intervention such as the counselor described is training to experience a sense of heightened but detached awareness of sensory and thought experience. Meditation often provides a way to cultivate a sense of inner calm, harmony, and transcendence that may be associated with spiritual growth (Miller, 1999).

Baer, Smith, Hopkins, Krietemeyer, and Toney (2006) identified five factors that foster mindfulness: (a) being able to perceive our emotions without reacting to them; (b) staying present with perceptions, sensations, thoughts, or feelings; (c) staying present with activities; (d) describing inner states with words; and (e) being nonjudgmental of our own experience.

Daniel Siegel (2010) offered an acronym for an accepting inner state: COAL—curiosity, openness, acceptance, and love. When we practice kind awareness in the COAL state, we merely note that a judgment has arisen and let it go. Badenoch (2008) defined mindfulness as "paying kind attention, on purpose, without grasping onto judgments, to whatever arises in the mind from moment to moment." All these definitions and practices can help the counselor explore the use of mindfulness intervention to balance Michael's needs with the needs and expectations of others.

Developmental Issues

The second question asked what important developmental issues could be addressed in counseling. Michael seemed to be involved in a developmental transition that encompassed career, personal, and family relationships. Erikson's "intimacy vs. isolation" psychosocial developmental stage best describes Michael's current dilemma regarding personal and family relationships. This stage takes place in young adulthood between the ages of about 19 and 40. During this period, the major conflict centers on forming intimate, loving relationships with other persons (Wiggins, 2003). Addressing the life span issues for young adults could help Michael recognize that his depressive symptoms might be a natural result of coping with intimacy issues, especially the loss of his relationship with his girlfriend.

Lines (2006) identified developmental areas that might warrant a counselor to move into a spiritual mode of counseling, including overcoming relationship obstacles (inadequacy in dealing with difficult relational tasks) and discovering one's inner self (finding inner resources to meet a challenge). These categories become evident during life span stages in which clients experience emotional, social, and psychological change.

The counselor needs to determine whether Michael's religious and spiritual beliefs are a healthy aspect of his life and a resource from which he can draw while he faces family and developmental issues. The counselor can use Clinebell's criteria, as cited in Wiggins (2003, pp. 113–114), by asking questions such as, "Do the religious or spiritual beliefs, attitudes, and practices of persons give the client meaning, hope and trust in the face of life's tragedies and improve love and self-acceptance rather than fear and guilt?"

Michael was experiencing a lack of self-worth and sense of control in the areas of work and career on the Wheel of Wellness. A career genogram would help him identify family career patterns and differentiate himself from his family members to recognize and deal with family pressure to meet high educational expectations. I would administer the Strong Interest Inventory and suggest further exploration using computer-assisted career-guidance programs, such as DISCOVER and O*NET.

Spiritual Development

Question 3 asked how Michael's spirituality and sense of connection to the church can be explored in counseling. Michael was in tears when he attended church and experienced an opening of the heart, demonstrating a feeling of connection to the church. "Faith, at all levels, is the search for an overarching, integrating and grounding trust in the center of value and power sufficiently worthy to give our lives unity and meaning" (Fowler, 1981, p. 5).

Fowler's stages of faith can create awareness of developmental tasks in spiritual growth. Most likely, Michael was in the Synthetic–Conventional faith stage where faith must provide a unifying means of synthesizing values and information and must serve as a basis for forming a stable identity and worldview (Fowler, 1981). At this point of development, a person might consider himself to have faith but has not examined his beliefs and values. Early adulthood is a powerful time for spiritual exploration and development. Referral to a young adult group at church might be helpful.

Enhanced use of meditation, acceptance of self, restoration of community, and a renewed sense of self-worth all are treatment goals for Michael. The wellness model can be used to focus on integrating the spiritual domain with his exploration of self. This integration can be accomplished using informal assessment methods during the clinical interview by asking questions such as the following: How important is spirituality or religion in your daily life? What things are most important to you? What gives your life purpose or meaning? What is your source of strength and hope? (Kelly, 1995).

Toward Self-Acceptance

Exploring Michael's definition of spirituality and his religion could strengthen his belief system and offer a source of support as he rides the waves of change. The counselor's intention to allow him to develop self-compassion and self-acceptance through mindfulness meditation is a positive intervention for integrating his developmental issues of spirituality, relationship, and career naturally without judgment. As a result, he was able to identify moments of connection and make choices to avoid getting caught up in the drama. The wellness model with spirituality as the core serves as a strong foundation to explore and embrace issues as they arise, unfold, and pass away.

References

Badenoch, B. (2008). *Being a brain-wise therapist*. New York, NY: W. W. Norton.

Baer, R. A., Smith, G. T., Hopkins, J., Krietemeyer, J., & Toney, L. (2006). Using self-report assessment methods to explore facets of mindfulness. *Assessment, 13*, 27–45.

Barnes, S. M., & Lynn, S. L. (2010). Mindfulness skills and depressive symptoms: A longitudinal study. *Imagination, Cognition, and Personality, 30*, 77–91.

Brown, K. W., & Ryan, R. M. (2003). The benefit of being present: Mindfulness and its role in psychological well-being. *Journal of Personality and Social Psychology, 84*, 822–848.

Fowler, J. W. (1981). *Stages of faith*. New York, NY: Harper & Row.

Hoffman, S. G., Sawyer, A. T., Witt, A. A., & Oh, D. (2010). The effect of mindfulness-based therapy on anxiety and depression: A meta-analytic review. *Journal of Counseling and Clinical Psychology, 78*, 169–183.

Kelly, E. W. (1995). *Spirituality and religion in counseling and psychotherapy.* Alexandria, VA: American Counseling Association.

Lines, D. (2006). *Spirituality in counseling and psychotherapy.* Thousand Oaks, CA: Sage.

Lynch, S., Gander, M.-L., Kohls, N., Kudielka, B., & Walach, H. (2011). Mindfulness-based coping with university life: A non-randomized wait-list-controlled pilot evaluation. *Stress and Health, 27,* 365–375.

Mason, O., & Hargreaves, I. (2001) A qualitative study of mindfulness-based cognitive therapy for depression. *British Journal of Medical Psychology, 74,* 197–212.

Miller, W. R. (1999). *Integrating spirituality into treatment.* Washington, DC: American Psychological Association.

Siegel, D. J. (2010). *The mindful therapist.* New York, NY: W. W. Norton.

Wiggins, M. (2003). *Integrating religion and spirituality into counseling.* Pacific Grove, CA: Brooks/Cole.

Witmer, J. M., & Sweeney, T. J. (1992). A holistic model for wellness and prevention over the life span. *Journal of Counseling & Development, 71,* 140–148.

 ## Reflections
Tracey E. Robert and Virginia A. Kelly

Wellness and spiritual well-being are connected and together provide a focus for this case and response. In addition, looking at multiple domains and Michael's development allows for an integrated approach to finding meaning and purpose in his life and healing from his losses. Helping Michael stay in the present rather than ruminate about the past or future creates space for him to reconnect to self and others. The wellness model helps him address his social, psychological, career, and spiritual issues. From a shattered, reclusive state he can move to become an engaged and curious client—helpful traits for positive outcomes. MBT can improve the counseling process in the following ways:

- It can reduce anxiety and depression caused by trauma, loss, and developmental transitions.
- It can provide a tool clients can use outside of the counseling process and for a lifetime.
- It can increase self-awareness, emotional regulation, and balance, providing clients with hope and optimism.

• • •

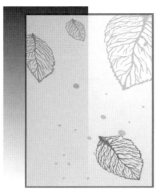

Chapter 26 Use of Prayer

Case
Sharon E. Cheston

Rob is a 40-year-old White male who is married and has two female children, ages 6 and 8. He arrived for counseling stating that he had been in therapy off and on for 15 years. In his first session, he reported suffering from recurrent depression and, when depressed, experiencing lethargy and self-critical thoughts. He said he wished he "was no longer on this planet" and questioned why God created him with this problem.

Rob is an ordained minister in a mainline Protestant church who has devoted his life to God. Before our counseling sessions, he was confused about why God would burden him with depression if he is devoted to serving God's people.

Background

Rob is the firstborn of three children. His father was a minister in the same Christian denomination as Rob, and his mother stayed home with the children and helped his father with his ministry. Both of Rob's parents are deceased. His sister, age 37, is a medical doctor who is working in Africa for the church, and his brother, age 32, is a professional football player.

Rob married Jeanne when they were in seminary together. She quit to start their family, but it was many years before they could conceive. In vitro fertilization helped them get pregnant. Rob blamed himself for their infertility, though there was no evidence that he was the reason.

Rob described his marriage as "dependable" when he is depressed and "good" when he is not. He expressed more positive emotion when he described his relationship with his daughters. He also reported feeling regret about "missing his time with them" when he is depressed.

As a child, Rob was required to attend church because of his role as the pastor's child. He never minded going to church but often wondered whether God was really "the wonderful being" described in the Bible.

One of Rob's earliest memories occurred when he was 10 years old. In his father's sermon, God was referred to as "He" multiple times and Rob remembered wondering if God really was a male, but he said nothing to his father to avoid the rage and condemnation he knew would occur if he brought up the topic. Rob had learned early that questions about God were usually dismissed with the use of a Bible passage.

Rob had learned in seminary that what was preached to parishioners was different from what was known by intellectuals. As a pastor, he struggled with how much of this knowledge he could reveal to congregants, who probably would see him as a heretic if he were to speak the truth and challenge their childhood teachings. Rob prayed many times a day but often felt that the prayer was a one-way conversation.

Incident

Rob was aware of the symptoms that indicated a depressive episode was beginning. Sometimes the symptoms appeared just before Christmas when the winter solstice decreases the amount of sunlight. Rob did not always experience depressive feelings when the sunlight decreased, but he had noticed a correlation between the amount of sunlight and his general mood. If a negative experience coincided with winter solstice, then depression was almost assured.

Rob was having a difficult time with the leadership of his small suburban congregation, specifically a man named Steve, who saw the world in a black-and-white dichotomy, like Rob's father did, but unlike Rob, who sees the grays but often does not see colors. Because depression had begun to cloud Rob's life, he sought psychiatric intervention and counseling. He arrived for counseling as an eager partner to improve his mental health.

Discussion

My work with Rob began with appreciation of his proactive work in recognizing his tendency to become depressed after winter solstice, seeking medication from his psychiatrist, and entering counseling as his mood moved toward depression. My primary goal was to monitor his affect and ensure that his mood stabilized and then improved as the medication became more effective.

This goal was easily attained because Rob was a willing client who carefully monitored his mood and proactively sought the help he needed. Rob saw this episode as an opportunity to learn a different way to respond to challenges, such as Steve's leadership in the church.

To understand how Rob responded to external and internal challenges, I decided the first therapeutic goal would be to have him tell about and explore this episode of "betrayal" and other instances when he felt betrayed by others who were seen as leaders. Rob immediately referenced his father's leadership in church and in his original family. For the first time, Rob had insight into the connection of others' rigidity and his discouraged feelings that often led to depression.

From this new understanding of how his depression was linked to his discouragement when others showed rigid beliefs, Rob saw how his relationship to God may model this same experience. He referenced his many experiences in which he felt that others used their church positions to "preach" half-truths to keep congregants dependent and thus further their self-importance. He openly spoke of how the Bible was constructed and women were misrepresented.

Rob's anger was evident as he unloaded years of what he called leadership abuse, starting with his father and ending with Steve. Bitterly, he spoke of his prayers not being answered. I took this opportunity to ask him to explain how he prayed and what he expected from prayer.

Rob's prayers included mostly petitions for God to intercede by stopping those in authority from abusing their power. He was disappointed when there was no change despite his prayers. These discussions were the most efficacious part of the counseling process. Rob explored additional types of prayer, including quiet listening with his heart and praying for those whom he found to be abusive.

Rob felt relieved of his many burdens. He began to understand the core source of his depression and was able to lessen its power over him. As his depression lifted, he became more confident and began to use the pulpit to teach others about God, not to preach to others. He called counseling "enlightenment," and indeed he felt "lighter" as he dropped his burdens.

Questions

1. Rob felt burdened by a darkness that settled in on him at various times, often when there is less light in the northern hemisphere where he lives. However, there was another darkness he struggled with. He expressed anger with God and prayed that this anger would be lifted. How could a counselor work with him sensitively concerning his prayer life and how he was praying out of anger, not love?

2. Rob felt powerless at times, yet as a church pastor, he held the power granted to him by his congregation. How could a counselor help him recognize his power and use it to enlighten others?

3. Rob believed that his prayers were not answered because he suffered from depressive symptoms, yet he had a successful career, a loving family, and a strong belief in God. How could a counselor help him recognize the answers in the prayers he offered?

Response
Tracey E. Robert

Many researchers have found that spiritual wellness and well-being correlate with low rates of depression (Robert, Young, & Kelly, 2006; Westgate, 1996). Using prayer in the treatment of depression has been found to be highly effective (Sperry, 2012), but integration of prayer into treatment requires caution and sensitivity on the part of the counselor (Cheston & Miller, 2011). According to the Association of Spiritual, Ethical, and Religious Values in Counseling's (ASERVIC's) competencies, counselors must feel competent in addressing spiritual and religious issues, be aware of their own views and beliefs, and be attuned to the client's worldview (ASERVIC, 2009). As Sperry (2012) stated, there are no evidence-based studies or guidelines on how to integrate prayer into therapy. Without the use of a professional protocol, many counselors choose to avoid this intervention or attempt to follow the client's lead (Hodge, 2007).

I commend the counselor in this case for a clear and thoughtful response that is well structured to support healing and spiritual wellness. Reviewing the case gave me the opportunity to assess my own beliefs and views about the use of prayer in counseling. I was able to reflect on the times during my practice when I considered integrating prayer into the counseling process. For me, prayer as a spiritual intervention showed potential for enhancing the working alliance. However, the ethical issues and techniques for integration of prayer were cause for concern. A careful and respectful conceptualization based on the client's worldview was critical, and letting the client lead was a helpful approach.

In Rob's case, the counselor modeled effective strategies and followed ethical guidelines. In responding to her questions, I am using the lens of Rob's overall spiritual well-being.

Assessing Prayer Life

In Question 1, the counselor asked how one could work with Rob sensitively concerning his prayer life. To use prayer effectively in counseling, the case conceptualization needs to be based on how the client prays (Cheston & Miller, 2011; Pargament, 2007; Sperry, 2012). Thus, a careful spiritual assessment of the type of prayer Rob used most often is important.

The use of a two-step assessment process recommended by Pargament (2007) could be helpful in (a) identifying how important spirituality is in the client's worldview and (b) determining how the client integrates this into his or her life. The initial spiritual assessment could be made through the use of tools—such as the Spiritual Assessment Scale (Howden, 1992); the Spiritual Well-Being Scale (Ellison & Paloutzian, 1982); and the Faith and Belief, Importance, Community, and Address in Care (FICA) instrument (Puchalski, 2000)—or with direct interview questions during the intake. The second step is important for the counselor to truly understand the role spirituality plays in the client's life and the type of prayer he or she may use. Prayer can be a useful tool for clinically assessing coping and psychological functioning (Sperry, 2012). In Rob's case, prayer is an integral part of his daily life.

Being aware of different types of prayer can be helpful to clients. Psychoeducation used as an intervention to describe the available types of prayer can provide the client with options and strategies for coping. Various descriptions of prayer types have been proposed. Seven types of prayer that might be used as counseling interventions are the following:

1. Petition—asking for something for self;
2. Intercession—asking for something for another person;
3. Confession—asking for forgiveness;
4. Lamentation—a cry of distress asking God for justice;
5. Adoration—giving praise and honor;
6. Invocation—a call of the presence of God to be with you; and
7. Thanksgiving—gratitude. (J. S. Young, personal communication, June, 2001)

Sperry (2012) described the following six types of prayer: petitionary, meditation, thanksgiving, adoration, confession, and intercessory. Prayers also have been described as inner, outer, and upward (Ladd & Spilka, 2002). Ways to use prayers in counseling include the counselor praying silently for the client in or outside of therapy, praying vocally with the client in session if he or she asks, and encouraging the client to pray for himself or herself outside of therapy (J. S. Young, personal communication, June 2001).

The counselor gently probed and discovered that Rob used mostly petitionary prayer, a type that focuses on asking God or a higher being for material or spiritual help. Rob stated that he constantly asked God to help with his depression and felt burdened by the weight of his illness. The counselor supported Rob's reaching out for help with the physical components of the depression, using medication, and addressing his tendency to have seasonal affective disorder during the winter months. She used this opportunity to offer him options for his prayer life.

Hodge (2007) found that many therapists use intercessory prayer—praying for others—outside of treatment with their clients. Sperry, Hoffman, Cox, and Cox (2007) found that mental health professionals' use of intercessory prayer is spreading. How the counselor uses this type of prayer would depend on the client case.

With Rob, the counselor suggested two types of prayer: intercessory, in which Rob prays for Steve, the person in his congregation who has created stress and conflict; and contemplative prayer, or quiet listening. Suggesting these two types of prayer provides interventions that allow Rob to restructure his view of his depression and stress and can increase his spiritual wellness and well-being. This reframe also can move Rob from anger to love.

Recognizing One's Power

In the second question, the counselor asked how one could help Rob recognize his power and use it to enlighten others. Rob struggled with his vocation and job beginning with his confusion about God and his beliefs in his early years. He appears to have "lost his way," further contributing to his depression.

Meaning and purpose in life is a key component of spiritual wellness (Briggs & Shoffner, 2006; Westgate, 1996). As Frankl (1984) stated, the existential emptiness of lack of purpose can be paralyzing. In recognizing his depression and coming to counseling, Rob took a step to explore the lack of meaning and feelings of powerlessness in his life. As his mood stabilized, he was able to start to restore and heal his spiritual well-being. As his perception of his spiritual health improves, he can become more confident and positive in his leadership. In prayer for the person who has challenged him, he has moved from being a victim to gaining strength and self-assertiveness. He is allowing his voice to be heard. The counselor stated that Rob is starting to teach instead of preach and thus share his knowledge and beliefs.

Exploring Rob's expectations of God's answers to his prayers and his discouragement helped him see how his personal beliefs were in conflict with his method of preaching. The counselor could help him see how his beliefs might be hindering his self-esteem by conducting a prayer review (Whittington & Scher, 2010). In clarifying what Rob was petitioning God for and what life events actually occurred, the counselor could help him identify the barriers to his petitions.

Rob's expectations may have been unrealistic, and a review of when and how he petitioned God could lead to possible solutions. In participating in the more reflective style of contemplative prayer, Rob allowed for time to listen to his own internal voice and became part of the process of prayer—more active than passive. This action could enhance his self-esteem and encourage him to share this positive aspect of praying with his congregation.

Life Review

In Question 3, the counselor asked how one could help Rob recognize that his prayers are being answered. To address Rob's overgeneralization and negative view of God's response, the counselor could suggest that he conduct a life review. This process would entail him creating a lifeline of events, both positive and negative. He could then use an adaptation of the TIC-TOC technique from rational–emotive behavioral therapy (Burns, 2008) to sort the events into two columns, positive and negative.

In reviewing his life to date, Rob would not be focusing on one single event—which often leads to overgeneralization—but on his entire life. In reflecting on the matrix he has produced, he can challenge his beliefs about how negative his life has been. Discussing this information with the counselor could enable Rob to recognize that many of his petitions may have been answered. He could start to look at how he could substitute a more positive view of his life.

The counselor can help Rob move from a negative view of his life to a more positive one and challenge his beliefs. Rob can begin to see hope and, as he stated, "be enlightened." The more positive his sense of spiritual well-being, the greater his job satisfaction will be (Brewer, 2001; Robert et al., 2006).

As Rob recognizes that he is addressing his challenges and becoming "lighter," his prayers may become less angry and self-critical. His spiritual wellness will increase, and, as a result, his depression will decrease.

References

Association for Spiritual, Ethical, and Religious Values in Counseling. (2009). *Competencies for addressing spiritual and religious issues in counseling.* Retrieved from http://www.aservic.org/resources/spiritual-competencies/

Brewer, E. W. (2001). Vocational Souljourn paradigm: A model of adult development to express spiritual wellness as meaning, being, and doing in work and life. *Counseling and Values, 45,* 83–94.

Briggs, M. K., & Shoffner, M. F. (2006). Spiritual wellness and depression: Testing a theoretical model with older adolescents and midlife adults. *Counseling and Values, 51,* 5–20.

Burns, D. D. (2008). *Feeling good: The new mood therapy.* New York, NY: Harper.

Cheston, S. E., & Miller, J. L. (2011). The use of prayer in counseling. In C. S. Cashwell & J. S. Young (Eds.), *Integrating spirituality and religion into counseling: A guide to competent practice* (2nd ed., pp. 243–260). Alexandria, VA: American Counseling Association.

Ellison, C. W., & Paloutzian, R. F. (1982). *Spiritual well-being scale.* Nyack, NY: Life Advance.

Frankl, V. E. (1984). *Man's search for meaning*. New York, NY: Washington Square Press.

Hodge, D. R. (2007). A systematic review of the empirical literature on intercessory prayer. *Research on Social Work Practice, 17*, 174–187. doi:10.1177/1049731506296170

Howden, J. W. (1992). Development and psychometric characteristics of the Spirituality Assessment Scale. *Dissertation Abstracts International: Section B. Sciences and Engineering, 54*(1), 166B. (UMI No. 9312917)

Ladd, K. L., & Spilka, B. (2002). Inward, outward, and upward: Cognitive aspects of prayer. *Journal for Scientific Study of Religion, 41*, 475–484.

Pargament, K. I. (2007). *Spiritually integrated psychotherapy: Understanding and addressing the sacred*. New York, NY: Guilford Press.

Puchalski, C. M. (2000). Spiritual assessment tool. *Journal of Palliative Medicine, 3*, 131.

Robert, T., Young, J. S., & Kelly, V. A. (2006). Relationships between adult workers' spiritual well-being and job satisfaction: A preliminary study. *Counseling and Values, 50*, 165–175.

Sperry, L. (2012). *Spirituality in clinical practice* (2nd ed.). New York, NY: Routledge.

Sperry L., Hoffman, L., Cox, R. H., & Cox, B. E. (2007). Spirituality in achieving physical and psychological health and well-being. In L. L'Abate (Ed.), *Low-cost approaches to physical and mental health: Theory, research, and practice* (pp. 435–452). New York, NY: Springer.

Westgate, C. E. (1996). Spiritual wellness and depression. *Journal of Counseling & Development, 75*, 26–35.

Whittington, B. L., & Scher S. J. (2010). Prayer and subjective well-being: An examination of six different types of prayer. *International Journal for the Psychology of Religion, 20*, 59–68.

 ## Reflections
Tracey E. Robert and Virginia A. Kelly

Close to 60% of U.S. adults say they pray at least once a day, according to the U.S. Religious Landscape Survey. Even many adults who are unaffiliated with a religion say they pray daily.

Prayer has been shown to be an effective counseling intervention for a variety of mental health issues. In Rob's case, prayer was used for treating depression, but various prayer types might be more appropriate for other concerns. A growing body of research supports the use of meditative prayer or mindfulness meditation for reducing stress and anxiety, coping with trauma and sexual abuse, and addressing addiction and chronic pain issues. Prayers of forgiveness and gratitude have been found effective in improving clients' cognition and behavior.

The types of prayer described in the response are predominantly from a Judeo-Christian perspective. The use of prayer from other belief systems (e.g., Eastern religions, Islam, Buddhism) should be considered depending on the client's worldview. With clients of the Muslim faith, for example, discussion of ritualistic prayer of adoration and connection to Allah can help them identify benefits and possible barriers to improved well-being.

Suggestions and cautions on integrating prayer into the counseling session would remain the same for all types of prayer. Counselors should be culturally sensitive and attuned to the client's belief system and prayer life and stay mindful of the risks and ethical issues involved. The use of prayer can benefit the counseling process in the following ways:

- It can provide comfort and connection and enhance the therapeutic relationship.
- It can provide support and help alleviate isolation and loneliness when dealing with depression, anxiety, and trauma.
- It can be used as a coping mechanism, strengthening the client's self-esteem and resilience.

• • •

Chapter 27

Group Work and Trauma

Case
A. Michael Hutchins

Teaching others to love is at the core of group work. Cornel West maintained, "But love is not a real small thing. Love is not just the key that unlocks the door to ultimate reality" (West, 2009). Love becomes the underlying source of integrating the cognitive, affective, behavioral, and spiritual aspects of who we are and our relationship to our community. This case study of a group of men with histories of childhood abuse and trauma provides a lesson in learning how to love and how to translate love into a way of being in the world.

Background: The Group Members

The counseling group, designed for men who experienced abuse and trauma, included the following men:

Alberto, a college-educated 32-year-old Mexican American, came to the group at the urging of his girlfriend. While in residential treatment for substance abuse, he began to acknowledge emotional, physical, and sexual abuse he had experienced as a child. His girlfriend shared that she would end their relationship if he continued his substance abuse and did not become more communicative. He was uncertain about how to communicate his feelings.

At 64, Tim retired from a career in government. He had been in an interracial marriage for 30 years and, with his wife's knowledge, had had a male lover for most of those years. Tim became a practicing

Buddhist at age 12. He recognized a pattern of sexual compulsivity and sought to explore its origins.

Having grown up in a wealthy Jewish family, Simon felt different from the other men in the group. A professional musician, he had been educated far beyond his parents. His father had always wanted Simon to be a doctor and still derided and verbally abused him. At 46, Simon had recently gone through a "very nasty" divorce and had been referred to the group to address his anger and depression.

Hama was a 37-year-old Iraqi refugee. Before coming to the United States, he had been a translator for a U.S. Army unit in Iraq. Before his work as a translator, he had an emerging career as a playwright. While serving as a translator, Hama was riding in a tank that hit a land mine. American soldiers were killed, and Hama was seriously wounded. He attempted to save his colleagues but was not successful. He was working in a Middle Eastern restaurant as a cook and attempting to write about his war experiences. His psychiatrist referred him to the group. He experienced isolation and fear. Coming to the group was a great challenge.

Tiago, a 50-year-old Brazilian-born American, came to the United States to attend medical school and built a successful medical practice. He recently had an extramarital affair and recognized that he was following a pattern that his father created. He also recognized that his father had been physically and emotionally abusive. Tiago's role in the family had been to "protect everyone" from being hurt. He processed the world intellectually.

George, a 49-year-old Maltese American bank manager, was the father of an adolescent son. He left a "loveless" marriage to explore an attraction to men. He described feelings of loneliness and sought to connect with older men. In counseling, George had begun to examine some sexual experiences he had as an adolescent with the local parish priest, a family friend. George acknowledged that he distrusted most people.

Group Formation

The group formed when these men were referred to address concerns related to childhood abuse and trauma. All had been involved in individual outpatient or inpatient counseling and were interested in coming to a greater understanding of how childhood abuse and trauma influenced their adult lives. They further wanted to transcend the life-inhibiting dynamics of abuse.

The group members agreed to participate for a minimum of 24 weekly 2-hour counseling sessions. They also agreed to participate in daily fitness programs and weekly community service activities. They all kept journals in which they wrote stories or poetry based on their group experiences.

The group members acknowledged that they were privileged to have the resources to participate in individual and group counseling. Participation in community service activities allowed them to use their privileged positions to give back to the community and to address some of their personal dynamics related to abuse and trauma. Participation in fitness programs further encouraged creating balance in all aspects of their lives.

In each session, members "checked in" and shared comments from their journals. The group leader's role was to facilitate group interaction. The session presented here (Session 12) focused on spiritual development and integration. The group progressed to the stage where members monitored the Gestalt norms (Zinker, 1977) introduced in the initial session.

A Framework

Before the initial group session, participants were introduced to a framework to be used throughout the life of the group. The framework distinguished among cognitive (thinking and believing), affective (core feelings), and behavioral processes. The focus for individual growth was on core feelings, the beliefs associated with these feelings, and the behaviors that result. Through the group process, members learned to articulate what occurred for them, increased their relationship and communication skills, and built a sharing community.

The framework included an integration model (Hutchins, 2009). The focus was on restructuring worldviews so that members could move through life-inhibiting feelings and thoughts, manifest congruent behaviors, and integrate messages of love and joy. When this integration occurred, group members experienced an aliveness of spirit. For many members, this integration was the core of spirituality. When group members became more integrated, the group became more connected and created a more spiritual community. The counselor's role was to assist in this process.

The Spirituality Session

In the previous session (Session 11), George spoke with hostility about the Roman Catholic church. He denied being angry and insisted that his hostility "made sense." Tim remained calm and timidly suggested that group members explore the differences between "organized religion and 'real' spirituality." Simon remained quiet before adding that music played a more important role in his life than religion.

Hama shook at several points during the session and became tearful. He reported that the discussion was "very painful" for him. Alberto listened to the discussion very carefully. He reported being "anxious" and stated that the church "covered up" the abuse of young men. Tiago appeared confused. He suggested that the others did not really understand the role of religion and spirituality in life. When Tiago shared his thoughts, the men got angry at him.

The group appeared to experience a great deal of dissonance, which provided the opportunity for direct and emotional discussion using the established norms. The group facilitator closed the session by inviting members to write about their experiences in their journals and shared that their reflections would provide the framework for the next session.

In Session 12, group members shared their journal reflections and sought to identify a theme in their writings. All members acknowledged that their experiences in Session 11 reflected the lack of connection that they experienced in their lives.

Simon and George expressed a lack of connectedness with any community or external force. Hama wrote a poem in which he described the terror and isolation he experienced. Simon acknowledged that he shared Hama's experiences of "being so different from the others." Alberto indicated that the isolation was within himself. Tim reported that, at times, he "felt a cold blue flame deep inside" and identified the flame as "loneliness." When Tim shared this information, Tiago began to cry and shared that "this group feels more like a family to me than anyplace else." Tim quietly suggested, "Maybe our theme is love." The group became quiet.

Discussion

Group counseling provides the opportunity for participants to create a spiritual community. The men in the group had lost touch with their capacity to access love and to connect with themselves and others. The experiences of abuse and trauma reinforced their lack of trust in the world and contributed to isolation and alienation.

Through group counseling, the men were beginning to take the risk of making connections. In the session discussed above (Session 12), the group was approaching the Norming Stage (Tuckman & Jensen, 1977) of group development. They created norms that worked for them and collaborated to move through difficult issues.

Although the men in the group were culturally diverse, common themes emerged. All had experiences of abuse and trauma and articulated that they had lost their passion for life and had difficulty making significant connections with others. When presented with the model in which love is the core of our being, all members acknowledged that they believed the model was theoretically possible but questioned whether they would be able to experience unconditional love. As they moved through the group process, they began to experience "moments" of connectedness in the group setting.

Another common theme was the experience of betrayal by organized religious structures. For some members, the mere mention of organized religion ignited anger, fear, and pain. Most often, the core feeling that came to the surface first was anger. The men could make cognitive distinctions between being "religious" and being "spiritual." All acknowledged the desire to have a rich spiritual life and shared that, for some, the experiences of religion had impeded the path to a spiritual life. Some members shared that organized religions could be paths to spirituality but other options existed.

Participation in the group process is a step in building a more spiritual community. Involvement in communities outside the counseling group also helps. All members shared the view that participation in the group and involvement in community organizations brought them closer to the experience of love.

Learning to balance "alone" time and "community" time was challenging for some, particularly those whose experience of abuse had been most severe. Group members expressed difficulties in trusting their own decision-making processes and in learning to trust others. As a result, they often were more likely to isolate and not engage in the lives of others. As the group sessions progressed, new patterns of connectedness emerged and the men became more willing to take social risks and to balance their time.

Initially, most of the men had negative views of themselves in the world. This lack of a positive worldview often manifested itself with the men neglecting to care for themselves physically. The members agreed to participate in fitness programs and to change their eating patterns to become healthier. They began to speak openly of the spiritual importance of physical and nutritional self-care and became supportive of each other in addressing these concerns. Tim frequently spoke of the "self-love" that comes from the practice of fitness.

Group members eventually began to address issues of sexuality and spirituality. Tim opened the discussion by exploring his "shame." George and Tiago made connections and shared authentically. Later in the life of the group, the discussion about sexuality was powerful.

The belief that love lies at the core of who we are as people is consistent with most spiritual traditions. If we are born into a loving world, unconditional love becomes the starting place for our lives. If love is our core feeling, then we learn that we deserve respect for merely "being." If we believe we deserve to be loved, we engage in behaviors that lead to connection and community. The men in the group articulated that they felt depressed, angry, afraid, hurt, ashamed, and lonely. The group counselor's challenge was to move through the blocks to the experience of love with the members in a manner that encouraged integration and integrity.

In a commencement address at Evergreen State College, bell hooks (1998) challenged the graduates "to change the world from love," and she further issued this invitation in her writing (2001, 2003). If we accept that invitation, we engage our clients in building a loving community in the group setting. We build a community where risks can be taken and old wounds healed. By its very nature, group work is community building.

Questions

1. What does the use of group work add to individual counseling for men who have experienced trauma and abuse?
2. How do the process and stages of group work contribute to the participants' healing?
3. Using the integration model, how could the group counselor integrate additional spiritual interventions into the process?

References

hooks, b. (1998, June 12). Commencement address, Evergreen State College, Olympia, WA.

hooks, b. (2001). *All about love: New visions.* New York, NY: Harper Collins.

hooks, b. (2003). *Teaching community: A pedagogy of hope.* New York, NY: Taylor & Francis.

Hutchins, A. M. (2009, December 14–17). *Using group work concepts as an integral part of reconciliation to understand and heal psychological trauma in response to violence.* PowerPoint presentation presented at the Global Reconciliation Pathways to Reconciliation Summit, Amman, Jordan.

Tuckman, B.W., & Jensen, M. A., (1977). Stages of small group development revisited. *Group and organizational studies, 2,* 419–427.

West, C. (2009, July 3). *Bill Moyers journal* [Public Broadcasting System transcript]. Retrieved from http://www.pbs.org/moyers/journal/07032009/transcript.html

Zinker, J. (1977). *Creative process in group therapy.* New York, NY: Vintage Books.

Response
Diana Hulse

The counselor in this case selected an integration model to guide his work. This model, which emphasizes the interactions among thoughts, feelings, and behaviors, served as his framework for helping group members understand their childhood abuse and trauma, transcend the dynamics of abuse, and learn about love. This conceptualization resonates with other group work models (Hulse-Killacky, Killacky, & Donigian, 2001). For example, the counselor invited answers to "Who am I?" "Who am I with you?" and "Who are we together?" Answers to these questions propel members toward activating Yalom's (2005b) therapeutic factors. Pairing the group counseling experience with members' participation in community service activities and fitness programs sets the stage for healing and spiritual growth.

The counselor's conceptualization and descriptions of the group process also connect well with a model presented by Orr and Hulse-Killacky (2006) in which voice, meaning, mutual construction of knowledge, and transfer of learning are introduced as key concepts for effective group work. The counselor clearly invited voice to help members begin the healing process—where, in a climate of openness and safety, each member is encouraged to speak, listen to others' stories, and begin answering the question "Who am I?"

As noted in the case, the counselor encouraged members to express the meaning they derived from the group—in the form of journal entries—and to share these meanings with others, thus furthering community building and demonstrating the potential healing that comes through mutually constructing knowledge. Through the expression of meaning and community-building activities, members began answering the question "Who am I with you?" Finally, the counselor attended to transfer of learning by helping members integrate instances of interpersonal connections. A significant example of this integration is observed in the member's self-disclosure, "This group feels more like a family to me than anyplace else."

Transfer of learning was a particularly salient concept for this group. My only recommendation for the counselor would be to maintain a focus on transfer of learning at the end of each session and as the group experience comes to a close. The importance of transfer of learning is highlighted in the *Schopenhauer Cure* (Yalom, 2005a) when Julius reminds us, "The group is not life; it's a dress rehearsal for life; we've all got to find a way to transfer what we learn in here to our life in the real world" (p. 302).

This statement is central to the goals and aspirations of these six group members. Often as groups come to a close, members want to linger by observing, "This was a special group. I will miss this group. I will miss everyone. I hate to see the group end." The counselor can certainly validate such statements while directing his members away from seeing the group as the end-all of the group experience. He can link examples of interpersonal learning in the group to life outside the group by asking members to answer the following questions:

- What did I learn about myself in this group?
- How did the relationships formed in this group help me learn about myself?
- How does my new self-knowledge help me reach out to others?
- How will I take what I have learned to my life at home, with friends, at work, in the community?

Taking time to close the group with answers to questions like the ones posed above ensures a stronger link between the power of the group process and how group members move forward in their healing and spiritual growth. Reflections after each session and at the group's end help members answer the question "Who are we together?" After all, it is the building and nurturing of relationships in the group that contribute to healing and strengthen the recognition that each member is part of something larger than himself. This recognition contributes to spiritual growth. Thoughtful and effective group closure provides members with a bridge to the outside world, options for joining other groups in the future, and help in recognizing how they can change the world with love.

Therapeutic Factors of Group Work

Question 1 asked what group work can add to individual counseling for men who have experienced trauma and abuse. Group work adds exponentially to healing through the expression of Yalom's (2005b) therapeutic factors. For example, evidence of universality abounds in the counselor's descriptions of this group, even as the men came from varied backgrounds and had different stories to tell. Universality is a core therapeutic factor because it begins to break down the wall of isolation and offer the possibility of connection.

Examples of instillation of hope are seen in the counselor's accounts of members' self-disclosures. Hope is a dramatic healing quality that can spur even the most skeptical group member toward the possibility of change as he gains the realization that loneliness and isolation do not have to be a foregone conclusion.

Interpersonal learning is the pièce de résistance in group work. In the context of relationships developed in the group, interpersonal learning helps members begin to slowly exchange earlier and entrenched behaviors and viewpoints with ones that acknowledge they have something to offer to others. Interpersonal learning is linked to altruism; as members begin to see value in themselves, they become willing to take steps to reach out to help others. Group members learn skills for being effective citizens and for operating in a loving manner toward others in their world.

The Healing Process

Question 2 asked how the process and stages of group work contribute to the participants' healing. The counselor took time at the beginning of this group to build connections through member similarities. Then, as members activated their voices and began to participate with one another, he invited them to engage in discussions about viewpoints that differed from their own. Here, he encouraged movement into what Frew (1986) called the control phase. This is the phase where members learn to articulate, "These are how my views are different from yours."

Navigating this control phase is essential for opening up new avenues for interpersonal learning and spiritual growth, and it provides a path to what Frew called the affection phase. As the counselor stays tuned to the here and now, he helps his members focus on how things happen and why things happen in the group. When the counselor attends to group process and the balance between process and content, he helps members gain confidence in putting aside their feelings of alienation, isolation, and distrust and replacing them with increasing levels of competence in expressing their authentic selves within a climate of safety and care. In this case, the counselor provided illustrations of member shifts from isolation to community, avoidance to self-awareness, focus on self to altruism, and dependence to interdependence. At the core of these shifts is interpersonal healing.

Creating a Spiritual Community

Question 3 asked how using the integration model the group counselor could integrate additional spiritual interventions into the process. Research has shown that spiritual interventions, such as meditation, yoga, a body scan exercise, and qi gong, have been effective in group work (Newsome, Waldo, & Gruszka, 2012). In his integration model, the counselor presented many examples of spiritual interventions. Connections to others are the key to creating a spiritual community. He fostered the presence of love through the significant act of relationship building because people learn in part through their relationships with others.

The counselor can continue to ask members to reflect on actions in the group: "What just happened?" "What did you observe in yourself?" "What did you observe in others?" Exploration of these questions moves members in the direction of seeing how learning with others comes to life in the work of the group. By keeping an eye on the process of how things happen, the counselor can continue to offer his members a glimpse into a world of relationships that not only helps heal trauma but inspires members toward spiritual growth.

References

Frew, J. F. (1986). Leadership approaches to achieve maximum therapeutic potential in mutual support groups. *Journal for Specialists in Group Work, 11*, 93–99.

Hulse-Killacky, D., Killacky, J., & Donigian, J. (2001). *Making task groups work in your world*. Upper Saddle River, NJ: Merrill/Prentice Hall.

Newsome, S., Waldo, M., & Gruszka, C. (2012). Mindfulness group work: Preventing stress and increasing self-compassion among helping professionals in training. *Journal for Specialists in Group Work, 37*, 297–311. doi:10.1080/01933922.2012.690832

Orr, J. J., & Hulse-Killacky, D. (2006). Using voice, meaning, mutual construction of knowledge, and transfer of learning to apply an ecological perspective to group work training. *Journal for Specialists in Group Work, 31,* 189–200.

Yalom, I. D. (2005a). *The Schopenhauer cure.* New York, NY: HarperCollins.

Yalom, I. D. (2005b). *The theory and practice of group psychotherapy* (5th ed.). New York, NY: Basic Books.

Reflections

Tracey E. Robert and Virginia A. Kelly

As the case and response demonstrate, the foundational concepts of group work fit well with the spiritual concepts of community and connection. Self-help groups that deal with mental health issues and faith-based groups that support members who are struggling with life challenges have proliferated since the 1970s. However, many training programs do not include spiritual content or focus in their group work courses, and spiritual content does not appear often in the group counseling literature. Many counselors do not feel that integration of spiritual or religious content or interventions is appropriate or fits in a group format, according to a recent survey of group workers. We think that group counseling with a spiritual focus can improve the counseling process in the following ways:

- The process supports development of a shared community and support of participants' belief systems.
- The discussion of spiritual values and beliefs can produce a climate of safety and connectedness to address isolation and loneliness.
- Our experience in practice has shown that engaging in psychoeducation with a spiritual focus in a group setting can produce more self-awareness and change.

• • •